EUROPEAN EDUCATION AND TEACHERS

Editor

Dr. Digumarti Bhaskara Rao
M.Sc., M.A., M.A., M.Ed., Ph.D.
Reader
R.V.R. College of Education
Guntur-522 006
India

DISCOVERY PUBLISHING HOUSE
NEW DELHI-110002

First Published - 2003

Reprinted - 2016

ISBN: 978-81-7141-702-5

European Education and Teachers

Published by:

DISCOVERY PUBLISHING HOUSE PVT. LTD.
4383/4B, Ansari Road, Darya Ganj
New Delhi-110 002 (India)
Phone: +91-11-23279245, 43596064-65
Fax: +91-11-23253475
E-mail: discoverypublishinghouse@gmail.com
sales@discoverypublishinggroup.com
web: www.discoverypublishinggroup.com

Printed at:
Infinity Imaging Systems
Delhi

To
my beloved
brother-in-law and sister

Mr. Veeramachaneni Venkateswara Rao
Mrs. Veeramachaneni Vijaya Lakshmi
Ravindra Bharathi Public School
Satyanarayanapuram
Vijayawada 520011
Andhra Pradesh

Preface

European countries have different educational set-ups and varied teacher education programmes. As much literature is not available on European education and teachers to people of developing states, this book is prepared in order to give all information in nutshell about the European education, the present status of education and teachers, the programmes that are in action to enhance the quality of education and teacher education, the aspects to be considered in education and teacher education, the factors to be considered to enhance the status and competencies of teachers, the strategies to be adopted in teacher training/education and recruitment, etc. This book will add many things to general education and teacher education programmes and policies. The readers can influence the educational activities in different angles.

—Bhaskara Rao Digumarti

Acknowledgements

I am
thankful to the
International Bureau of Education
for reproducing the papers
contributed to the 45th session of the
International Conference of Education
for the benefit of
educational enterprise

I am also
thankful to the
European Consultation Committee
and OECD.

I am
greatful to
Dr. Julieta Savova
Mr. Jose Antonio Fernandez
Prof. Maurice Galton
Mr. Y. Brunsvick
Mr. J.C. Tedesco
for their valueable
contributions

—Editor

Contents

PART— I

EDUCATION AND TEACHERS IN CENTRAL AND EASTERN EUROPE

Dr. Julieta Savova
Consultant, International Bureau of Education

I. Countries in Transition

A. Political, economic and social aspects of development

For the countries in Central and Eastern Europe, the first half of the 1990s has been marked by a *large number of dynamic and dramatic events*. The transition from a totalitarian towards a democratic social order has involved a chain of political, economic, social and demographic changes with an impact on education.

Comparative data on the political dynamics of these changes indicate that, after the beginning of the period of transition, *some common trends* have been observed in almost all countries:

— the adoption of new constitutions;
— the irreversible destruction of the monopoly of one-party systems;
— a multiplication of new political parties and movements;
— great political changes at parliamentary and presidential levels, often leading to frequent parliamentary or presidential elections;
— frequent changes of government leading to inconsistency in State policies and in the definition of priorities;
— the re-emergence of nationalistic tendencies.

During recent years the political tendency in most Central and Eastern European countries has been a turn to the left (with the exception of the Czech Republic). This has brought the left wings back on to the political stage in an entirely new socio-political and economic context. Such a shift has not necessarily led to the termination of already initiated reforms and certainly not a return to the totalitarian regimes of the pre-1989 period. This shift is, however, very indicative of the process of events in Central and Eastern European countries today, five years after the first critical steps towards reform had been taken.

Against the background of these common trends, there is still evidence of some *differences* in the political dynamics within the countries of the region. Some of the major ones are:

— differences in the actual commencement of the radical changes. The Vishegrad Four (Poland, Hungary, Slovakia and the Czech Republic) initiated their changes earlier than the other countries;
— different rates in the renewal process, the greatest impetus being evident in Central Europe and the greatest inertia in the Balkans and in the former republics of the Soviet Union, especially in Central Asia. Countries involved in armed conflicts (the countries of ex-Yugoslavia, some former Soviet republics) faced particular problems;
— different levels of political consensus—or more precisely lack of political consensus—on essential issues of national priorities and development;
— different models of government, depending on the national constitution.

This political picture would not by itself have accounted for the nature of the changes taking place in these countries after 1989, if it had not been accompanied by *economic trends* during the same period. The majority of the latter are totally new, unknown and have had a dramatic influence. More often than not, countries have been shocked by them and ill-prepared.

Economic developments within the countries of Central and Eastern Europe have witnessed a sudden decline in productivity immediately after the changes in 1989.[1] The gross domestic product (GDP) indicator has been rapidly declining. Despite these clearly noticeable common trends, there have also been differences in economic developments in each country. Considerable economic hardship can be reported during the transition period in Armenia, Azerbaijan, Tajikistan, Georgia, Moldova, etc. The situation has not improved even today. However, a careful comparison of the rates of economic decline indicates disparities which are very evident in Moldova, Tajikistan and Uzbekistan. The Baltic countries also display similar inconsistency in economic deterioration, 1994 being the year when they reached the bottom. During 1991-94 the average level of production was reduced by more than 50 per cent.

Bosnia and Herzegovina, Croatia, the former Yugoslav Republic of Macedonia and Yugoslavia have been marked by different trends in their economic development. The common feature among them is the general collapse of GDP with different durations in each country.

Comparative analysis of the countries in transition has shown *similarities* in the following areas:

— there was a common trend towards economic decline (most evident in Armenia, Belarus, Georgia, Moldova, Tajikistan, etc.).
— a tendency to have a high inflation rate; at its most dramatic in Albania, Yugoslavia.
— an upward trend in unemployment;
— a worsening balance of payments.

The *differences* lie in the following:

(a) the rate of economic decline; these rates are different not only for each country, but also in terms of the dynamics within each country from 1990 onwards;
(b) in observing the first noticeable signs of economic recovery in the countries in transition;
(c) in the rates and degrees of success in overcoming the negative tendencies during the transition period, such as in the areas of unemployment, poverty, crime, etc.;
(d) in the depth and scope of structural reforms: differences in establishing and expanding the private sector (the Czech Republic, Hungary and Poland are more advanced than the other countries.).

It was in 1994 that the data for economic development began for the first time to show positive changes. Despite the unreliability of certain data and the difficulties in data comparison due to different methods used in gathering them, economic growth has indeed been reported since 1994.[2]

The countries of Central Europe have been able to take the most rapid steps to control the decline in their GDP. The Czech Republic has been very successful in its economic measures. Poland is an example of a country adopting swift tactics to overcome its economic shortfall and has managed to contain the situation.

An interesting development in comparative terms is visible in Romania, Slovenia and Albania. Apart from wide differences in the rate of economic decline in terms of GDP (Albania had by far the greatest figures of economic collapse: 27.7%), there has been some success in overcoming it since 1993 and noticeable growth in GDP.

Apart from changes in GDP, there were also changes in levels of inflation, although in a number of Central and Eastern European countries the rate still remains high.

But even in the most rapidly recovering economies (the Czech Republic, Poland, etc.), GDP is still below that for the period prior to 1989 (it being understood that this is not the only indicator for measuring economic growth). Financial stability is far from achieving the desired levels and in some countries radical measures have been taken to rescue the national currency (Yugoslavia, 1994-95). In the majority of countries experiencing transition there has been modest success in gaining control over inflation; although some countries were not very successful at all. The monetary strategies for reforms in most countries have proved insufficient and have been unable to bring order to the violently disturbed financial market, principally because they were not backed up by the relevant structural reforms and were accompanied by drastic liberalization of national economies.

The year 1994 also marked the beginning of the growth of total real incomes. This tendency, however, should be interpreted with great care because the period of transition radically increased the gulf between rich and poor, and impoverished the greater part of the population. (Moldova, Tajikistan, Ukraine, etc.).

Together with the moderate rates of economic growth since 1994, the countries in transition have been unable to find the right balance in decisions concerning:

— the degree of government intervention in the transition from over-centralized economies towards market economies;
— the implementation of new laws, and harmonization of the existing laws with European legislation;
— the speed in the change of ownership, which is rapid in most Central and Eastern European countries, the Baltic States, etc. and relatively slow in Bulgaria and Albania.

The year 1994 was also when there was a tendency to achieve at least partial control over the high levels of unemployment in Central and Eastern European countries, although unemployment rates vary to a remarkable degree. The serious structural changes in the economies of all countries undergoing transition have led to sweeping changes in employment: whole sectors have disappeared; others are working with a big reduction in capacity.

Since the statistical data are not completely reliable (e.g. data may be available only for the officially registered unemployed, but never for hidden unemployment; or there are data on unemployment with no specific information on duration), firm statements concerning low unemployment rates (particularly concerning the ex-Soviet countries) cannot be made.

The labour market is characterized by decreasing employment in the State sector, although it has still remained dominant. There continues to be evidence of artificially subsidized inefficient employment: for example, in many countries of the former USSR, it was considered unwise to shut down certain factories and to make the employees redundant, but preferable to retain them on long-term unpaid leave. This decreases the State's expenses on social security, but gives rise to numerous other problems.

Different again is transition towards *alternative employment* in various countries—e.g. the private sector—including employment in the education sector.

The private sector is itself a new phenomenon for the countries in transition and is developing at different speeds. The structural framework of unemployment is also influenced by different forces:

— the most typical tendency is a decrease in unemployment among people with higher education (Bulgaria,[3] Poland); unemployment among people with secondary or primary education is rising;
— youth unemployment is a widespread phenomenon and the rates are high;
— an increase in the duration of persistent unemployment, i. e. the emergence of long-term unemployment where the job loss might last on average for more than a year;
— differences in unemployment rates among minority groups. Members of minority ethnic groups are potentially in more danger of losing their jobs.

The social and demographic implications of the above-mentioned economic climate are to a large extent logical and natural, some of them being the following:

— a rapid decrease in the standard of living, which had been kept artificially high prior to 1989. The percentage of people living in poverty has increased very rapidly since then. About one-third of the population in the Central European countries have been affected by these processes, while in the rest of the region the number is even higher.[4]

— economic reforms have not been accompanied by adequate social reforms and protection of the population; the system of social security has found itself unprepared to meet the challenges of the new situation. During the first four years of transition, the total number of jobs lost came to more than 8 million, whereas the number of registered unemployed in Eastern Europe even now amounts to 7.5 million.[5]

— incomes show drastic declines and any increase since 1994 has been substantial only for those already in high-income groups, leaving grounds for acute social diversification and polarity. Income disparities have become a threatening phenomenon. There has been a rapid increase in the number of people living below the socially accepted minimum level of income. Part of the population is being labelled as the new poor' (according to the Azerbaijan report).

— social disintegration is also displaying dangerous tendencies.

The demographic characteristics in this context indicate that there is an evident tendency towards a steady decline in birth rates and some countries report negative population growth (e.g. Bulgaria, the Czech Republic, Hungary, Romania, etc.). It is very disturbing to note that death rates are increasing, including those for infant mortality, in parallel with a decrease in life expectancy. Almost all countries are reporting these tendencies. In many countries, the number of terminated pregnancies exceeded the number of births. (Bulgaria, Moldova,[6] the Russian Federation).

Some former Soviet Republics of Central Asia still report high birth rates, despite predictions that births will decrease during the coming years. Family planning has little tradition here, if any, yet the levels of births observed before 1989 have little chance of being re-established.

B. Educational implications

The profound political, economic, social and demographic changes that have taken place in Central and Eastern European countries since 1990 have had an impact on education in general, as well as on teachers in particular.

The steady decrease of GDP up until 1994 had an unfavourable influence on education because the total budget figures for education, allocated from GDP, have not been relevant to the real needs of the education systems (Table 1).

The educational budgets in some countries (Belarus, Moldova, the Russian Federation, Ukraine, etc.) are far below those of other developed countries. Recent years have witnessed budget increases for education in some countries alongside decreases in others. A decrease in the percentage of GDP allocated to education immediately places limitations on the prospects for curriculum innovations, enrichment of teaching materials and, thus, on raising the quality of teaching. Of course, this also affect teachers' salaries.

TABLE 1 : Educational Expenditures

Country	GDP %	Total of national budget%
Albania		8.2
Bulgaria (1995)	4.1	14.1
Czech Rep. (1995)	5.9	16.6
Estonia		16.0
Hungary	6.6	8.9
Latvia		12.97
Poland (1993)	5.6	10.3
Romania (1994)	3.9	13.0
Slovakia (1994)	6.3	
Slovenia		16.3

The education system and teachers have suffered directly from the implications of all negative aspects of the process of transition—increased inflation, decreased income, rising unemployment (including youth unemployment).

On the other hand, it is as a result of the changes that had not been experienced prior to 1989 in countries undergoing transition that *new responsibilities* have been assigned to teachers, no matter how unprepared they were to assume them. Re-evaluation of the national curriculum, the design of new national educational standards and assessment of the quality of education imply teacher involvement on a large scale, especially if these reforms are accompanied by decentralization of educational administration. These priorities demand high-quality teaching and require the professional level of the teaching staff to be raised. An analysis of teachers' roles in Central and Eastern European countries shows that they need a new type of motivation, as well as specialized training, if they are to comply with the new requirements whose scope is still expanding. Teachers are expected to be actively involved in these changes, to be critical in their thinking and evaluation, to generate new ideas and to participate actively in educational management. Most Central and Eastern European countries have placed strong emphasis on these trends (Bulgaria, the Czech Republic, Hungary, Poland, Romania, the Russian Federation, Slovakia, etc.)

Thus, *education* has all at once been singled out as one of the most powerful driving forces in finding a way out of the social and economic crisis; this is not regarded as idealism or over-estimation of the actual potential, but rather as a significant pre-condition for national growth through the search for perfection in education and empowerment of the teacher. Education can, therefore, play a crucial role in any country's efforts out of the crisis, or in providing at least a partial solution for the unemployment problems by adapting people quickly to the new working conditions, as well as raising educational standards for the younger generation. All this cannot be achieved without the commitment of teachers. As comparisons show, in those Central and Eastern European countries where changes in the quality of teachers are evident and they have an awareness of their new mission, the reforms have been more successful.

C. The social context of professional development: school and society

In Central and Eastern European countries, despite variations in contemporary opinions about the position and the role of the school and of teachers in society, enough evidence exists to regard them as *agencies of social transformation and change.*[7]

This dimension is of significant importance for a deeper understanding in order to anticipate the newly assigned roles of schools and teachers—one of the factors promoting change-in countries where the reform processes are politically charged and the economic situation lays a heavy burden on society.

Awareness of the importance of the school and teachers in the transformation processes in the countries undergoing transition and of the expected passage to the coming century (when education will no longer be viewed as 'locked' behind the institutional walls of basic education, but rather as 'lifelong' education[8]) makes us consider the design and implementation of a model interrelating education and society, which will allow for successful fulfillment of the mission assigned to schools and to teachers, and thus accelerate reforms in society.

In all these countries, there is a well-defined need for a *new image of schools and teachers* which would correspond to their role of actively involved partners in the profound changes taking place in society on the road to democracy, promotion of national identity within the broader concept of a European identity and cultural diversity.

The development of a new model for the social structure in order to respond to the challenges of both the transition period and the coming century should be based on: democratic leadership; freedom and responsible citizenship; tolerance and respect for others; personal growth and enrichment; and active participation in changes. All of these will *require a new type of relationship* between school and society, between teachers and the other partners on the social stage.

If, in the past, party ideological functions had been allotted to schools and teachers, whereas in the new socio-political context they are expected to create a favourable environment for the adequate education and training of the young generation, for the exercise of democratic citizenship, for tolerance and for encouraging the new culture of peace.

Under totalitarian regimes schools and teachers were 'sealed off' from novelty and outside experience, from unconventional and provocative ideas, while any new ventures were only tolerated in externally prescribed contexts. Schools and teachers functioned according to the so-called limited work-place autonomy. Today, schools and teachers are expected to be wide-open to positive and effective developments, to promote innovations and to initiate them, and to assume a really broad professional autonomy.

The unemployment situation also poses new requirements for

education and teachers since they are responsible for the training and retraining of young people. The high level of youth unemployment calls for the implementation of new programmes envisaging measures to overcome it. The need for lifelong education becomes an important new guideline. Although in some Central and Eastern European countries practical differences and difficulties have been encountered, national and international sources state that various retraining programmes are available for the unemployed.

The need to introduce new types of relationship between school and society can be expressed in economic terms as well. The school as an educational institution trains young people for their encounters with the 'professional world'. Training which is relevant to the demands of the economy is a major task for education today. Flexibility and adjustment to structural changes taking place in the economy are the challenges that education must face. A proper balance between theory and practice in training can be sought through offering training and qualifications in the actual professions that the labour market demands, such as the public services that have expanded in all of these countries.

Negative demographic growth also calls for specific measures. The predictions made in these countries for a further fall in birth rates provoke an urgent reassessment of the emphasis on education and the adoption of corrective strategies for upgrading its quality. **Education for all can** no longer be seen in terms of providing equal access to all educational establishments. Today, education for all means 'quality' education for all. Closely connected to this broad interpretation is the requirement of education that is relevant to economic changes and demands, which implies greater flexibility and response to personal preferences and social needs.

D. The new educational paradigm

The new type of school needs a new type of teacher as much as the new type of teacher needs a new type of school. This formula supports and confirms the findings of UNESCO's International Commission on Education for the Twenty-first Century that education in the next century, which is not geographically or politically defined, has four essential features:

— learning to know;

— learning to do;
— learning to be;
— learning to live together.

The provision of proper conditions for the successful implementation of these four principles would define the new image of education and the status of the teaching profession.

Free access to education for all, high quality education, relevance to existing needs (both individual and social), and accountability are the requirements of modern education.

Education is a powerful factor in the formation and development of the personality. It builds up individual abilities, attitudes and personal qualities, and trains young people for their future roles in a renewed and democratic society where freedom and responsibility make up the two facets of individually and socially valued behaviour. Education is also a significant factor in the democratization of society by encouraging the transmission of shared values and by social integration through generating and encouraging people's educational and professional growth.

A comparative overview of the directions and principles of reform in the education systems of the countries experiencing transition, including reforms of the school itself, as well as in teacher training and their qualifica-tions, has indicated that the new type of relationship between the State and the school should aim at abolish-ing the remaining elements of the dichotomies expressed by: 'authority/collaboration', 'competition/co-operation', 'superiority/prejudice and acceptance'. In a situation where the State embodies 'authority', 'superiority' and 'prejudice'—and is the sole winner—there is little room, if any, for 'partnership', 'co-operation' and 'adaptation'.

Changes in the relationships of the 'school/State' type do not take place easily or rapidly, especially during transition periods pervaded by instability. Thus, creating a new balance between centralization and decentralization, redistributing power so that greater responsibility is accorded to lower administrative levels, and ensuring real autonomy for schools and teachers, will be long-term processes. The role of teachers in these processes will be irreplaceable.

The new role of education and the strengthening of its influence in the transformation processes in the countries undergoing transition pose special requirements and place new emphases on the teaching

profession. The teacher today should be:
— sensitive to change;
— open to innovation;
— tolerant of differences;
— committed to her/his profession;
— able to demonstrate respect of others and of himself/herself;
— empowered;
— highly accountable for what he/she does;
— more sensitive and responsive to individual and social expectations.

The new requirements placed on education and teachers are not limited to any region or country. They are based on commonly established beliefs and can serve as an argument in the shift from one educational paradigm to another (Table 2).

Table 2 : Old educational paradigms and new educational paradigms

Old educational paradigm	New educational paradigm
Domestic (narrow centred, one-sided)	International (European, global, pluralistic)
Homogeneous (monocultural) educational diversity)	Heterogeneous (cultural and
Economic security and economic demands	Personal growth and satisfaction
Dominance of quantitative measures in the evaluation of results	Importance of qualitative measures in the evaluation of results
Over-centralized management	Decentralization trends in terms of management
Low responsibility at the bottom	Balanced share of responsibilities
Symbolic participation in decision-making at school and teacher levels	Redistribution of power and real participation

The conclusions to be drawn from the above analysis direct our attention towards the need to:
— redefine the role of education, educational institutions and

teachers in the transformation process taking place in these countries—it is growing and becoming more complex.

— revitalize the school and all other educational institutions in order to make them more sensitive to changes and to become active partners in these changes.

— rethink the model of the teaching profession, so that it plays a vital part not only in transmitting knowledge but also in inculcating values and in renewing society.

II. Legislative Reforms in Education

The transition period in the countries being analysed is characterized by dynamic legislative activity. In almost all countries new constitutions have been created and adopted. Upon this new legislative foundation, the rest of the laws are being recast. They concern literally all fields of social practice—political, economic and social. Such intensive legislative activity has no parallel in recent history. Comparative analysis reveals *certain similarities:*

1. It is being carried out in all countries undergoing transition, though at different speeds and on different scales;
2. It affects key areas and is directed towards underpinning the present transition and avoiding any return to the totalitarian period;
3. It guarantees the new priorities;
4. It is directed towards a new type of management and the development of a new model of interaction between institutions and people;
5. It foresees radical and simultaneous changes in many areas over a short period of time.

The educational aspects of this picture does not differ notably from the above description of the reforms undertaken in these countries since 1989. Changes in education accelerated at the beginning of the transition period and provided a legislative framework and grounds for subsequent reforms. These educational reforms cover the system at all levels and in all its dimensions. They are aimed at new priorities and are oriented towards a new type of management, including a shift from centralization to partial decentralization, where the administrative authority and responsibilities are distributed in a more balanced way at different levels. Some other similarities in Central and Eastern European countries can also be observed, such as: including parents and other social actors in decision making processes at different levels; creating opportunities for non-governmental organizations, societies, foundations, churches and private persons to run schools.

According to one of the acquired classifications[9] of different reforms (not specifically educational), the following types can be identified:

1. Corrective reforms;
2. Modernization reforms;
3. Structural reforms;
4. Systemic reforms.

Systemic reforms in education are based upon giving a new meaning to and a redefinition of basic principles and interrelations in the education system and in other social systems. They concern fundamental aspects of education, including the teachers, who are the most powerful internal agents capable of influencing success or failure in the implementation of reforms.

A comparative analysis of reforms in education in *transition countries* and their legislative basis shows that:

— Education is considered as an essential factor for achieving the goals of democracy;
— The majority of Central and Eastern European countries are oriented towards systemic reforms (Birzea) requiring profound changes in educational legislation;
— A primary 'thrust' (Kotasek[10]) in educational legislation can be observed after the beginning of the key political, economic and social changes in the transition countries (after 1989);
— The newly passed educational laws, or amendments to the old ones, are irregularly scattered in time (from 1989 to the present). Already in 1990, the Czech Republic, Hungary and Romania were the first countries. They were also the first countries to adopt new laws or to have amended existing laws. In 1991, four more countries—Bulgaria, Latvia, Lithuania and Poland—adopted new educational laws. A year later (in 1992), Albania, Estonia, the Russian Federation and the Ukraine joined them. In 1994, Belarus, Hungary and Slovenia adopted their new

educational legislation. The Czech Republic, after separating from Slovakia, adopted a new educational law in 1995 and so did Romania once again. Some of the former republics of Yugoslavia—Croatia, Bosnia and Herzegovina and the former Yugoslav Republic of Macedonia introduced amendments and supplements to their inherited legislation;

— Legislation has been carried out in an atmosphere of intense activity, particularly after the first parliamentary elections in most countries;

— The new educational legislation sets out new macro-frames for the development of the education systems, drawing them nearer to Western European models, at the same time as maintaining the traditional characteristics of each national education system;

— Comparative analysis also shows that the new educational legislation includes many regulations concerning teaching and teachers without, however, making them in many cases a subject of a separate legislative act or a special law on teachers and the teaching profession. Raising the social status of teachers, fostering their active participation in social changes, empowering them—achieving all this requires special legislative activity. Thus, in 1994, Poland emphasized designing a separate law for teachers, although this draft has not yet been adopted at parliamentary level. In Slovakia (1995), a document on teachers' status is under preparation. In Romania (1995), special amendments for teachers are being introduced as additions to the present law on education. In the Ukraine, some amendments to the educational law are also under discussion;

— The new laws of education—often passed at the beginning of the transition period in circumstances of some perplexity; in the presence of great dynamics in change; in the absence of broad consensus; faced with inconsistency in defining national priorities, etc.—were processed for 'urgent revision' and complements very soon after their adoption. This can be observed by the number of countries that are making amendments and complements to their recently-passed educational laws;

— The new educational laws have not been developed in a package together with other laws concerning educa-tion. This often leads to conflict between different laws.

A comparison among the analysed countries shows that:

— there are common trends in the development of education in the Central and Eastern European countries;

— educational reforms affect all sectors of education and they envisage simultaneous changes (educational structures, curriculum, management, teachers and teaching);

— irregularity in the rapidity of reforms in the various educational sectors can be observed. Changes connected with teachers have developed rather more slowly than had been expected.

Mention deserves to be made of the fact that there exist a number of normative acts (decrees, regulations, etc.) concerning teachers and the teaching profession. Amendments to the existing laws made in individual countries also include new regulations for teachers. In the Russian Federation, for example, 60 per cent of the articles in the law of education are under revision. In Bulgaria, Romania, etc., new amendments concerning teachers are also being made to the existing educational laws. Finally:

— a discrepancy between so-called intended policy,[11] rhetorical policy and implemented policy affects teachers directly;

— educational reforms demand better financing. They are at present taking place in a situation of limited resources. This affects the strengthening of teachers' positions and their social status.

III. Teaching as a Profession

There has been a long-term debate concerning the teaching profession. As usual, this has involved *two extremes.* At one end stands the concept of the teaching profession as a 'full profession', while the other promotes the opposite idea. The *paradox* of these contrary concepts lies in the fact that all attempts to associate the teaching profession with the adjectives 'full' or 'semi' spring up from a common starting point, based on the descriptive explanations of what is known as the 'ideal profession' (Weber, 1947; Millerson, 1964; Lortie, 1969; Hoyle, 1969; Bergen, 1986, etc.). As we deal with a broad continuum of opinions on what the status of the teaching profession is, on the basis of which are constructed a variety of social ideologies or beliefs, it can either be viewed as an 'occupation', a 'semi-profession' or a 'full-profession', depending on what ideological stance or belief is adopted.

A. A model of the ideal profession

If we want to present a rich panorama of the characteristics of the so-called 'full profession', there is a listing which ranks them in the following way:

First, a profession renders a unique, definite and essential service to society. Only people in a particular profession render that service. For instance, only lawyers practice law. The service rendered must be considered sufficiently important to be available to all people in a society.

Second, a profession relies on intellectual skills in its performance. This does not mean that physical actions and skills are not required, but rather that the emphasis in carrying out the work is on intellectual skills and techniques.

Third, a profession is preceded by a long period of specialized training. Because professional work requires special intellectual skills, specialized intellectual training is needed. General education, such as that represented by a bachelor's degree, is of value, but not considered adequate. The specialized training covers a substantial period and may not be obtained in 'cram' courses or through correspondence schools.

Fourth, both individual members of the profession and the professional group enjoy a considerable degree of authority. Professional groups regulate their own activities rather than having outsiders establish policies and enforce adherence to standards. Whereas factory workers have very limited decision-making power and are closely supervised in the performance of their work, professionals are expected to take most of their own decisions and be free from close supervision by superiors.

Fifth, a profession requires its members to accept personal responsibility for their actions and decisions. Along with having a high degree of freedom and autonomy, the professional must shoulder a large measure of responsibility for his or her performance. Since the professional's service is usually related to the human welfare of individuals, this responsibility is an especially important one.

Sixth, a profession emphasizes the services rendered by its practitioners more than financial rewards. Although the personal motives of an individual professional are not necessarily any higher than those of another worker, the emphasis of the professional group is on public service.

Seventh, a profession is self-governing and responsible for policing its own ranks. This means that there are professional sub-groups who perform a number of activities aimed at maintaining the high quality of services and looking after the social and economic well-being of their members. These self-governing groups set standards of admission and exclusion for the profession.

Eighth, a profession has a code of ethics that sets out acceptable standards of conduct for its members: For a professional group to regulate the quality of its service, it needs a code of ethics to aid it in enforcing high standards.[12]

This kind of approach, however, outlines the 'static' image of a profession. Its fundamental drawback lies in its inability to outline a clear and full picture of the development of an occupation or semi-profession, when an occupation or semi-profession is in a position of 'gaining' professional status. We are by no means denying the possibility (or arguing against the value) of creating an *invariant model of the 'ideal profession'* which might serve as a comparison for other occupations claiming 'full' professional status. The model, therefore, cannot and should not be placed outside the broader social context where any activity (occupation or semi-profession) could be re-evaluated in terms of becoming a 'full profession'. On the other hand, this model should not be confined to a single profession and this is even more necessary during transition from one social system to another, because the social requirements for the teacher and his/ her profession are extremely high.

In the period of transition from totalitarian to democratic society and models of development, new expectations and requirements for education, schools and teachers have appeared, all of them being regarded as significant factors in social transformation and change. The need for this reconfirmation of the importance of teachers, schools and education in periods of transformation in the development of transition countries is reinforced by the challenges of the twenty-first century, when the educational picture is expected to be extremely diverse. For instance, it is possible to predict:

— greater heterogeneity in the school population (a wider range of abilities, interests and backgrounds in the classroom);
— explosive growth in the quantity of information, and hence of curriculum content;
— competition from alternative sources of information, especially the mass media, which may convey contradictory values;
— the introduction of new teaching methods at school, especially resulting from the advent of the new information and communication technologies;
— the opening up of the school to the outside world, which will confront teachers with a variety of expectations and conflicting judgements.[13]

The teaching profession possesses all the basic features of a 'full' profession, despite some specific features that characterize it. It provides a service which is *fundamental* to society because everybody attends school. Being a successful teacher depends to a great extent upon the degree of developed intellectual skills attained during the process of specialized training required by the profession. Teachers are autonomous, although their autonomy—as with any autonomy—is specifically limited.

Teachers have been assigned a high degree of responsibility because society relies on them for the education and training of children. Teachers have, on their part, assumed responsibility for the well-being of all children.

Teaching, like any other profession, has self-governing bodies. A code of ethics regulating professional behaviour is not an unfamiliar thing among teachers and very often manifests itself as 'common sense'. This does not mean that its importance as a regulator should be underestimated.

B. Certain myths about the teaching profession

Although everyone who is committed to the teaching profession needs no persuasion that it is a fully recognized one, we would like to point out the existence of certain myths that erode its image. The implications of these myths can be encountered in almost all Central and Eastern European countries.

It is a Myth that *the teacher is born for the profession* and his/her education and training therefore take less time compared to other professions. This myth is grounded in the belief that anyone who is preparing to become a teacher will have learned everything they need to know during their own formal education and training. Some people tend to forget that teachers never stop learning and that lifelong education in all its forms, as well as in-service training, are essential. Learning to teach is a lifelong process.

Another 'Myth' is the idea that *teachers have very little freedom and seldom take part in decision-making concerning their profession.* In fact, teachers enjoy a vast amount of work-place autonomy and, despite all ideas to the contrary, make decisions everyday—decisions for the whole class or the individual student, decisions on curriculum design, etc. (In Poland, 30 % of the school curriculum is designed by teachers themselves). This makes them unique decision-makers, mainly on instructional matters.

We should point out here an issue of extreme importance—the levels of professional autonomy and decision-making. It is not a myth that teachers' participation in major decisions concerning them is minimal. Nor is it a myth that teachers feel more like technicians than actual decision-makers and professionals; involvement in educational policy making has been symbolic and is hardly ever carried out.

Contemporary events have brought about changes in the teacher's expectations in terms of their active participation in decision-making at higher levels of the administration and in taking initiatives in a context of broad professional autonomy. In other words, teachers should be encouraged and given access to the government of the teaching profession. This is one way of raising their status in society and especially in transition countries. The need for renovation, with the active participation of those who educate future generations, is an imperative exercise in the times we live in.

Another 'Myth' is the statement that *the teaching profession has no code of ethics* as, for example, is found among doctors and lawyers. The professional code of ethics is present 'behind the scenes' and has its impact not only on the quality of the services but also on the behaviour of teachers, both in and outside the institutional relations involving them. The social expectations and imperatives of the type *'He is a teacher and is obliged to do that'* or *'He is a teacher and therefore must never do that'* are sometimes far stronger than those placed on doctors and lawyers. The teacher always re-mains a teacher, even in the day-to-day social conscience.

It is not a myth, however, that in Central and Eastern European countries, where the role of teachers and the expectations placed on them are becoming more complex, teachers and the teaching profession are underestimated. Their social value seems to be assessed in an ambivalent manner, which makes them feel isolated and underestimated. In other words, what teachers face is many obligations *versus* little attention and support.

Different studies made in Central and Eastern European countries since 1990 resolutely indicate that in many of them (with variations, but with no exceptions) teachers are said to be underestimated, isolated, neglected and rejected. This sad fact has had a negative impact on the professional code of ethics of teachers.

C. Contradictions of the teaching profession

The teaching profession displays a number of specific characteristics and contradictions, some of which are presented below (Bennet & Le Compte, 1990; Arrends, 1988).

A multi-dimensional character

The teaching profession includes a multitude of varied tasks. It is not limited to instruction and testing, to evaluation, to curricular and extra-curricular activities, or responding to children with special needs, or working in conjunction with parents. The teacher is all this and much, much more.

Simultaneity

In the teaching profession, many of the activities are complimentary and take place at one time. This kind of simul-taneity refers to both teachers and students. At any moment, different activities are being carried on simultane-ously.

Disparity

All teaching activities, including instruction, are 'patchy' and deprive the teacher of going into a subject in depth, of concentrating and focusing on a single issue or idea, on one student or on one aspect of the profession. The pre-arranged schedule of teachers and the pre-set order of their activities add to the lack of coherence in action and of immediate results.

Isolation

Isolation is both the great advantage and a drawback of the teaching profession, especially during instruction. Upon closing the classroom door, the teacher becomes 'sovereign'. Being strongly constrained in time and space, though, teachers have little opportunity to share their experience with colleagues and to compare themselves with others.

Unpredictability

Most events that relate to teachers and their profession are abrupt and unanticipated. Such events are very difficult to predict or are often not subject to forecasts.

Lack of tangible results

The teaching profession distinguishes itself from other professions in its cumulative nature. The results, including student achievement, are a product of the influence of many factors—the teacher being only one of them—are delayed in time and come to fruition far later than the actual efforts put into them.

D. The special features of teaching

The teaching profession requires an extremely high degree of involvement and self-commitment. Due to the very complex nature of the activities performed, the workload and the pressure of everyday communication with different groups of people—students, parents, administrators, representatives of the community, etc.—the teacher is constantly under stress and at the risk of 'burnout'.

The current changes in the modern school—an increase in the number of poorly motivated students; heterogeneous working conditions; parent and institutional pressure; the low status of the profession; the increasingly complex demands made upon it; discontent about the conditions for professional improvement; and inadequate salaries—make the teaching profession extremely stressful.

The reasons for stress and of 'burnout' can be sought in different directions (Le Compte, 1990; 1987), but the principal ones among them are the following:

— the gap between what teachers expect of the profession and the harsh reality encountered inside and outside the school. Beginning

teachers face stress from the administrative routine and school bureaucracy, and their lack of experience in coping with a multitude of tasks. As a rule, teachers are thoroughly prepared in the area of their subject, but very little or not at all prepared for working with different types of student, for conducting effective classroom control, for co-operating with parents, etc.;
— the on-going comparison with representatives of other professions in terms of career, opportunities for promotion, working conditions and salaries;
— the many-sided, even conflicting, expectations placed on the teacher by different groups of people;
— the lack of real control within the profession, connected with the feeling that the causes of dissatisfaction cannot be changed;
— a strongly female environment has a specific negative impact on working conditions;
— specific working conditions that lead to overload and exhaustion;
— frequent reforms and changes to the curriculum and subject matter;
— the risk of illness, such as chest complaints or nervous problems;
— the continuous raising of demands upon teachers, who receive little or no outside help or support.

This list is incomplete, since new factors appear and some old ones disappear. The factors mentioned in this list are, however, sufficient to give even a partial glimpse of the complex nature of the many factors causing stress and 'burnout' in the teaching profession.

Results from studies in almost all transition countries have been reporting low morale in the profession due to the factors listed above. Statistics from Bulgaria, the Russian Federation, Ukraine, etc., indicate that teachers are the group most exposed to illnesses of the nervous system or lung diseases. From this point of view and without exception, teachers occupy one of the lowest positions among professional groups specially monitored for health risks (in the Czech Republic—in group 10 out of fifteen groups, in Bulgaria—in group 14 out of fifteen groups). In some countries (Bosnia and Herzegovina, Croatia, the Russian Federation, Ukraine), teachers may have to wait for months to be paid.

IV. The Impact of New Information Technologies on Teaching

The teaching profession has been modified as a result of changes in education and society. For Central and Eastern European countries *two main lines of change* have been observed. On the one hand, they result from the political, economic, social and other transformations. On the other, they concern the challenges to teachers and their profession presented by the new century, which will be characterized by the major role to be played by high technology.

In Western European countries, the boundary between the industrialized and the high-technology society can be registered and assessed relatively accurately because the transition is being carried out peacefully and naturally. In Central and Eastern European countries, however, this 'boundary' is too vague and the transition too diffuse. For teachers and the teaching profession in these countries, the two lines of change co-exist and blend in a specific way compared to the Western European model. Teachers in transition countries are forced to destroy old stereotypes, to master new forms of professional adaptation and new standards of professional attitudes because they have been assigned an active role in the process of transition and in the establishment of new models of social development. On the other hand, they are obliged to be 'open' to the anticipated changes brought about by high technology and to the implications of the twenty-first century.

Stepping into the new era of information technology imposes the need to redefine teachers' roles. This has become more complex and demands specialized training and qualifications, which, in turn, lead to changing the paradigms of pre-service and in-service teacher training (in some Central and Eastern European countries the national standards for teacher education include special courses in new information technology—for example, in Bulgaria).

Teachers are no longer the only source of information for the students or, indeed, the most important one. What they are expected to be today is to serve as mediators between the students and varied sources of information and to act as counsellors and consultants. They are also responsible for organizing a proper environment for the personal development of each student and for stimulating the learning and learning-to-learn process, and thus being able to manage the impact of information effectively. Teachers also train their students and prepare them for work in the information technology environment, and yet preserve and value the essence of the one-to-one relationship. In other words, the *personal and professional mission of the teacher is reinforced.* The importance of teacher/student relations is further emphasized in working with computers, CD-ROMs, multi-media and other information technologies.

With the new information technologies entering education the teacher[14] will be able to:

— successfully prepare young people in terms of knowledge, skills and attitudes, for the challenges of the information century and the technological society.
— facilitate the adaptation of young people to the world of work, to the reality where advanced technological environments will be dominant and lifelong education will be based on technological advantages;
— educate students and develop their personality, not only as citizens within their own country, but as citizens of Europe and the world, and to develop their critical thinking and their skills to live in and further develop democracy.

Technological advancements in education and their use as teaching tools will lead to the internationalization of education, because making use of the new information and communication technologies means:

— mastering universal languages;
— becoming part of world technological advancement aimed at people's well-being;
— re-discovering the real value of person-to-person communication, of interpersonal relations in terms of sharing and caring, which has no analogy and cannot be replaced even by the most sophisticated media.

New information technologies are changing the world we live in and changing us as well. They demand changes in education and will assist teachers in changing themselves.

The role of teachers in an environment pervaded by information technology is altered with respect to their acting as organizer of the students' learning process, and teachers themselves becoming active learners. The school, as the place to learn, now implies active and interdependent relations between two types of learners—*the learner-student and the learner-teacher*.

These changes are tied to the need to reconceptualize the role of the school—seen as a learning environment in which *the teacher is a continuous learner* (Ryan & Cooper, 1988, etc.).

The introduction of new technologies in schools brings about:
— curricular effects; .
— instructional effects;
— social effects.

All of these affect the domain of change in the teacher's role. The prescribed scenarios stating that introducing new technology will lessen the role of the teacher and restrict the need for a teacher in the classroom does not seem likely to happen. There is enough evidence to prove the contrary. *New information technologies demand enhancing and strengthening the role of the teacher*.

An analysis of the processes of introducing new technology in education in the countries in transition shows *similarities* with other countries. Among them, the most significant are the following:

— *the curricular dimension*—new subjects are being introduced '(e.g. computer studies) mainly in secondary schools. Specialized education in mathematics and information technology is becoming widespread. Applied mathematics is becoming a larger component of the subject area. New extra-curricular activities are promoted with an emphasis on computer skills and computer literacy.

— *the instructional dimension*—teachers in various subjects are using computers in their work and thus enriching their instruction in terms of information, attractiveness and pupil motivation. Software packages for instructional purposes are being developed or introduced in many of the Central and Eastern European countries (Bulgaria, Croatia, the Czech Republic, Hungary, Poland, Romania, Slovenia).

— *the social dimension*—there is a noticeable change in students' attitudes.

Some of the specific features and difficulties encountered are:

— the need to introduce new technology or information technology precedes the degree of readiness on the part of the teachers and schools to adapt to it;
— there is a strongly expressed wish for the provision of computers in schools and very little concern about their effective use. If we were to compare the countries under discussion with Western European countries in terms of the provision of computers, it is likely that we would discover the number of computers in schools in Central and Eastern Europe (though not necessarily of the latest technology) to be greater than that in Western countries. An important finding would also be that the computers available are not being used effectively;
— teachers for the most part still prefer traditional teaching methods, including the 'chalk and talk' paradigm. Teacher qualification and training is far from adequate for working with the new technological environment;
— there is unevenness in the provision of computers or modern technology in schools—while some schools benefit from this technology, others do not. ('Technology discrimination', Ryan & Cooper.) Schools in villages are for the most part deprived of computer facilities;
— there is unequal application of modern technology and training in its use in different parts of these countries. Due to constant financial problems, schools and teachers cannot equally benefit from the advantages of information technology.

V. The Social and Demographic Characteristics of Teachers

A. The number of teachers

The teaching profession is one of the largest. This fact needs no explanation, given the need of society to educate all its children and the implication to provide compulsory schooling. The number of years of compulsory schooling varies and in transition countries it is within the range of eight to ten years.

With the change in the number of years of compulsory schooling, it is only natural that the number of teachers will change, being influenced by many other determinants, like the birth-rate, student/ teacher ratios, time allocated for each subject in the curriculum, etc.

A decrease in the number of teachers entering pre-school education[15] has been observed in almost all countries, and the greatest reduction is reported in Poland and Bulgaria. This trend remains stable. Since 1992, there have been even more countries where pre-school educational establishments and the number of teachers in them have decreased. Among the main reasons worth mentioning are the following:

— a steady decline in the birth-rate in transition countries. In some countries (e.g. Bulgaria, Moldova, the Russian Federation, etc.) the number of pregnancy terminations exceeds the number of births: Moldova[16]—100 births vs. 110 pregnancy terminations; Bulgaria[17]—41.5 births *vs.* 52.4 pregnancy terminations per 1,000 women;
— budgetary reductions for education, including pre-schools;
— the non-compulsory character of pre-school education;
— high unemployment and the increasing impoverish-ment of people.

As far as the number of teachers at the first level is concerned,[18] transition countries show different trends. Teachers in Armenia, Belarus, the Czech Republic, Romania, the Russian Federation, Ukraine, etc., have increased in number since 1990, whereas their number has decreased in Bulgaria, Poland, etc. (until 1992).

The reasons for this can be found in the changes of birth-rate levels—for example, in the Russian Federation the birth-rate during 1987-89 and the transition to four-year elementary school has led to an increase in the number of students, teachers and schools. Since then, there has been a decrease due to a declining birth-rate during 1990-93 and various other structural and content changes—in the teacher/student ratio, in the curriculum, etc.

As far as teachers at the second level are concerned, there has been a significant increase in the last few years, evident in Armenia, Bulgaria, Hungary, Poland, Romania, etc. In some countries, there has even been an increase in the number of students and teachers in general education and a decrease in vocational education. In countries where the pre-service training of teachers for the pre-school level is carried out within secondary education, the number of teachers and students in those establishments has decreased (the Czech Republic, Poland, the Russian Federation and Slovakia). An interesting exception is observed in Romania where there has been an increase in the number of teachers trained outside the university system.

Examining the reasons, we can draw attention to the following:

- the changed role of education and its social significance as an conomic value (in all transition countries);
- the extension of the network and variety of schools at the second level, including private schools. In many countries (Moldova, Poland, Romania, the Russian Federation, Ukraine, etc.) new types of schools are being opened—lyceums, colleges, grammar schools—which provide greater job opportunities. Some countries (e.g. Poland) have created schools run by non-governmental organizations.

B. Sex differences

A comparative analysis of the available data (incomplete and not presented in detail due to lack of reliable sources) on the socio-demographic characteristics of teachers in transition countries shows *a very stable tendency towards feminization of the profession at all levels.* Compared to the tendency of feminization worldwide (57% of women teachers at the first level; 45% of women teachers at the second level), in Europe in general we are confronted with higher figures:[19] 1991-77 per cent women at the first level and 59 per cent at the second level.

In all Central and Eastern European countries (where the data exist, mainly up to 1992), the profession at pre-school level is almost totally feminized. Figures show 100 per cent feminization in Albania, Bulgaria, the Czech Republic, Estonia, Hungary, Romania, the Russian Federation; and for Slovenia—98 per cent, the former Yugoslav Republic of Macedonia—97 per cent, Yugoslavia—94 per cent. This is a tendency which is common for Western European countries as well and feminization of the teaching profession at this level is also almost total.

The almost total feminization at this level supports the sterile and traditional concept about the profession being a typical 'women's profession'. Such a stereotyped view of the teaching profession reflects unfavourably on its image.

In some countries (e.g. the Russian Federation), there is a tendency towards regarding pre-school establishments more and more as educational ones, rather than traditional child-care institutions. This kind of orientation can bring a more precise differentiation to the role and functions of teachers at this level.

The sex structure of teachers at the first level also shows clearly expressed trends towards feminization, though the figures are lower compared with pre-school data. In all analysed countries, the teaching profession at this level has been feminized and the range in figures is between 55 per cent for Albania (1990) and 92 per cent for Slovakia and Slovenia (1992). Feminization of the teaching profession at this level is also high in the Czech Republic—83 per cent (1994, OECD data).

At the second level, OECD data are also significant. Within this level, some differences can be noticed. Feminization has a higher trend in general comprehensive schools and this tendency is clearly seen in the countries with available data. The highest figures are for the Baltic States—Estonia, 83 per cent; Latvia, 76 per cent (1992).

Feminization in vocational schools is relatively low, but over the last few years it has been growing. In the Czech Republic, for example, from 39 per cent in 1991, it has gone up to 56 per cent in 1994 (OECD data, 1994). In Bulgaria, Slovakia and Slovenia feminization in 1992 reached 55-56 per cent. We may then conclude that there is a better balance in the sex structure in vocational schools.

The teacher is a major factor in the process of socialization of young people and feminization of the profession can distort young people's notions. Furthermore, it can underline stereotyped views about the teaching profession being a woman's profession, therefore reducing the chances of men being attracted to it. A vicious circle is what we see in reality—men are very reluctant to enter the teaching profession. Vacant teaching posts for men in schools are being taken over by women which leads to high rates of feminization. This again creates further grounds for the impression that men are being 'pushed out', thus leaving the field of education 'reserved' for women only.

Strengthening the role of the teaching profession in modern societies needs active participation by both men and women in the transformation process. The unprecedented rates of feminization should be regarded not only as a phenomenon inside the profession and, as a consequence, in education, but as a broader phenomenon with greater social implications.

C. Age structure

The age structure of teachers also calls for special analysis. Constant throughout Europe is *the ageing of the teachers.* In half of the observed European countries (both Eastern and Central, and West European coun-tries), the principal primary education teachers age group is 30-39. Exceptions are primary school-teachers in Romania where the largest number are between 20 and 29 years old. This tendency is illustrated by Table 3.

Table 3 : The age structure of teachers in the Czech Republic (%)

	below 24	25-29	30-39	40-49	50-59	60 and above
Total	3.7	11.7	30.0	27.3	21.5	5.8
Male	1.9	8.4	24.2	22.6	29.2	13.7
Female	4.2	12.5	31.5	28.3	19.6	3.9

In Bulgaria the data shows marked ageing of teachers. In the Russian Federation more than half of the teachers have more than twenty years of teaching practice, which is further evidence of ageing among teachers.

The weak process of renovation in the teaching profession is closely connected with the negative flow of young people into it. Some of the young people who have already entered the profession are constantly seeking ways out of it and looking for job opportunities elsewhere. The older teachers, on the other hand, remain firmly rooted in the profession. The chances of a mid-career change are very limited for them.

D. Job opportunities in education

There is a widespread opinion that education and schools offer only a single-career pattern—that of a teacher. Careful analysis of the profile of educational institutions and the activities typical for them reveals the existence of a great diversity and a broad variety of jobs.

By way of example, in Hungary[21] and Lithuania[22] the various teaching posts are:

Hungary—pre-schoolteacher, primary school-teacher, subject teacher, art teacher, youth-care teacher, speech therapist, psychologist, guidance teacher, etc.

Lithuania—pre-school teacher, elementary teacher, subject teacher, vocational teacher, vocational lecturer, special education teacher, social pedagogue, ethnic minority school-teacher, etc.

In other countries (e.g. Bulgaria), several new occupations have been introduced—career adviser, psychologist, pedagogue, assistant teacher—and although they are not 'purely' teaching jobs, their job description makes provision for the occupant to benefit from teacher's rights.

In Croatia, the Czech Republic, Poland, Romania and Slovenia the 'display' of job opportunities inside the teaching profession is also quite wide, thus broadening the potential opportunities for more job options.

A comparative overview on the options in teaching indicates that Central and Eastern European countries exhibit a widening of the career patterns by adding new posts in education, inside and outside teaching. But, without any doubt, practice varies in different countries and is not subject to direct comparison.

With the emergence of the private sector in education the opportunities to find more job options increase (the data from the Czech Republic, Hungary, Poland, etc. show rapid growth of the private sector in education). The impact on job opportunities, however, is not very great and the likelihood of getting a job in the State sector still prevails.

The rate of broadening of the career pattern horizontally and vertically is still very slow compared to those in Western European countries, where there is a greater variety of opportunities. Promotion schemes for teachers vary to a certain extent, but educational level, acquired qualification and the length of service determine promotion in most cases.

As far as available working places in education are concerned, some of the countries in transition have reported existing vacancies (Armenia, Azerbaijan, Bulgaria, the Czech Republic, Moldova, Poland, the Russian Federation, Slovakia, Ukraine, etc.). In the Russian

Federation, for example, the percentage of unfilled posts is as follows, given that teacher provision for the school year 1994/95 is higher than that of the previous years:23 1990–3.2 per cent; 1991–3.3 per cent; 1992–2.9 per cent; 1993–3.0 per cent; 1994–2.7 per cent.

In Poland 4.3 per cent of full-time teachers are lacking teacher qualifications (9.3 per cent—basic vocational schools; 6.4 per cent secondary and post-secondary vocational schools; 3.9 per cent—primary schools) for 1995.

In the Czech Republic (OECD report, 1995), 7 per cent of primary teachers are unqualified and are equal to the number of employed pensioners in the profession. In the same country, about 45 per cent of foreign-language teachers are unqualified—a fact that raises the question of the quality of teaching staff, as much as about the potential number of qualified teachers required. In the countries compared, the greatest demand is for foreign-language teachers (Central European countries, Romania, Bulgaria, ex-Soviet countries, etc.), for mother-tongue teachers, mathematics teachers, informatics teachers, etc. It is very disturbing to note the lack of qualified teachers in rural areas.

This professional group as a whole is not in any danger of losing jobs compared to other categories. In the Czech Republic, for example, teachers represent 0.8 per cent of the total unemployed. In Bulgaria, unemployment among teachers is relatively rare. A more typical phenomenon for education is unfilled vacancies, not unemployment.

Within the education systems of transition countries, non-certified teachers are very often recruited for posts vacated by retired teachers or for newly created posts. In some countries (e.g. Central Europe, Bulgaria, etc.), where after recent changes Russian was no longer a compulsory subject in schools, retraining programmes for Russian-language teachers have been launched. This kind of measure proved insufficient to solve the problems of the great demand for foreign-language teachers. In Poland, for example, coping with the problem has accelerated the setting up of three-year teacher-training colleges for foreign-language teachers.

Vacancies in education exist due to:

- — low salaries and low attractiveness of the teaching profession for people with degrees in foreign languages, informatics, etc., because they can easily find jobs in other, highly paid, sectors;
- — limited promotion opportunities compared with other sectors;

— unattractive working conditions, especially in rural areas, including transport difficulties, lack of adequate teaching materials, remote locations, etc. Another typical phenomenon in these countries is teachers who work in two or three shift schools (in the Russian Federation, 35 per cent of the schools have two or more shift schedules).
— changes in the curriculum and the introduction of new subjects without a sufficient number of teachers trained to teach them.

E. Social status of the teaching profession

Despite variations in the Central and Eastern European countries, *the teaching profession still has a relatively low social status.* This is confirmed by the results of various studies among teachers and other professional groups, by the results of sociological studies, ministerial analyses, etc.

There is a clearly expressed internal differentiation of prestige in the teaching profession. Teachers in lower grades have lower status than their colleagues at higher levels. For the higher levels, even the term 'teacher' is not used; 'professor' is the appropriate term (the Czech Republic, Poland, Romania, etc.). Taken as a whole, the image of the teacher has been seriously damaged in this way.

This phenomenon should not be attributed to the present period, but during the transition it has become extremely acute due to the ups and downs of social developments, and the growing bitterness among teachers about the underestimation of their problems—the problem of the low status of the teaching profession making worse the problems of education as a whole.

In Central and Eastern European countries the following *paradox is observed. In these countries, education is stated to be among national priorities but is not actually receiving priority financing.*

In almost all transition countries teachers' salaries are lower than salaries in other sectors, in spite of the rise in salaries since 1990, which, however, are constantly eroded by inflation.

In most Central and Eastern European countries *no special policy for guidance and encouraging youth to choose the teaching profession* exists (there are some exceptions—Poland, for instance).

Societies seem to be ambivalent in their expectations and evaluations of the teaching profession. In this respect, a serious gap between intended and real policy is observed, which is reflected on the teaching profession and demoralizes the teachers.

The available data, concerning both general entrance to higher education and entrance to the teaching specialities, though gathered in a non-systematic manner, shows that in most countries under analysis the number of applicants for teaching specialities is either growing irregularly or decreasing. In some countries, people are streaming out of higher education (in Moldova the number of universities is growing while the number of university students is decreasing). Ukraine also shows a decrease of applicants for universities: 1990—205,000; 1993—148,000; and at higher technical institutes: 1990—191,000; 1993—172,000. In Azerbaijan there is a similar phenomenon and the number of university graduates has decreased: 1993—18,000; 1994—16,098.

But in the Russian Federation there is a totally different trend. University applicants are increasing in number. Particularly in the teacher-training institutes, 2.4 applicants competed in 1995 for each place, which is more than in 1994. The total number of students at tertiary level has also increased. The quality of applicants has increased and applicants with higher academic levels are entering teaching specialities.

In Central European countries the number of students at tertiary level is also increasing steadily. Only in Slovakia there is very little increase, which became evident after 1992.

Bulgaria presents an unusual picture for the academic year 1995/96: 70 per cent of secondary school-leavers were admitted to university or higher education institutes. This increase is rather large for 'paid' higher education.

In the Czech Republic, the demand for higher education and teacher-education faculties is several times greater than the places available at this level (OECD report, 1995).

Although we may view the cases of an increase of university students as: (a) further democratization of the higher education system; (b) the opening up of the system of higher education both in response to social demands and to individual preferences; (c) greater participation in education, therefore in the changes in society, etc.; this trend is not typical for all analysed countries, even more so because teacher education does not only take place at the higher education level.

One possible explanation for the low status of pre-school and primary school teachers, and the unattractive image of their profession, is linked to the traditionally established model of pre-school teacher education in a number of transition countries during the period before 1989 (in Belarus, the Czech Republic, Moldova, the Russian Federation, Ukraine, etc.), which relegates it to institutions outside higher education.

The duration of teacher preparation in these institutes is usually two or three years, the academic level is lower compared to university education and training focuses mainly on practical aspects of the profession. The comparison between the training of pre-school or primary-school teachers and secondary-school teachers at university level does not favour the first group of teachers. Maintaining this training model today adds to the stereotyped image about the teaching profession as lacking the characteristics of a 'full profession'.

By way of analogy, a factor of influence on the status of teachers and the image of the teaching profession is their role as intermediaries (Hoyle, 1989, etc.) between the interests of the State or society and the students or their parents. The role, thus assigned, does not allow autonomy within the profession, as is the case with other professions, and the teachers are regarded merely as 'deliverers of the State curriculum'. .

To upgrade the status of teachers and the image of the teaching profession, a number of countries have adopted the model of either directly including the pre-service training of pre-school and primary school-teachers into university level education or associating it with university education (the case of teacher-training colleges in Poland, the Czech Republic, etc.). This model aims at raising the academic level of pre-school and primary school teacher training, therefore, placing it closer to that of secondary school-teachers. It also allows for a higher degree of academic expertise in mastering the subject matter.

Another measure undertaken by the countries in transition is the emphasis laid upon the significance of the professional development of teachers, which is seen as a factor in further raising their status. Enriching professional skills, extending career patterns for horizontal or vertical promotion (in Bulgaria, for example, a network of foreign-language teacher-trainers has been created)—these are only some of the concrete actions taken. In conditions of considerable expansion of the role of the teacher, raising the status of teachers is an extremely important part of educational policy. This would imply influence on the processes, connected with the political and social changes with the aim of making a successful transition to democracy.

Taking into consideration all the different indicators influencing the status of the teaching profession, we can confirm the hypothesis that it is not sufficiently high and special measures are required to raise its level. Some of the measures taken so far have proved insufficient and ineffective. The Report of the Joint ILO-UNESCO Committee of Experts on the Application of the Recommendation concerning the Status of Teachers, Geneva, 1994, underlines the need for urgent action to raise the status of teachers and of the teaching profession. In our recommendations, we attempt to suggest such strategies and actions.

F. Working conditions: recruitment, probation year, induction

The teachers' employer is the principal of the school and the school is, through legislative regulations, a legal entity in most Central and Eastern European countries. Cases where the employer is different are specifically mentioned in normative acts which differ for each country. Still another difference lies in the principal's freedom to select teachers.

The school principal is appointed in two main ways: centralized or decentralized, and the most frequent method applied is the centralized one. The requirements for principals vary in different countries. While in the Czech Republic, the requirements are for seven years of experience in the profession and successful performance in a competition for the post, in Bulgaria, the requirement for professional experience in the field has been lowered to two or three years, due to the large number of vacant posts—over 900 in 1995. Principals are also appointed through competition, for the post. The terms of appointment for principals also differ—from temporary to permanent appointment.

Typical of all analysed countries is the practice of keeping the requirements for, teacher appointment very 'nebulous', which can be witnessed by the large number of unqualified teachers in schools; in other words, control over entrance to the profession is rather vague due to the reasons already mentioned.

The system of a probation year and the system of induction for beginning teachers (Vonk; 1994) is not well developed in Central and Eastern European countries. In some countries, the system existed several decades ago and was subsequently abolished.

The lack of a system of specifically developed measures and the non-existence of mentors (tutors) is compensated by other measures, such as a system where the amount of time spent on concrete work at school as teaching practice or compulsory teaching experience before certification (not after) can also be regarded as a kind of probation, though its real meaning is not the same as traditional probation and induction.

There are grounds to view temporary teacher appointment (one or more years) as another substitute (a distorted equivalent) of probation. Sadly, permanent teacher appointment is not in any way connected with the development and implementation of a specific policy for teacher encouragement and support, or the monitoring and registering of their progress and difficulties—factors which constitute the essence of probation.

In some countries in transition the period of probation is applied not only to newly qualified teachers, but to teachers who often change schools. In the latter case, the period of probation can be used rather as a measure of 'rejecting' unsuitable teachers (i.e. an eliminatory strategy) rather than as assistance to beginning teachers (a constructivist strategy).

In Romania, administrative provision has been made for temporary teachers that can be interpreted as induction. In Slovenia, there exists an already developed and implemented induction system. Provision is made for specialized training courses and professional support during the first year (by appointing mentors, etc.).

G. Pupil/teacher ratio and the teachers' workload

A characteristic trend in Central and Eastern European countries is a decrease in the pupil/teacher ratio (see Table—4). However, it would be premature to interpret this trend only from its positive aspect, i. e. improving the working conditions in terms of teaching. Behind this tendency there obviously ties the decreasing number of students, due to the circumstances already explained, but one of the serious reasons for the decrease is connected with the artificial retainment of part of the present teaching force in villages or remote rural areas. Problems with schools and teachers resulting from dramatic falls in the number of pupils in such regions have been reported from almost all countries. In the Ukraine,[24] for example, there has been a radical fall in the birth rate, mainly among village women. The problems with the so-called 'small complex' schools for most of the analysed countries are very grave and the policy of preventing their closure has influenced decision-making on the maintenance of both the schools and the teachers employed there. Usually, this implies a steady reduction of class size and the teacher's workload, as well as a parallel decrease in the pupil/teacher ratio, in some cases going to extremes, e.g. a teacher/pupil ratio of 1:5 or 6 or 7. In this case, *education performs its function of social protection of teachers but causes serious economic problems* which boomerang on the teachers and result in low salaries, difficulties in providing funding for minimal size classes, lack of teaching materials, etc.

The tendency to reduce the teacher's workload and maintain it at a lower level cannot be regarded as entirely positive, because it is not linked with an improvement in working conditions. It only protects teachers artificially against unemployment and has grave economic consequences.

Table 4 : The pupil/teacher ratio at the first level, 1992

Country	Pupil/Teacher ratio	Country	Pupil/Teacher ratio
Albania (1990)	19	FYR of Macedonia	20
Belarus	16	Moldova (1991)	18
Bulgaria	14	Poland (1994/95)	16.3
Croatia	19	Romania	21
Czech Republic (1994/95)	16	Slovakia	22
Hungary (1991)	12	Slovenia	18
Latvia	10	Ukraine	17

Source: UNESCO statistical yearbook, 1994; OECD reports; national sources.

H. Teachers' salaries

One of the most sensitive and on-going topics of discussion

concerns teachers' salaries. In the analysed countries, *teachers' salaries are considerably lower than salaries in other sectors.* Despite the salary rises awarded in all transition countries, the high rates of inflation have kept teachers among the least-monitored professional groups.

Data from a study carried out by Leclerq (1995)[25] indicates that in Hungary in 1990 salaries in education were 30 to 50 per cent lower than those in other sectors. In the Russian Federation, one-third of teachers have been forced to exist at survival level and salaries are 30 per cent lower than those in industry. In Romania, the average teacher's salary is US$80—almost the same as in Bulgaria.

By way of example, a comparative analysis (for 1994) on the average monthly rise in salaries in education and in other sectors of economy in the Russian Federation has shown educational salaries significantly lagging behind in the growth (Table—5). The same tendency is typical not only of the Russian Federation [26] but of the other countries as well.

Table 5: Average rise in salaries in education compared with salaries in other sectors, the Russian Federation, 1994 (January = 100%)

	Feb.	Mar.	Apr.	May	Jun.	Jul.	Aug.	Sep.	Oct.	Nov.	Dec.
Other sectors	**144.8**	**164.8**	**186.2**	**189.5**	**221.0**	**221.8**	**232.8**	**253.2**	**264.9**	**281.6**	**345.2**
Education	**114.8**	**127.7**	**125.8**	**139.9**	**150.5**	**150.5**	**144.3**	**178.1**	**194.7**	**195.5**	**216.9**

In Poland,[27] teachers are also in a low-paid group. The average salary in education has decreased by 66.7 per cent compared to 1989. In 1993, teachers' salaries represented only 70 per cent of the salaries in other sectors.

In Hungary,[28] a new salary scale has been introduced since 1994 based on qualification and length of service, resulting in a 20 per cent salary rise.

In the Ukraine,[29] the teachers' salary equals 81.4 per cent of the overall average wage in the State sector and, although in the mid-1990s teachers' salaries more than doubled, the rise has been constantly eaten up by inflation. Again in the Ukraine, 10 per cent of the teachers have left the education sector due to low salaries.

In Estonia,[30] five salary categories have been introduced among the teaching staff, the 'first category' being the highest. These categories are based upon teacher evaluation with indicators being taken into consideration, such as: the applicant's educational background; teacher training; length of service; teaching experience; and job performance.

In Azerbaijan,[31] there are still gender inequalities in payment; women receive 70 per cent of men's salaries.

In Bulgaria,[32] teachers' salaries, despite current rises, have remained significantly below salaries in other sectors. Among the fifteen groups categorized by economic activity, teachers remain in group 14 according to salary. Attempts have been made to move the teacher group up (to group 11) in the national classification.

Although growth in salaries has been stable in the Czech Republic,[33] and there is a relatively constant salary proportion amounting to 2 per cent of GNP, salaries in education still remain at 95 per cent of the average salary for the country. Among fifteen sectors observed by category of economic activity, average salaries in education are ranked in tenth place.

Extremely grave is the situation in Armenia, where the average teacher's salary equals US$5. In Armenia,[34] a new certification system is under preparation designed to ensure transition into a new system of teachers' salaries; only during the period 1 September to 15 October 1994 about 3,200 teachers left the education service.

The social situation of teachers is disastrous in terms of salary in those Balkan countries involved in military conflicts (e.g. Bosnia and Herzegovina, Croatia), where salaries have been replaced by consumer coupons. A similar picture can be observed in the Ukraine and some other countries.

The dissatisfactory picture outlined above can have irreversible consequences. Abandonment of the teaching profession or simply ignoring it as a career option is clearly visible in almost all analysed countries. The most commonly given reasons are financial and the greater career opportunities outside education.

I. Support for the teacher's professional development

Despite the very limited data concerning the design and support of social arrangements for the professional development of teachers, we may conclude that transition countries are favouring different kinds of establishments.

In Bulgaria, over the past four years, resource centres for foreign-language teachers have been set up in all major cities with the assistance of the British Council. The existing teacher centres (an establishment existing long before 1989) are undergoing reform and one of their future major activities envisages teachers' professional development.

In Poland,[35] pedagogical libraries have been growing intensively. The establishment of a network of 358 centres (forty-nine libraries at the *voivodstvo* administrative level and 309 affiliated centres) is a major accomplishment and can also be interpreted as a measure to stimulate teachers' professional development.

In a number of countries (Poland, Bulgaria, etc.) special centres for distance learning are being created with the active participation of non-governmental institutions, universities, etc. These are centres promoting the use of modern media in the classroom and are expanding a nationwide network.

In Estonia[36], in close co-operation with Finland, training centres being set up. They aim at compensating for the lack of a training tem for vocational teachers.

The teachers in the analysed countries are obtaining support through teachers' professional associations. Teachers are invited to join them on a voluntary basis.

Professional associations empower teachers, stimulate their self-awareness and belief in the social significance of their profession and encourage them to contribute their expertise when participating in decision-making. Such associations created on a professional basis are entitled to a vote in discussions and decision-making regarding changes in the curriculum and textbooks.

Teachers' unions deserve special attention. They were set up and functioned actively in the transition period in some countries (not all countries have reported the existence of teachers' unions). We could relate them to the organizations and associations which aim at teachers' professional development and support, but we should not overlook the special place they have in education. In some transition countries (Bulgaria, Poland, the Russian Federation, etc.) all teacher protection activities, including strikes, have been organized by the unions. In the Russian Federation, the first half of 1995 witnessed the greatest number of protest actions in favour of education, when compared with other countries.

The professional societies and associations, the organizations of subject teachers and teacher unions place different emphases on their varied activities. They are, however, always deeply concerned about teachers' welfare and the raising of their status, as well as the image of the teaching profession.

The activity of these organizations, though varying in scope and aims, is rather wide and includes:

— keeping teachers informed;
— sharing ideas and motivating teachers;
— helping members to learn more about teaching and governing the profession;
— achieving better working conditions;
— participating in collective bargaining;
— making teachers a more coherent professional group;
— making teachers feel more powerful and affiliated, etc.

It is very important for teachers to develop a sense of solidarity. That is why it is necessary for professional associations and organizations to stimulate teachers and to accelerate their activities. A sense of belonging to a single group makes teachers feel empowered. Unified models for the further development of professional associations and unions cannot be found in any Central and Eastern European countries. Their functions often overlap. Some teachers' unions focus mainly on syndicate problems. In their efforts to adopt modern European models of union structure, other unions, especially in Central Europe and Bulgaria, deal extensively with teachers' professional development. Still others are politically oriented.

Owing to the existing internal political and social contradictions in transition countries, the teachers' unions encounter problems of the following nature:

— undefined membership (not defining a clear scope of action);
— lack of co-ordination and co-operation;
— frequent inter-union conflicts;
— unsustained actions;
— lack of skill to participate in constructive discussions with government officials, etc.;

Some of the challenges[37] facing both teacher organizations (associations) and teacher unions are:

— limited sources of financial support;
— shortage of adequate skills;
— lack of outside understanding;
— lack of interrelations and co-ordination, etc.

Whatever the difficulties affecting teacher societies and unions, they will in the future be playing a considerably significant role and will become even more influential on professional grounds. Their activities should involve more teachers, thus giving them a chance for a stronger voice in their professional affairs. Of course, they could also play an anti-constructivist role, especially if they decide to 'leave' the professional domain of actions and become politically affiliated.

J. Evaluation of teachers

Without going into terminological explanations and disputable details, we would only mention that the problem of evaluation is not only a problem of the teachers themselves, but also a problem for the school, for education as a whole and, despite the fact that it is a crucial point, it has not yet been adequately resolved in the analysed countries.

There exist three basic models of teacher appraisal: inspectorial, 'peer review' and 'line management'. They have not been equally represented in the on-going process of evaluation in transition countries.

Traditionally, the *inspectorial model* has been widespread. Teachers are subject to inspection at different intervals. In spite of certain drawbacks—such as 'externally imposed' criteria, denying the teachers status as professionals, underlying the isolation of the teacher, etc. (Wilson[38], 1994)—this model is based on the officially recognized professional expertise and competence of evaluators and has been applied to a different extend in all transition countries. (Bulgaria, Croatia, the Czech Republic, Hungary, Poland, Slovakia, Romania, the former Soviet countries, etc.).

Line—management models are also traditionally represented, although in transition countries they can be further linked with that particular level of inter-school hierarchy in which the principal (or vice-principal) himself evaluates the teacher. This model has been applied in evaluating school principals as well, though at rarer intervals.

The line management model, applied as organizational and procedural evaluation of teachers 'from the inside' has advantages. It is based upon knowledge about a particular school and teachers, about the level of student achievement (performance), about the concrete conditions of work in the school. It allows more precise observations and registration (reflections about the progress and difficulties of the teachers, and current and effective measures to support them). It can also facilitate evaluation of teacher training needs and have an actual constructivist and stimulating function.

While the first mentioned model is more often connected with summative evaluation, the second one gravitates towards formative evaluation, though both are present in the second practice.

Peer review (management), in terms of evaluation at internal school level, has not been used extensively as an official evaluation procedure where evaluation results will be used for the promotion of teachers.

Whatever the model of evaluation, the purpose is to foster teacher's professional development, to define in clearer terms their in-service training needs and to monitor and register their progress. Regretfully, a 'left-over' of the old system of evaluation is fear and distrust towards appraisal and evaluation, especially when carried out at higher levels. It is believed that evaluation is not always performed with a positive attitude, hence the numerous complaints against concrete evaluations. For Central and Eastern European countries, *evaluation* (not only teacher evaluation) could be subject to further perfection. The problem of quality control in close relation with evaluation has not been satisfactory solved.

In different countries evaluation includes different numbers of summative and formative elements. For example, in Estonia evaluation of teachers registers their job performance. In the Czech Republic special emphasis is laid upon teacher accountability.

There is a noticeable orientation to evaluate teachers by their students' achievements, ignoring the fact that achievement is a result of many factors. The teacher is only one factor, although undoubtedly very influential, and the significance of this factor should not be overestimated.

The clear tendency towards performance-based evalua-tion[39] requires teacher's evaluation within the context of :

— the instructional process;
— classroom management;
— interpersonal relationships; and
— professional responsibilities.

Although this orientation of evaluation is observed in transition countries, consensus has not yet been reached as to what should be evaluated in the teacher. Evaluation usually takes place in an instructional context. Emphasis is mainly placed on one side of the professional role of the teacher (instruction). Underestimation of the last two elements has been observed.

VI. Teacher Education and Training :
Challenges and Changing Patterns

One of the key areas in the changes taking place in education is related to teacher training models. If teachers are not offered education and training adequate to the new reality, they will not be able to participate effectively in the changes taking place. *Active participation in the changes happening in today's world with a view to the world of tomorrow is an essential issue.* Contemporary teacher education and training will enable teachers to recognize their new mission and responsibilities when facing the challenges both of the transition to democracy and of the twenty-first century.

As with other dimensions of the teaching profession, teacher education and training in the analysed countries shows as many similarities as differences, irrespective of the unified models inherited from the period prior to 1989.

A. The structure of teacher education: achievements and failures

A comparative analysis of the systems of teacher education and training in transition countries draws some interesting lines of development and tendencies; there have been *significant structural changes* and the emergence of new establishments (Bulgaria, the Czech Republic, Poland, the Russian Federation), alongside elements dating from the period before 1989 that have been retained. Innovation is especially true for the teachers choosing career opportunities in pre-school or primary school education (Bulgaria, the Czech Republic, Moldova, the Russian Federation, Slovakia, Ukraine). *The main trends are:*

— an effort to create a multi-level structure within teacher education and training (the Russian Federation, etc.);
— enlarging the number of teacher education institutions by providing it in higher technical universities, academies and newly set-up colleges;
— the creation of international universities and other establishments for teacher education and training (Bulgaria, Poland, the Russian Federation, etc.);
— fostering the role of non-governmental institutions in teacher training;
— a lack of real planning based on the need for teachers, which is demonstrated by noticeable teacher shortages.

The Central and Eastern European countries are swaying between two extremes. In the past, all university graduates had an equal chance of receiving certificates for the teaching profession because pedagogy, psychology and methodology were a compulsory part of university (or higher education) courses. Exceptions were confined to the 'purely scientific' or applied specialities, e.g. nuclear physics, bio-technology, etc. Now teacher qualification is provided only for those students who take elective courses in psychology, pedagogy, methodology, etc. Thus, with no factual study of the demands for teachers and inflexibility on the part of universities to respond to these demands, all the pre-requisites are present for a deficiency of one type of teacher and an excess of another type. In other words, the democratic principle of free choice by the student is not always compatible with market research on teacher demand.

B. The content of teacher education and training

The minimum required areas have been agreed upon for teacher education and training—psychology, pedagogy and methodology. These have recently been enlarged to include such subject areas as sociology, communication, etc. However, with the academic autonomy of universities and higher education institutes, there has emerged a trend towards underestimating teacher education and training with regard to psychological and pedagogical knowledge and favouring subject training.

There has been an increase in the number of courses offered, including teacher qualification courses. In the Russian Federation, for example; new areas of teacher training have been introduced—social pedagogy, applied psychology, ecology, economics, political studies, cultural studies, etc. There has also been expansion in teacher training programmes (in Slovenia, over 600 programmes have been submitted by seventy contributors for 1993/94).

Teacher education has been reformed with respect to creating new types of teachers (e.g. Estonia).

In teacher education theory is still dominant and academic skills and knowledge are favoured, compared with practical skills. All countries report a lack of practical training, which is quite insufficient.

The concept of lifelong education has not yet been sufficiently applied in teacher education, although serious steps have been taken in respect of the professionalization of teacher training. Nevertheless, there is still room for the illusion that everything teachers need to know in their future job can be learned at the university.

The development of positive attitudes towards the teaching profession is still underestimated. The significance of the four types of teacher attitudes—attitude towards self, attitude towards children; attitude towards parents and peers; attitude toward subjects—is often overlooked.[40] These attitudes in different blends form the 'effective teacher', building up a feeling towards the profession.

C. Organization of teacher education and training

The special selection of applicants for teacher qualification courses (specialities) is almost absent, with the exception of countries like the Czech Republic, Bulgaria, Poland, Romania, etc., where special selection for pre-school teachers and elementary school-teachers is still in practice.

In a great number of countries *training of school principals and other educational management staff is regrettably neglected.*

Elsewhere, in Bulgaria, the Czech Republic, Poland, Romania, the Russian Federation and Ukraine; the training of one and the same category of teachers is provided at different levels (at the university level or at a lower level)

Changes within the system of teacher education and the innovation processes take place slowly and lag behind changes in other areas of education. There is an impression of conservativeness and inertia in the system of teacher education and training.

D. The choice of teaching as a profession

A comparative review, of national reports from transition countries, as well as various studies related to the choice of teaching as a profession, reveal a *typical picture* far most of them, which has the following features:

— in only a few countries is special emphasis laid upon promoting, teaching as a profession (in the Russian Federation, the new core of psychological and pedagogical disciplines offers three modules, one of which is career guidance; in Poland, teaching career guidance is provided through institutional activities which are directed toward systematic presentation of psychological and pedagogical knowledge to the students and organizing practical sessions which are conducive to operational application of this knowledge in school situations);

— the teaching profession is not chosen by the best students or applicants (Armenia, the Baltic states; Bosnia and Herzegovina, Bulgaria, Moldova, Poland, Slovakia, Ukraine; etc.). This fact poses severe questions about the quality of future teachers. Exceptions, among many others, are Azerbaijan; the Russian Federation, Slovenia, where 'teaching positions are given only to exceptional graduates as there is a large pool of trained teachers[41].

— special selection for teacher specialities is not carried out at tertiary level (with the exception of pre-school and primary school-teacher selection in Bulgaria, the Czech Republic, Poland, Slovakia, etc.). In these countries, traditional entry examinations, psychological tests or speaking tests are also administered.

E. Teacher education institutions

The great diversity of institutions of teacher education and training is evident[42] in all countries in transition.

The secondly school teacher-education pattern

In a large number of Central and Eastern European countries, pre-school teachers are still trained at the upper secondary level (the Czech Republic, Moldova, Romania, the Russian Federation, Slovakia, Ukraine, etc.). In Poland, this type of establishment has recently been closed, as in Bulgaria. At present, there are some new experimental forms of profiled classes in secondary schools for training assistant teachers. In Romania, for example, 74 per cent of the pre-school teachers are being trained in pedagogical lyceums.

The post-secondary teacher education pattern

In a number of countries in transition, teacher education and training at semi-higher institutes have been maintained (a pattern that existed before 1989) and offer courses for pre-school and primary school-teachers-e.g. Bulgaria. In Slovakia, training of the same category of teachers is offered at two-year post-secondary schools. In Estonia, teacher-training colleges for primary and music teachers function at this level. In the Russian Federation, there are 362 secondary special training educational establishments—277 vocational schools and 85 colleges. The number of colleges has increased two-fold since 1992. The number of students at vocational schools and colleges has decreased.

The university teacher education pattern

Within the structure of this pattern there are also evident differences between countries. Teacher education and training exist in several variations in higher education establishments:

— traditional universities (in all countries);

— pedagogical, universities (Belarus; Bulgaria, Estonia Moldova, Romania, the Russian Federation, Ukraine, etc.). In the Russian Federation, after restructuring the system of teacher education and training, twenty-eight pedagogical institutes were given the status of universities;

— higher education pedagogical schools (Poland, etc);

— other institutions of higher education (technical universities, academies, etc.).

Within these patterns, especially at university level, there are differences due to their organizational structure:

— teacher education and training in faculties of education (for primary and other teachers) exist in former Soviet countries, as well as in Bulgaria, Romania and some Central European countries;

— teacher education and training at colleges for teacher education forming part of universities (in the Czech Republic, Poland);

— teacher education and training at other faculties in universities (subject-based training in these faculties). The faculties of education ensure courses in psychology, pedagogy, etc.

Unconventional patterns

There are teacher's universities broadcast on the radio and television (Bulgaria, Poland). Distance education centres have been established (Bulgaria, Poland).

F. Curricular patterns

Comparative analyses of the countries in transition from the point of view of the content of the programmes for teacher education and training also show *great variety. The common part in these programmes concerns.*

— studies in the educational sciences (psychology, pedagogy, sociology, management, etc.);

— subject based studies (depending on the chosen speciality). There is a trend towards education and training in two specialities at university level (the Czech Republic, the Russian Federation; Slovakia).

— subject methodology;

— teaching practice.[43]

The established pattern of teacher education and training in two specialities was, until recently, more typical for the post-secondary education model. It enlarges the job opportunities and responds more adequately to the needs of the 'small schools' where one teacher may have to teach two or more subjects.

The time allocated for the study of the different components of the programme is different, not only among the analysed countries but inside the countries, because this depends largely on where teacher education and training take place. In Poland, for example, the teacher education standard envisages 90 hours of psychology, 90 hours of pedagogy and 120 hours of subject methodology.

In the case of Bulgaria, it is worth mentioning that national standards for teacher education and training have been developed (Decree of the Council of Ministers, 1995), which envisage 60 hours of pedagogy, 60 hours of psychology, 60 hours of new information technology, 120 hours of subject methodology. The theoretical module comprises all these and is added to a practical module containing 150 hours. Some universities are not ready to accept this standard. As mentioned above, due to academic autonomy teacher education and training are underestimated in their psychology-pedagogy dimension. Some universities even go to extreme reductions of time envisaged for these important areas of knowledge. This trend can be observed particularly in the Czech Republic and Bulgaria.

G. The structure of programmes for teacher education and training

Training programmes have various structures and are based on different organizational models:

— *concurrent model,* where all components of teacher training are run in parallel (subject based training, psychology and pedagogy courses, subject methodology, etc.). The combinations between these disciplines also differ;

— *consecutive model*—the component courses are taken only after subject matter training has been completed. In transition countries, different combinations are again in evidence. This model is typical for secondary school-teacher education and training;

— *integrated model* (interrelation and integration of theoretical and practical training), which are typical of pre-school and primary school-teacher education and training;

— *modular model* (encountered in Central European countries, Bulgaria, the Russian Federation, etc.). In Russia, the new core of psychology and pedagogy disciplines includes three modules: orientation module, theoretical and methodology module, and activity module.

— *distance model* (a new type for all countries in transition)—has been established in Bulgaria, Poland, etc.

All of these models exist in the countries undergoing transition, but their implementation depends upon the national traditions and the new priorities recently set up.

H. The duration of teacher education and training

The duration of teacher education and training depends not only on the national model, but also on the type of schools existing within the education system.

The span is between two and five years almost everywhere. For example:

— *pre-school and primary teacher programmes* have a two-year duration at post-secondary level (the Czech Republic); four- to five-year duration at upper secondary level (the Czech Republic, the Russian Federation, Ukraine); and a three- to four-year duration at university level. In cases of extra-mural study for students who have completed a two-year programme, the duration is three years (Bulgaria, the Czech Republic, Poland).

— *primary school-teacher programmes* have three-to four-year durations; three years in post-secondary educational establishments or colleges (Bulgaria, Poland) and four years at university level; .

— *secondary school-teacher programmes* have five-year durations and offer M.A. degree programmes for general subject teachers in all countries in transition.

— *vocational teacher programmes* are extremely diverse in terms of education, training and duration; There is no preliminary preparation outside the subject education and training (Estonia). On-the-job teacher preparation is a frequent pattern and is similar to apprenticeship schemes or education and training at other higher education institutes outside universities or higher pedagogical schools (four- to five-year programmes at polytechnics or other institutes).

— *special three-year programmes for teachers. of practical subjects* (Bulgaria, the Czech Republic).

In Central and Eastern European countries, *there is a trend towards:*

— extending the duration of teacher education and training (despite some differences);

— 'raising' education and training to a higher level—with more balance between theory and practice;

— expanding the list of specialities;

— enlarging the 'paid education' sector;
— the active participation by non-State universities in teacher education and training;
— the development of accreditation mechanisms and the introduction of State standards for teacher education and training.

VII. In-Service Teacher Training

The uniqueness of the present period for transition countries (and education in them), marked by new political, economic and social developments, means that *the further upgrading of in-service teacher-training systems (INSET) is a priority. INSET becomes a major factor in the professional growth* of teachers, and is related to lifelong education and enhancing their role as participants in these changes.

The main task and aims of INSET can be identified among the following:

— to help improve the school, seen as the primary permanent nucleus whose members are engaged in a common educational project;
— to provide teaching staff with professional resources that foster skills closely connected with their teaching practice, and thus to respond to the needs of the education system and of the profession;
— to create and foster teacher participation in the design and development of training plans, and in the exchange of experiences;
— to promote specialized training for teaching staff' in areas where such specialities are lacking;
— to re-train teaching staff (vocational education);
— to devote special attention to the training of trainers.[44]

A comparative analysis of the systems of INSET shows *great diversity* between and within countries. Within this diversity, *some similarities* may be identified:

— INSET represents an important part of educational policy in transition countries. This is evident from the numerous legislative documents adopted after 1990 several of which contain regulations concerning teacher education and in-service training

(Bulgaria, Romania, the Russian Federation, Slovakia, Slovenia).

— for INSET purposes and needs, separate institutions have been set up (very often irrespective of existing traditions), though variations within countries can be noticed (Bulgaria, Romania, Poland, the Russian Federation, Slovenia). This tendency has both positive and negative aspects. The emergence of different systems of INSET indicates awareness of the need to respond to a diversity of situations, coupled with diversity in the training of teachers to cope with these situations. It is also a proof of the realization that a .separate structure could play a different role in education other than existing institutions within the education system. In other words, educational policy meets practice face to face.

Some of the *negative sides of INSET* relate to the separation of INSET from initial teacher training. Particularly where universities are the major institutions for initial teacher education and training (PRESET), and due to their academic autonomy, there is a lack of co-operation and co-ordination between PRESET and INSET institutions.

In some countries in transition (e.g. Romania), the concepts of further development of INSET presuppose their future activity taking place within the institutions responsible for initial teacher education and training. This is envisaged with regard to better links and internal coherence of programmes and a real increase of INSET programmes compared with initial teacher education and training.

There is no *single model of INSET.* In most countries INSET is integrated in different institutions at central, regional or local levels. In several transition countries, there is a vast restructuring of INSET under way.

The following features are typical of developments:

— INSET for teachers is centrally organized in cases where there are national INSET institutions. The system of INSET is decentralized into regional, district or school level, or functions at the university level.

— In a large number of transition countries, efforts are now being devoted to the revival of school-based INSET (Slovenia, etc.). In various countries, there is a difference in the correlation between centralized and decentralized INSET. In some cases

(Romania), administrators are being trained in national institutes and teachers in 'teachers' houses'.

— INSET programmes are designed within the institutions themselves, but where financing is still on a central budget, programmes have to be approved by ministries of education.

— INSET programmes provide a larger number and variety of courses. Many new areas are being covered—management, information technology, etc.—as well as new dimensions of subject areas that have emerged recently. There is still dissatisfaction on the part of the teachers with the quantity of INSET programmes (the Czech Republic, Hungary). Poland reports a reduction of some INSET programmes.

— The variety of private providers of INSET is becoming greater, including non-State organizations, foundations, etc. (Bulgaria). Prejudice and lack of confidence in competition between State and non-State institutions still prevails and problems arising from the recognition of certificates issued by private providers seem difficult to resolve. One basic reason for these phenomena is the absence of standards in initial and in-service teacher education and training in many of these countries.

— Joint INSET programmes have been launched—especially for foreign-language teachers (Bulgaria, Poland, Romania, the Russian Federation). Other subject teachers taking part in joint programmes are not as well represented as the group of foreign language teachers.

— INSET continues to be regarded as either a compulsory or a voluntary activity. In Estonia, for example, refresher courses for teachers in the former Soviet school system were mandatory. Now it is left to the discretion of teachers. In Bulgaria INSET training is mandatory when there are changes in curricula; at present, even inspectors in the regional ministry structures are involved in retraining during INSET-based courses. In many cases, however, attending INSET courses is left to the choice of teachers or educators. It is believed that teachers have to be aware of their own responsibility for professional development, whereas the school is obliged to provide the proper conditions for their permanent upgrading. In most transition countries, it is very typical that INSET programmes have both a mandatory and a voluntary character. In the Czech Republic, where the former INSET system was abolished in 1991 and not replaced with a new one, a survey carried out among teachers indicates that 90 per cent of them were willing to pay for such training.[45] In other words, there is a recognized necessity for professional development, even when it is not directly tied to promotion opportunities, which is symptomatic of the personal involvement of teachers in this important issue.

— School-based INSET is not very well developed in most countries. It is often considered that INSET initiatives should arise at central or regional levels.
— Teacher mobility, especially in INSET programmes offering teacher exchanges, is not very widespread. There is a larger amount of exchange of teachers among transition countries than between transition countries and Western Europe. More opportunities for teacher exchange already exist in Central European countries. Bulgaria has a significant amount of experience with teacher exchanges. Given the limited number of subjects concerned by teacher-exchange programmes, it would seem desirable to broaden the scope of the subject-teacher categories involved in these exchanges. The issue of teacher exchanges, with its three main principles—bringing pupils and teachers from schools in different countries into contact with one another, parity and reciprocity; working together—has a large potential that remains untapped.[46]

Up to now, INSET programmes for teachers working with children with special needs have not been well developed and the same is true of special INSET programmes for teachers working with pupils from minority groups (immigrants, refugees, etc.). Some transition countries are suffering from the lack of such programmes (Armenia, Azerbaijan, Bosnia and Herzegovina).

VIII. The Social Partners of the Teacher

Teachers in the countries in transition have daily encounters and communications with different categories of social partners, who can be classified into *two major groups: the traditional and the non-*

traditional.

Among these, parents occupy a special place. However, due to the drastic impoverishment of large sections of the population, the high rate of unemployment and the difficulties in coping with current hardships, a great number of parents have been forced to adopt 'survival strategies', which oblige them to neglect the problems of the school. This category of parents does not entirely abandon social partnership with teachers and the school, but the role they perform in supporting changes in school and in the teachers' role is, in fact, too passive. This is further confirmed by observations and surveys, both among parents and teachers and by current studies and analyses of reports prepared for ministries of education (Belarus, Bulgaria, Moldova, Ukraine).

The transition period reinforces the emergence of a peculiar PARADOX: on the one hand, such periods call for enhancing democracy expressed through the joint participation of teachers and parents in the renovation process; on the other hand, owing to the difficulties faced by large sections of the population and to the alienation inherited from the totalitarian past, parents are playing a less active role in the changes affecting schools and teachers. This phenomenon is observed with different intensities in almost all transition countries. Apart from this consequence, another reality is also evident—parents are becoming more critical towards the school, the teachers and the changes being implemented. (For example, Slovakia reports the lowest recognition of teachers' efforts by parents. Parents of pupils at secondary vocational schools are the most critical towards their children's teachers. The Bulgarian situation confirms this attitude.) Thus, the current relationships between the social partners are not in favour of assisting teachers in managing the educational changes required by society.

The transition period has to face yet another problem. Awareness of the need for participation by parents and other large social groups in effecting reforms results in the need to take measures to promote effective dialogue. One way is to initiate and increase the participation of teachers and parents, as well as businesses and communities, on school boards. In setting up school boards and enlarging their functions, transition countries already had considerable experience from the period prior to 1989. Today, however, school boards have to respond to the new context and to assume the new roles assigned to them in the present circumstances, to overcome and eliminate old stereotypes of hierarchical subordination and to act as governing bodies in their own right. School boards provide opportunities for teachers, parents and the community to co-operate in their efforts to promote and guarantee the success of reforms, to control the outcomes and monitor the school's financial matters, to provide external support and to contribute to the welfare of the school and its pupils. Involving teachers in the work of the school boards enables them to co-ordinate both external and internal efforts towards accepting and managing various aspects of school-related processes.

The period of transition also gave birth to the so-called *parent/teacher associations* (PTAs) and other voluntary organizations at national, regional and school levels (Bulgaria, the Czech Republic, Estonia, Hungary, Poland, Slovakia, etc.). PTAs take an active part in the public announcement and discussion of urgent educational problems and facilitate dialogue between central government educational institutions and the teachers and parents, thus serving both professional and social interests. They also assist teachers in their role of managing changes. In some countries (Hungary, Slovakia), the existence and functioning of PTAs is guaranteed by law or by special legislative measures.

In transition countries non-governmental and non-State *organizations,* which act as partners to teachers in educational changes, are growing in number. They assist teachers in offering programmes for professional development and exchange through the financing of initiatives, through providing funds for the purchase of new equipment for information technology, through buying educational publications, etc.

The contribution of the *cultural environment and institutions* to the schools was not lost in the period of transition, but has been seriously altered due to chronic financial deficits and the 'survival strategy' adopted by these institutions.

Among their different social roles, teachers in transition countries are now also employed in the *private sector.* Although not very large and its interests in education not widely based, the private sector nevertheless makes its existence noticeable and affects education. In a large number of transition countries, specific laws have not yet been passed to stimulate investment and donations to education by private business, hence its slowness in becoming an active partner of the teacher and the school. In Bulgaria, for example, specific economic regulations have been introduced which ensure real participation by private businesses in educational changes. Special acts regarding the relationships between schools and private businesses have been put into practice.

The mass media are also increasingly becoming real partners to teachers through involvement in educational problems. They are becoming powerful and helpful accomplices in disseminating information on education and shaping social attitudes towards change. The mass media play an active role in the distance education of teachers, thus enriching the ways in which their professional development can be fostered. In almost all countries, special bulletins and newspapers dedicated to education are published.

Some of the more general trends in the relationships between the teacher and other social factors are as follows:

— in the transition period, the traditional social partners of the teacher have remained the same, but the characteristics of the relationship between them is different. The teacher has not been sufficiently prepared to co-operate with traditional partners under the new circumstances, when attitudes have changed and expectations grown;

— new social partners for the teacher have emerged and have increased in number, thereby enlarging the scope for their action;

— the teacher has to stimulate the involvement of the other partners, not only on instructional matters, but in uniting and directing group interests towards achieving the global changes taking place in and outside the school;

— due to the modified place and position of education within the value system of society, the teacher is facing new problems of co-operation with both new and traditional partners;

— there is still a lack of understanding of the need for teachers and other partners to work together as a team. Teamwork aimed at the well-being of pupils, teachers and schools establishes and strengthens partnerships.

IX. Teachers in Difficult Professional Situations

It is typical of the countries in transition that they are *multi-cultural.* Different ethnic minorities live there and this compounds the role and functions of the teacher. In the Russian Federation, there are 89 regions and 120 ethnic groups, with the result that 90 languages are taught in schools. In the Ukraine, where the total population is 52.1 million, the Ukranians represent 72.7 per cent and the Russians 22.1 per cent; numerous other nationalities and ethnic minorities, like Belarusians, Jews, Moldovians, Bulgarians, Polish, Hungarians, Romani, Greeks, Tartars, Germans, etc., constitute 5.2 per cent of the total population. Very similar is the picture in Moldova, where the *high diversity of ethnic groups* is expressed in the following way: 64 per cent Moldovian; 13.8 per cent Ukrainian; 13.5 per cent Russian; and 3.5 per cent Bulgarian.

In the Baltic countries, great diversity is also typical and the number of Russians living there sometimes exceeds the numbers of other ethnic groups. Mixed ethnic minorities also coexist in the former Yugoslavia.

The same diverse ethnic picture is exhibited in Hungary, Poland and elsewhere. Hungary has distinguished itself by some of the most radical decisions concerning the recognition of the rights of ethnic groups in its constitution.

This is a phenomenon which has a powerful impact on teachers and presents them with new tasks. *Multicultural education* becomes an important feature of education in transition countries. The principal task is to promote equality and equity in education, among the urgent imperatives set by UNESCO, and calls for specific measures in teacher education and in INSET programmes towards: (a) the European dimension in education; (b) interculturality; and (c) multicultural equality and equity.

In the majority of transition countries, learning the mother-tongue has been introduced for bilingual children in an effort to guarantee the constitutional rights of ethnic minorities (Bulgaria, Hungary, the former Yugoslav republic of Macedonia, Moldova, Romania, Ukraine, etc.). A difficult problem which must be tackled at the same time is the insufficient component in teacher education for developing teachers skills in order to work with minority children and to respond to their practical needs. One possible explanation is the lack of any tradition in this area, especially during the period prior to 1989. Promoting mutual understanding, cross-cultural relations, tolerance towards differences, self-respect and respect of others, living in a culture of peace—these are only a few of the major tasks that teachers of minority children face. These are also the activities that UNESCO has stressed.

Some of the countries in transition have been involved in armed conflicts since 1989 and are faced with the hardships of overcoming the grave consequences (Armenia, Azerbaijan, Bosnia and Herzegovina, Croatia, etc.). In Slovenia, for example, 17,500 displaced pupil refugees from Bosnia and Croatia were placed in school in 1992/93. Some 3,892 of them were accommodated at reception centres, while another 5,000 were not even registered. A 'bridge' curriculum has been specially designed for them upon agreement with the two minorities and 420 teachers were involved in its implementation, 92.4 per cent of them from Bosnia and Croatia.

Teachers in these countries are obliged to participate in the restoration of burnt-out schools and destroyed equipment.

As a result of the violently disturbed school routine in these countries and the extremely difficult working conditions, *symptoms of demoralization* are evident among teachers. Very often they are forced to apply 'survival strategies'. Special attention should be paid to this problem in terms of undertaking concrete surveys and educational studies of this 'new' category of teacher. These efforts are largely supported by UNESCO. In these countries, the working and living conditions of teachers should be the subject of a separate analysis. In this way, adequate strategies and concrete actions could be devised in an effort to overcome the negative consequences.

Among the main problems and contradictions observed in the areas that have been subject to a comparative analysis are *an increase in the number of children with special educational needs and the inadequate and insufficient provision made for them.* School equipment is extremely out-of-date and, in most cases, completely unsuited to their needs. In the Russian Federation, for example, more than 40 per cent of children suffer from chronic diseases and the number of children suffering from illnesses of the nervous system is growing. Their total number had already reached 7.5 million, which means one child in three, whereas special education is provided for only 350,000 children. The number of handicapped children is also increasing and, to this very ominous statistic, we have to add the number of children growing up in difficult conditions in a context where there are a decreasing number of boarding houses.

Within the Russian Federation there are 600,000 orphan children who, for different reasons, have no guardianship. This leads to excessive numbers of them in child institutions and boarding houses. At present, only 15 per cent of the children leaving child-care institutions and boarding houses continue their education in secondary or higher professional schools. This is far below the average percentage for Russia and places them in the category of educationally deprived young people.

The common problems in the analysed countries with respect to the specific role of teachers in extreme situations are the following:

— the large number of teachers working with children with special educational needs due to low pupil/teacher ratios and the lack of specialized training for most of them;
— the increasing need for the provision of special teaching, as well as the necessary materials, accompanied by the shortage of funds to finance or purchase them;
— the need to reconstruct the network of special schools which had been neglected prior to 1989. There is a desperate need to build up new types of establishment, to design special programmes and to create an appropriate environment for teacher/pupil relationships;
— the need to select special teachers for this type of educational establishments in a context of a general shortage of teachers.

In a number of countries new teacher education specialities have been introduced (Hungary, Poland, the Russian Federation) aimed at preparing more teachers to work with children with special educational needs. In Bulgaria, too, alongside the existing provisions in special education, new ones have been introduced, including social workers trained to deal with deviant behaviour among children.

Conclusions

The reference paper on *'Education and teachers in Central and Eastern European countries'* clearly states that education and teachers are among the major factors in the social transformation of contemporary societies. Fostering the mission of teachers in order to stimulate their active participation in the acceleration of democratic processes and in building up 'a world acceptable for all' is among the most important priorities.

This paper has identified a number of common issues related to teachers and their profession:

— Changes in both the education system and the teaching staff are taking place in a dynamic political, economic, social and demographic context subject to a lot of constraints;
— In most Central and Eastern European countries, educational reforms began with active legislative steps. New educational laws have been passed, but separate laws for teachers have not yet been developed. Instead, a lot of other normative acts or amendments to the educational laws concerning teachers have been adopted;
— In all countries, education is a high priority area and there is an awareness of the importance of teachers as a professional group concerned by the transformations in society. Teachers are expected to be actively involved in the democratization process but, as a profession, they are not highly valued by society. The social status of teachers is relatively low compared with the status of other professions, which calls for specific measures in order to raise it;
— Feminization of the teaching profession is very marked in all Central and Eastern European countries. A profession enjoying low social status and employing a large number of women attracts few men;
— Ageing of the teacher population is observed in most countries;
— Teachers' salaries are low compared with those in other sectors, which causes great dissatisfaction among teachers and does not stimulate a sense of belonging to an important professional group;
— Support for the teachers' professional development is widening, but is still not enough to encourage teachers to play an active role in decision-making processes outside the field of their subject;
— The development of partnerships and a sense of solidarity through

professional organizations, associations and unions of teachers still needs to be accelerated;

— In most Central and Eastern European countries, professional career patterns for teachers are not well developed and there is a clearly expressed need for their enlargement. Promotion arrangements are not well defined;

— The quality of teacher education is considered to be relatively low and insufficient, especially in terms of professional and practical training. There has been an increase in the number of the teacher-training programmes, but the emphasis is still mainly theoretical;

— Different patterns of teacher education exist and the duration of training varies widely;

— In-service training, as a major factor in professional growth, requires further upgrading;

— Lifelong education of teachers is becoming one of the major issues in all Central and Eastern European countries.

References

1. This draws upon data and analyses in: Economic Commission for Europe, *Economic survey of Europe in 1994-1995.* New York; Geneva, United Nations, 1995, p. 69-203. It also relies on all accessible reports (*Human development report* for each country), as well as on national sources.
2. Economic Commission for Europe, op. cit. All available national reports on *human development for 1995* have been used: Armenia, *Human development report, 1995,* Yerevan, UNDP, 1995; Azerbaijan, *Human development report, 1995,* Baku, UNDP, 1995; Bulgaria, *Human development report, 1995,* Sofia, UNDP, Ministry of Foreign Affairs, 1995; Macicj Juszezynski, ed., *Human development report, Poland '95,* Warsaw, Split Trading, 1995; Republic of Moldova, *National human development report,* Chisinan, 1995; Ukraine, *Human development report,* Kiev, UNDP, 1995.
3. Bulgaria. *Human development report,* 1995, op. cit.
4. Economic Commission for Europe, op. cit.
5. Economic Commission for Europe, op. cit., p. 109.
6. According to data included in Republic of Moldova, *National report on human development,* op. cit., 79% of the population was below the poverty level in 1992.
7. K. Bennett and Margaret D. LeCompte, The way schools work: a sociological analysis of education, New York; London, Longman, 1990.
8. International Commission on Education for the Twenty-first Century, Report of the Commission: preliminary synthesis, Paris, UNESCO, 1995.

9. C. Birzea,. *Educational policies of the countries in transition: secondary education for Europe,* Strasbourg, Council of Europe, 1994.
10. Symposium on 'Educational reforms in Central and Eastern Europe: process and outcomes', Prague, 4-7 October, 1995, Strasbourg, Council of Europe, p. 44-80. (Papers by Leclercq, Halasz, Kallen, Kotasek.)
11. J. Samoff, *Education for what? Education for whom?* Paris, Unesco, 1994.
12. K. Ryan & J. Cooper, *Those who can, teach,* Boston, Houghton-Mifflin, 1988.
13. M. Galton & B. Moon, eds., *Handbook of teacher training in Europe:* issues and trends, London, David Fulton, 1994.
14. M. J. de Vries, ed., *General report of the Symposium on 'Science and technology teacher training: what training for what type of teaching?'* Paris, 1994. Strasbourg, Council of Europe, 1994.
15. UNESCO *statistical yearbook,* 1994. Paris, UNESCO, 1994.
16. Republic of Moldova, *National report on human development,* op. cit.
17. Bulgaria, *Human development report,* 1995, op. cit.
18. UNESCO *statistical yearbook,* 1994, op cit.; *Cesky Statisticky Urad Statisticha rocenka Ceska Republiky,* Prahe, Vydal Cesky Spisovatel, 1994; Poland, Ministry of Education, *Education in a changing society,* Warsaw, TEPIS Publishing House, 1995; OECD, *Review of the educational system and policy in the Czech Republic: background report,* Prague, 1995; UNESCO, Division of Statistics, *Special survey of primary education teaching staff: levels of qualification and age structures,* Paris, 1992.
19. UNESCO *statistical yearbook,* 1994, op. cit.
20. UNESCO *statistical yearbook,* 1994, op. cit.
21. ' Act L XXIX of 1993 on public education of the Hungarian Republic, Budapest, 1993.
22. *General concept of education in Lithuania,* Vilnius, 1994.
23. *Gazeta obrazovaniya* (Moscow, Ministry of Education), June 1995.
24. Ukraine, *Human development report,* 1995, op. cit..
25. J. LeClercq, *Teachers in a context of change in Central and Eastern Europe.* Paper presented at the Symposium on 'Educational reforms in Central and Eastern Europe', Prague, 1995. Strasbourg, Council of Europe, 1995.
26. *Gazeta obrazovaniya,* op. cit..
27. Maciej Juszczynski, ed., *Human development report,* Poland '95, op. cit.
28. Hungary, *National report on education presented at the forty-fourth session of the International Conference on Education,* 1994, Budapest, 1994.
29. Ukraine, *Human development report,* 1995, op. cit..
30. Estonia. *The development of education in Estonia, National report presented to the forty-fourth session of the ICE,* 1994, Tallinn, 1994.
31. Azerbaijan, *Human development report,* 1995, op. cit.
32. Bulgaria, *Human development report,* 1995, op. cit.
33. OECD, *Review of the educational system and policy in the Czech republic,* op. cit.; OECD, *Pilot project on regional co-operation in reforming general secondary education,* Paris, 1996.
34. Armenia, *Human development report,* 1995, op. cit.
35. Poland, Ministry of National Education, *The development of education in Poland in 1992-1993,* Warsaw, 1994.

36. Estonia, *The development of education in Estonia,* op. cit.
37. B. Granger, *The role of NGOs in public policy development,* Fort Collins, Co, Colorado State University, 1994.
38. J. Wilson, *Appraisal of teachers in: teacher training in Europe,* London, David Fulton, 1994.
39. R. Bartman, *Guidelines for performance based evaluation,* St Louis, MO, Department of Elementary and Secondary Education, 1990.
40. Ryan & Cooper, op. cit.
41. Azerbaijan, *Human development report, 1995,* op. cit.
42. Galton & Moon, op. cit.
43. These findings are the same as those of F. Buchberger, *in:* Galton & Moon, op. cit.
44. Buchberger, op. cit.
45. OECD, *Review of the eudcational system and policy in the Czech republic,* op. cit.
46. EAT, Teaching for exchanges : aims and ways of teacher training, *in :* ERGTSE, *A secondary education for Europe,* Strasbourg, Councii of Europe, 1993.

Bibliography

National reports presented at the forty-third (1992) and forty-forth (1994) sessions of the International Conference on Education organized in Geneva by the International Bureau of Education.

Forty-third session

Bulgaria. *The development of education 1990-1992, national report of the Republic of Bulgaria.* Sofia Ministry of Education and Science, 1992.

Czech and Slovak Federal Republics. *Development of education 1990-1992.* Bratislava, 1992.

Poland. Ministry of National Education. *The development of education in Poland in 1990-1991.* Warsaw, 1992.

Russian Federation. *The development of education, national report from the Russian Federation.* Moscow, Ministry of education, 1992.

Slovakia. *Development of Education 1992-94.* Bratislava, Institute of Information and Prognoses of Education, Youth and Sports, 1994.

Slovenia. *The development of education in the Republic of Slovenia 1990-1992.* Ljubljana, Ministry of Education and Sport, 1992.

Ukraine. *Development of education in Ukraine in 1990-91.* Kiev, Ministry of Education, 1992.

Federal Republic of Yugoslavia. Yugoslavia Commission for UNESCO; Ministry of Education and Culture. *Development of Education in the Federal Republic of Yugoslavia, 1990-1991.* Belgrade, 1992.

Forty-fourth session

Reports on the development of education have been used presented by the following countries: Armenia, Bulgaria, Czech Republic, Estonia, Hungary, Poland,

Romania, Russian, Federation, Slovakia, Slovenia, Ukraine.

In addition, recent documents sent to the IBE or to the Bulgarian National Commission for UNESCO in December 1995 by the following Member States have been used: Albania, Belarus, Bulgaria, Estonia, Latvia, Romania, Russian Federation, Slovakia, Uzbekistan.

Other sources:

Arends, R. *Learning to teach.* New York, Random House, 1988.

Association for Teacher Education in Europe. Working 4: Information and communication technology for teacher education. In. Libotton, A., ed. *Visions and realisations.* Brussels, ATEF, 1993.

Birzea, C. *The process on educational reform of the countries in transition.* Speech given at the symposium on 'Educational reforms in Central and Eastern Europe: processes and outcomes', September 1995. Strasbourg, Council for Cultural Co-operation, 1995.

Carte blanche of the reform of education in Romania. Bucharest, Ministry of Education 1995.

Cole, M., ed. *Education for equality.* London; New York, Routledge, 1989.

Symposium on 'Contents and methods in secondary education: a secondary education for Europe', Porsgrunn, Norway, October 1993. *General report* by Francine Dugast Portes. Strasbourg, Council of Europe, 1994.

Economic development of Slovakia in 1994. Bratislava, 1995. (Study prepared on behalf of the United Nations European Economic Commission for Europe).

Foucher, M. *The faces of Europe: a secondary education for Europe.* Strasbourg, Council for Cultural Co-operation, Council of Europe, 1995.

Galton, M.; Blyth, A., eds. *Handbook of primary education in Europe.* London, David Fulton, 1989.

Holly, M.L.; McLoughlin, C.S. eds. *Perspectives on teacher professional development.* London, The Falmer Press, 1989.

Joint ILO-UNESCO Committee of Experts on the Application of the Recommendation concerning the Status of Teachers. *Report.* Geneva, ILO, 1994.

Lawn, M.; Grace, Gerald, eds. *Teachers: the culture and politics of work.* London, The Falmer Press, 1987. (An Open University book)

Lawson, R., ed. *Changing patterns of secondary education: an international comparison.* Calgary, Alberta, The University of Calgary Press, 1987.

Ministere de l'enseignement. *Le systeme de l'education.* Bucharest, 1994.

Osnovnoye itogi 1994-1995 ichebnogo goda I piti v obnovleniya obrazovaniya v Rossii. Moscow, Ministerstvo obrazovaniya Rossii, 1995.

Poland. Ministry of National Education. *Education in a changing society.* Warsaw, TEPIS Publishing House, 1995.

Quality and accountability: the programme for development of the education system in the Czech Republic. Prague, Ministry of Education, Youth and Sports, 1994.

Rogers, R., ed. *Education and social class.* London, The Falmer Press, 1986.

Romania. *The new education law in Romania.* Bucharest, Public Information Department, 1994.

Seminar on 'School legislation: dialogue on the reforms in Central and Eastern Europe', Brussels, December 1993. *General report* by Cesar Birzea. Strasbourg, Council for Cultural Co-operation, Council of Europe, 1994.

Symposium on 'Science and technology teacher training: what training for what type of teaching?' Paris, March-April 1994. *General report* by M.J. de Vries. Strasbourg, Council for Cultural Co-operation, Council of Europe, 1994.

Ukrainian Economic Trends. *Monthly update.* August 1995.

UNESCO. *World education report.* Oxford, OUP, 1995.

Wilson, J., ed. *The effectiveness of in-service education and training of teachers and school leaders.* Report of the fifth All-European Conference of Directors of Educational Research Institutions, Triesenberg, October 1998. London; New, York, Taylor & Francis, 1989.

World statistics in brief. New York, United Nations, 1993. (Statistical pocketbook.)

*Reference paper prepared for the European Consultation to the 45th Session of the International Conference on Education, 1996.

Country : International Bureau of Education UNESCO, Geneva, Switzerland.

PART — II

EDUCATION AND TEACHERS IN WESTERN EUROPE

Mr. Jose Antonio Fernandez
Consultant International Bureau of Education

I. Introduction

Current social changes have an enormous impact on education, which is why for decades there has been little doubt in Europe regarding the essential need for change in education. This has been expounded by experts, solicited by societies and promised by politicians. Change has taken the form of teaching and political/administrative reforms in practically all countries inside and outside the European Union. In some countries, the reforms have not achieved a consensus, while in many others dissatisfaction with the results of one reform have merely heralded another. Politicians are criticized for the lack of success of the reforms, which is blamed on the insufficient resources allocated and/or the weak motivation or low capability of the teachers.

The slowness of educational change in relation to the changes occurring in the economic and socio-cultural areas has been associated in some circles with a diagnosis of teaching staff, in which emphasis has been placed on aspects which are considered to be symptomatic of the difficulty of facing up to the challenges of change. The contradictory situations in recruitment as well as ageing and feminization at the basic levels of education are considered in Europe to be clear manifestations of a decline in professional *status* compared with the recent past. One of the best European specialists in the subject was already saying a few years ago: *'Never has Europe had to face so great a challenge and still less one which finds its teaching bodies in so profound a state of dismay, if not disgruntlement'* (Neave, 1992).

The educational co-operation programmes sponsored by the European Commission since 1976, which have matured in the SOCRATES and LEONARDO programmes (in which several European countries that are not members of the Union participate), are clearly intended to place educational change in a European framework. The increasing flow of persons, information and experiments produced by the projects and joint actions undertaken under these programmes have been involving thousands of teachers and future teachers, who will be given the opportunity in this way to compare and combine their points of view on educational practice within a European framework.

This is the background against which the thoughts outlined in these pages are situated. The intention has not been to describe in detail all the factors involved in teaching—which are fully familiar to all participants at the preparatory regional meeting for the 45th session of the International Conference on Education—but rather to highlight a few aspects which appear to be more relevant as a means of stimulating the debate on ways of strengthening the role of teachers in educational change within a context of general social change.

The paper is divided into five chapters. *Chapter—I* considers the more significant features of current social change, analyzed from the point of view of and in relation to the world of education, and more particularly of teachers.

Chapter—2 analyzes some of the challenges faced by education systems, schools and teachers as a result of current changes.

Chapter—3 reviews the various social attitudes or diagnoses concerning the school system and teachers.

Chapter—4 comments on government-led reforms and on changes initiated by teachers in schools.

In *Chapter—5,* we summarize the hypothesis of a strategy for change where the teachers are the protagonists, which runs throughout the study.

Explanatory note

We would like to give readers of this document an explanation for the features which might be thought to be missing, such as the few direct references to countries or the lack of statistical annexes.

With regard to the first of these points, we have tried to avoid the risk of omissions, inaccuracies or imprecision which are unfortunately inevitable when dealing with such a vast range of countries. Exceptions to this rule have been made only where a concrete example provides a better understanding of the idea conveyed.

Statistical tables have been omitted for two reasons. Firstly, the analysis of the relationship between teachers and social change does not easily lend itself to the use of statistics. As the readers will see, when statistics are given it is merely to show how unreliable they are as evidence of the notions they are supposed to prove.

Secondly, a serious problem arises when it comes to comparing statistics concerning teachers in European countries. It is by no means easy to analyze the complicated national statistical series relating to the numbers of teachers and students. For the same year, the figures for these numbers can vary by many thousands, depending on the source. For instance, from one year to another pre-school teachers may or may not be included among primary school-teachers. Part-time teachers may either be included in the statistics as if they are full-time or be reduced to a full-time equivalent. Private school-teachers may or may not be included in the figures, or one year's statistics may omit data for a particular community, region or country. Thus, before any comparisons can be drawn between periods and/or countries, all the data have to be analyzed very carefully to see whether they are, in fact, comparable. The sources consulted have been the *World Education Report,* 1991 and other UNESCO statistical data, the OECD's *Education at a Glance* and, for countries of the European Union, the *Key Figures of Education in the European Union* (published each year by the European Commission in several languages). On the precise point of the number of teachers per level and per country, the 1994 European Union report, which contains data for the 1991/92 academic year, continues to warn of the difficulty of obtaining comparable data and of the methodological problems involved with interpreting the data.

For both of these reasons, then, it has been decided not to include any statistical tables, which would require explanatory notes for many of the countries and still be unable to shed any specific light on the topic under discussion. We would refer instead to the National reports presented to sessions of the ICE and to UNESCO, OECD and European Commission statistics, with which readers are already familiar.

II. Some Features of Global Change

A. The complexity of current change

Every generation may have the impression that it is emerging from an organized and stable world to face a threatening future. This aspect of the matter has to be taken into consideration, especially as we approach the end of a century and the end of a millennium. It would appear, however, that the present appreciation of change can be compared to none other in the past. The objects we use daily, the geopolitical structure of the world, the basic way all societies are organized are changing, as is our vision of the world, of the earth's eco-system and of the universe. The first original feature of the present, therefore, is that there are now many millions of people who are rationally aware of the practical changes occurring in our time, unlike in the past, when changes were identified only after the event and not by contemporaries.

There are no ready-made explanations

Although the society of the future has been analyzed extensively, analysts recognize that it is not easy to build a theory to explain a process in which we are all immersed. There have been many attempts and much research, but *few theories are specific, comprehensive or rigorous enough to provide an interpretative framework for understanding new history. After twenty years of efforts and speculation to produce a theory of the 'new society', there is considerable uncertainty as to what that society is* (Castells, 1994).

While change affects all aspects of daily life in the developed countries and of some sectors of the so-called emerging countries, its impact differs from one country, institution or individual to another. As pointed out in the European Commission's recent White paper (1995), *Teaching and learning: towards a cognitive society,* while current changes open up wonderful prospects for some sectors or individuals, for others they create insecurity and uncertainty and signify unemployment and social exclusion. For that reason, opinions and attitudes regarding today's changes tend to vary considerably. The disparities in the *social accounts* of this process of transformation are due to its complexity and to the maladjustments and loss of continuity it causes. This diversity of opinions reappears in education not only in the form of differences of appreciation from one sector to another (such as parents, teachers, students or businessmen), but also in the actual dynamic of the school system, which is where the tensions between diverging demands and expectations are materialized.

Globalization: the global village and individual villages

What is most striking at first sight is the advocacy of a common direction or 'final destination' for all countries and peoples in the world. As a combined effect of the scientific and technical revolution and of the abrupt end of the international political order prevailing for the last fifty years, profound changes are occurring in the workings of the international system, giving rise to the phenomenon of 'globalization'. This is a complex phenomenon, of which very different aspects may be identified.

The world is an eco-system: For the first time, the world is being perceived by millions of people as an eco-system. In only four centuries, we have gone from a cosmic view whereby the earth and the solar system were everything, to a direct vision (via satellites, probes, telescopes and television screens) of the unsuspected vastness of the universe, within which 'we are' but one tiny, vulnerable speck.

The world is a single market: Although the world is a stage where all have a role to play, it is dominated practically unilaterally by enterprises of the triangle made up of the United States, Japan and the European Union and other countries of Western Europe (Groupe de Lisbonne, 1995). The trend towards increasing internationalization has been generating institutions responsible for regulating functions which used to be controlled by national governments and bilateral agreements, or, for instance, by the International Monetary Fund and the World Trade Organization.

Is the 'global village' a world civilization or culture? Generated and fed by the communications media and culture industries, and in recent years borne along by the `information superhighways', an embryonic global culture is beginning to take shape in simple views of science, human history, the present and the future. This cultural sub-stratum is a collection of opinions, fashions, attitudes and values which are shared by thousands of millions of people, who, in all the corners of the earth, are consuming the same cultural products. As tends to happen with all current changes, the mere possibility of a global culture arouses contrasting opinions and feelings both inside and outside Europe. Beyond the different interpretations, however, there is no denying what nowadays appears to be an unstoppable process of cultural globalization.

'Villages' claim an identity: The reverse of economic and cultural globalization is the affirmation of national identity and, in the case of Europe, of identities which have been subordinated to national States over the last two centuries. The affirmation of regional cultures may either tend towards *openness,* featuring cultural co-existence and/or hybridization, or it may turn into plans for *anti-modern identity-building* (Ramonet, 1993; Touraine, 1995). As has been highlighted in recent United Nations world conferences, the cultural factor is becoming a new demarcation line *between* the positions of different countries and blocs of countries. Cultural factors have moved to the centre of the international political stage, giving rise to a view that future conflicts will be *'a clash of civilizations'* (Huntington, 1993).

The world united by Internet is profoundly unequal: There are hidden economic factors behind cultural and religious confrontations. Post-modern globalization has abandoned whole countries and regions of the world to their fate. Extreme poverty, wars and the despair of millions have brought about angry reactions among individuals and communities, who do not accept that Internet cables should take precedence over pipes for drinking water (Pisani, 1995). The emerging new world is undoubtedly much less homogeneous and therefore less 'governable' than it appears (UNESCO, 1995).

Integration by blocs: the European Union: This is an example of regional integration, which serves the dual purpose of protecting the economic interests of countries belonging to the bloc and fulfilling certain functions of political regulation which counterbalance purely commercial dynamics. Although the construction of Europe comes from further back and has other causes, the European Union's expansion is now part of the process of globalization and clearly plays a mediating role between the global market, member countries of the Union and other regional blocs and organizations of the United Nations system.

The crisis of national States: National States are caught up in the complex combination of globalization, the affirmation of regional and local identities and the emergence of blocs of countries with common cultural or commercial interests. As a result, all the European countries, some sooner and some later, have been redefining their role and the attribution of responsibilities in basic areas, such as macro-economic variables, industrial development or educational policies. Because it is so strongly anchored in the history and traditions of each country, formal education continues to be a national responsibility, an aspect which has been endorsed in article 126 of the Treaty revised in Maastricht. As we shall see later, globalization has made the challenges to education increasingly universal. Besides globalization, the search for closer territorial and cultural ties and identities further challenges the traditional role of national States in education systems.

B. The transformation of society and personal lives

Change affects not only the way States are ordered, but also the way societies function and the way individuals live their lives. Three aspects may be highlighted.

The changing socio-cultural environment

The economic landscape of the world is changing fast and the same effect is visible in every country and every region. Some *regions and towns* are losing their traditional industries. Many enterprises, which appeared to be part of the landscape of so many small places in Europe, either merge, move or disappear. Both *old and new institutions,* like the procedures by which society is regulated and which have been long established in European civilization and culture, have been seriously affected by current changes, including the family, social security, the machinery of democracy, systems of values, schools, political parties, businesses, trade unions and the labour market. Change is practically the only idea which is socially sustainable. Innovation is considered good in itself. Educationists are well aware that if they are to 'sell' good policies, they have to say they are new.

The emergence of women: a case of two

Alongside the two paradigmatic phenomena of the modern era (ecological awareness and the globalization of human affairs), which refer us back to the common origin and destiny of mankind, the third key factor, through its specific impact on general change, and on account of its significance for the education of new generations and of the teachers themselves, is the emergence of women in the organization and functioning of advanced societies. The fate of women still tends to vary considerably in the different 'neighbourhoods' of the global village, since even in Western societies there has been a re-emergence of discrimination and 'machismo'. Because it touches on the very essence of human life, the new awareness will take dozens of years to become established throughout the world and much longer still to take shape in social practices, but the trend appears irreversible. The new collective awareness, however patchy it may be, has already begun to change family life, life at work, and social and political activity. From now on, the *present and future* of mankind (a single world on a small planet) will be *a matter for two* to decide.

NIT (New Information Technologies) and the knowledge revolution

Practically all analysts agree that the explosion of knowledge lies at the root of all change. *The generation of knowledge and information processing are the basis of the new socio-technical revolution* (Castells, 1994). As far as European education systems are concerned, the significance of the new role of information and the radical challenge it offers to the work of educators and to the organization of learning are obvious. The material support and the main symbol of current change are the *new information and communication technologies*. At the same time, it is worth distinguishing between different aspects of the problem, which are sometimes confused in the debate about schools and, in particular, about relations between teachers, schools and NIT.

Television and computing : Some of the most conspicuous tools and objects of our daily lives are *televisions, video recorders, fax machines, photocopiers and the personal computers*. Either singly or together, these objects have been transforming our lives much more rapidly than the Roman plough, the printing press or the steam engine did in their time, since they have invaded the workplace, the bedroom and the kitchen, children's games and the way children construct their private worlds. We already know that there is no single purpose and that the effects of each of the tools gathered under the common 'NIT' label are different. This distinction, which is inherent in the nature of each tool, between the passive attitude of the television viewer and the unavoidable activity of the computer user, is particularly significant for education (Tedesco, 1995).

The revolution occurring now is the spread of 'multimedia', in other worlds the various permutations between these media, including telecommunication over a telephone line or by satellite signal. *The emergence of a multimedia world (with sound, words and pictures)* *constitutes a change which is comparable to the first industrial revolution,* according to the European Commission's White Paper (Commission Européenne, 1993) *Growth. Competitiveness. Employment.* While the flow of images and messages between networks already provides an underlying thread in our social structure, technological advances are bound to make information a key ingredient in all areas of human activity. One of the cultural upheavals of the post-modern era is precisely the fact that worldwide networks are gradually replacing local systems and mechanisms, including schools, in the socialization of individuals.

One example of this trend is illustrated by the *millions of teachers and 70 million European children and youths,* of different national cultures and languages, who attend classes every day in education systems jealously bent on defending their national and regional identities, while nourishing their imaginations with the same music, the same films, the same computer games as are being consumed by their peers all over the world, with whom some are beginning to communicate over the worldwide information web - though perhaps not entirely for didactic or scientific purposes. Whether NIT are admitted into schools or not, their effects are imprinted in the minds of both teachers and students, who are themselves the products of the audio-visual and computing world.

Information, knowledge and thought : Knowledge applied to knowing, developing and applying new forms of knowledge is the key to present development. *No information society is possible without the microprocessor and recombinant DNA.* The concern for knowledge is not related to its material and technological basis. From the point of view of the likely evolution of learning methods, and hence from the point of view of the change in education systems, the epistemological revolution which is occurring is more important than the utilitarian aspect of knowledge (or know-how).

Never before had so much study gone into so many aspects of the act of knowing and ways of stimulating it in oneself and in others. Even so, it may be said that its study has only just begun. Evidence of this is the fascinating insight into *false rationality, fragmented thought and thought of the context and complexity* offered by Edgar Morin (1994). The knowledge of knowledge has already become a 'transdiscip-line' (Morin, 1986). At first monopolized by philosophy and later by psychology, the 'theories of knowledge' and forms of learning have been invaded by sociologists, linguists and cyberneticians, and more recently by some theoretical physicists and biochemists (Najmanovich, 1994). Some of the terms used by scientists to emphasize the need for and benefit of inter- or transdisciplinarity are quite suggestive. *The break-up of disciplines, illegitimate scientific concubinage, original pairings, fringe contacts between borderline and/or marginal scientists* (Albertini, 1992, p. 207) are supposed to be some of the keys of basic scientific advances, such as molecular biology.

On the other hand, some scientists are trying hard not only to understand, but also to attach a *meaning* to the dimensions and faces of reality. Hence, the *new cognitive style,* replete with non-linear, multi-dimensional hypotheses, chaos theories and fractals, gazes without bias into the dark and even irrational corners of human experience, which invariably arouse so much interest, as may be appreciated by the massive recourse to extra-scientific techniques and institutions.

C. Conclusion

The social changes outlined in this chapter are put forward as a justification for criticizing teaching practices or for placing teachers before challenges which exceed their capabilities. At times, teachers may feel puzzled at some of the views of the world of the future, which range from ingenuous to triumphalistic. Fantastic tales about the *'information superhighways'* jar with the daily experience of many teachers, even in the fine schools of the richest countries, where they still have to wade through administrative red tape for access to a documentation centre, a photocopier, a video recorder or a fax machine.

To sum up, three general considerations are offered to educators:

- The first refers to the complexity, depth and multidirectional nature of current changes, which are not predetermined and which may be oriented one way or another. For this reason, this process of transformation is a wonderful opportunity for the regeneration of education systems. The extent of the overall changes occurring offers a challenge to educational change, while its complexity and openness call for caution and tolerance, equally removed from utopianism and catastrophism.

- The second consideration is more in the form of a question: If knowledge and the knowledge of knowledge lie at the nerve centre of current change, then why are education systems not occupying the centre of the social stage?
- Lastly, just as there is no *single way of thinking,* there is no *ideal school,* no *single professional profile* of a teacher, no *one best way* of transforming a school system. In order to cope with this historic period of uncertainty and searching, it seems essential to adopt a strategy based on experimentation and a combination of policies.

III. Social Change as an Opportunity to Arrive at a New Educational Consensus

A. The point of view of the teachers and other players

Twenty years ago, in 1975, a study arising from the debates of the thirty-fifth session of the International Conference on Education (also on the role of teachers) began by saying: *In a changing world education has to take a new turning* (Goble & Porter, 1977). What is this turning which education has to take? How should the education system and teachers behave as part of the changing general environment? The replies to these questions vary, both in theory and in practice. But, whatever the effects of the clash of opinions and the states of mind of the different players, one thing is certain: twenty years after the thirty-fifth International Conference on Education, even though many things have changed for the better in European education, the need for a 'turning' is now felt even more than in 1975.

In the following sections, we review the objectives and standards which change has inspired among the more influential social sectors and which, in one way or another, govern the development of education. We approach them from the point of view of strengthening the role of teachers in the process of change.

B. Adapting to the economy: a significant development

The notion of the failure of 'educational products' to adapt to the needs of business came to Europe from the United States. Institutions and experts connected with advanced sectors of the economy have been suggesting that education and training should be adapted to economic requirements. The central role played by the economy in our societies has been fully transferred to the field of education.

European political views on education and training in the 1980s and early 1990s highlighted the economic aspect of societal change in two further ways. It was argued that education and training systems had to change because both the European Union as a bloc ('Europe dedicated to quality') and individual countries, regions and businesses needed to become more competitive in world markets. On a personal level, it was argued that young people in particular had to be increasingly skilled in a labour market requiring new qualifications and/or capacities, but offering few jobs.

In all European countries, this approach has been a key factor in the criticism levelled at schools and at teachers and in guiding opinion along the way of reform. In this sense, one of the basic ideas of educational reforms has been that education should be more responsive to the requirements of the economy.

While these views on adaptation originated in business circles, they were eagerly taken up by politicians and educational authorities. Many teachers, both in general education and even more so on the technical side, have taken up the challenge and have participated in national and European programmes aimed at bringing schools and business closer together, at ensuring the transition to an adult working life, or simply at providing an introduction to the economy and to the world of work, as expressed in several reports by OECD (1992) and the European Union (Commission Européenne, 1995). The programmes have led to scattered experiments across Europe, which are commendable 'educational versions' of the notion of creating links between schools and business.

But it is precisely the 'popular' versions of this popular approach which arouse the rejection of or scepticism towards change on the part of much of the school system. This point lies at the heart of the present dissent in education, because it is also related to the suspicion of hidden neo-liberal intentions. In teacher training colleges, in-service training centres and in the schools themselves, applying economics to education is one of the aspects most contested by educationists and teachers in general. Many have the feeling that the historical achievements of education and educationists are going to be thrown overboard, while others believe that an exclusively economic view tends to divert attention from other aspects of change, which are just as relevant for education or even more so than mere economic changes (Cuadernos de pedagogia, 1996).

The economic approach still carries a great deal of weight in the educational policies of European countries, as may be appreciated from the national reports submitted at the forty-fourth session of the International Conference on Education (1994). There are clear signs at present, however, that the reductionist tendency is weakening and that a promising convergence of viewpoints is emerging among the more lucid representatives of business and education. Several national reports highlight other purposes served by schooling, apart from preparing youngsters for work. As we shall see below, the recent White Paper of the European Commission (Commission Européenne, 1995) will probably be considered a landmark in this transition towards a more general interpretation of the educational challenges arising in the present climate of change. It is instructive to see how ideas have matured in organizations, which in the course of a few years have moved from wanting to adapt education to the economic environment (ERT, 1989) to the notion that even the economy requires fully-developed personalities, and therefore to advocating general culture and character-building as the objects of all education and training (ERT, 1995).

These developments carry a double risk for the education system. On the one hand, there is the risk of not believing in the *good intentions* of the 'converted', especially since the call for general culture goes hand in hand with the expression of serious doubts regarding the ability of schools to convey it. This mistrust is believed to be due to the climate of mutual suspicion or indifference prevailing between education and business, according to some European studies (ERT, 1989) and many press reports.

Secondly, there is the risk of a certain *reversal of roles* resulting from the slowness with which everything happens in education. Curiously enough, while the businessmen who began advocating closer links between schools and business are already changing their minds, some political and educational authorities are still pursuing the idea of adapting to the economy, while, as an effect of democratic alternation, a new batch of politicians are unearthing old arguments. In addition to this time gap in attitudes, there are the views of parents who, aware of the difficulties their children have in finding work, exert pressure on the school system based on expectations which are no longer in tune with the rediscovery of basic needs by business (Prost, 1990; Neave, 1992; OECD, 1990).

There are some signs of positive change, however, precisely thanks to programmes linking schools and business. Ideally, all the parties involved (including families, whose influence has grown thanks to their increased participation in schools) should look beyond the dialectics of mistrust and belated discoveries and build instead on the basis of the present convergence of views, seeing it as a great opportunity to bring about the desired change so long unfulfilled owing to disagreement. For the first time in the history of education, when it seemed as if everything was becoming economic, the economists themselves are arguing that general culture and knowledge of life can provide a common basis of ability for learning to work, to live and to co-exist (Tedesco, 1995). Might this not lead to a new consensus regarding what teachers should know and be able to do? In this respect, the educational debate would become centred again on educational activity itself, and teachers can recover the role of protagonists in their own sphere of activity, which is much more promising than the social role sought in the past.

C. The information society as an opportunity for redefining the purposes of the school system

Teachers frequently have the feeling that the way current changes are referred to constitutes a threat against them. External criticism and the internal malaise of education systems are due to a great extent to the real or imagined malfunction of academic institutions in relation to changing society. In some cases, it is a question of normal resistance to change and the fear of departing from established routines. In other cases, the introduction of change by the authorities is perceived by teachers as a pretext for detracting from their acquired rights or as an ideological argument for undertaking specifically oriented reforms. Generally speaking, social change is portrayed as a set of challenges which exceed the administrative and professional scope of individual teachers and even of individual schools. In fact, very few primary or secondary school-teachers see social change as a great opportunity for reforming the school system.

On the other hand, a common paradox nowadays is that public opinion considers that the knowledge society is largely being constructed outside formal education. There is an impression that 'discoveries' and 'progress' occur in other networks, such as those linking dispersed scientific researchers and connected to technological and economic development. The education system as such does not feel involved in the debate on the knowledge of knowledge and even less in its implications for the transformation of the school system. According to most of these views, the prevailing practice would be what the Faure Report called 'maintenance education', which in itself is increasingly difficult to achieve on account of the versatile way knowledge is developing.

This separation between education and the development of knowledge is also apparent in the little use the school system makes of the results even of educational research. The amount of research conducted into teaching and the school system has led to an exponential increase in the number of records in bibliographical data-bases. Educational research groups, networks and associations are being set up in every country, as well as on a European and international level. A significant quantity of theoretical and practical knowledge has been accumulated in recent years on all aspects affecting the teaching/learning process. Several researchers (Escudero Munoz, 1991; Albertini, 1992; Neave, 1992; OECD, 1990; Fullan, 1991) have, however, highlighted a number of problems. The first of these is the little use made of available pedagogic knowledge by teachers and schools in general, which some even go as far as to describe as an absurdly small proportional use by schools of available research. While a lot is known regarding the content of desirable educational change, much less is known about the ways and means of bringing about change, whether at the personal level in teachers, or in teams or in whole schools. This aspect is also being studied (Escudero Munoz, 1991) and the results so far indicate that there are subjective barriers and resistance to change (due to the beliefs, prejudices and mental make-ups of teachers and other players, based on their own learning experience), as well as barriers brought about by administrative structures, which do little to stimulate and much to hold back the desire or ability to change on the part of individual teachers and schools.

It also appears that educational researchers are frequently gathered into circles of 'mutual readership or audience', usually within a specialized sector, with few contacts with other fields of research. Furthermore, despite growing transnational co-operation, research communities tend to be national in character, and are frequently linked with specific universities. While there are no comparative studies available, it may be said that in most European countries there does not appear to be any significant exchange between business R&D on learning theories and methods (where the literature is already plentiful) and educational R&D. A glance at the bibliographic references of either sector is suffcient to see that there is little communication between them, although the education system is beginning to take a clear initiative in this respect.

A promising tendency pointed out by some analysts (Albertini, 1992), and which is confirmed by the education reviews of several countries, is for direct research to be undertaken by teams of teachers, often as part of action-research activities. These teams are looking into 'anticipatory learning' and 'new styles of learning' (Escudero Munoz, 1991; Esteve et al., 1995; University of Valladolid, 1995; OECD-CERI, 1992) and may be pioneers in the task of connecting the school system with the many places and networks where knowledge is being produced. Within this tendency, it is worth noting the growing link between action-research teams, the research teams of teacher training centres and those of the schools and faculties where teacher instructors are being trained. These links can be a means of overcoming the tradition of using teachers and schools as mere passive laboratories. The research results produced are easier to transfer, based on real experiments, and supply material to reviews consulted by the educational communities of every country. Establishing closer links between schools and action-research teams of teachers is a way of strengthening the connection between research and educational development, a necessary condition for schools to participate in shaping the knowledge society.

D. What are the citizens of our time expected to learn?

Over 70 million children, adolescents and young people go to school every day in the countries of Western Europe. Although no reliable statistical data are available, several million adult students take part in the varied range of educational activities offered by institutions and establishments. Both they and the teachers, trainers and organizers have to know exactly what knowledge and skills are required.

Every country has tried to find the answer by introducing curricular reforms. The European Commission (Commission Européenne, 1995) has taken a step forward by venturing to propose *basic curricular guidelines* for the general education of Europeans. Being well aware that the development of curricula is a matter for member States to decide, the authors of the White Paper have undoubtedly sought their inspiration in national studies or white papers or in recent laws and regulations. As may be appreciated, there is a promising convergence with the guidelines offered by the *World Conference on Education for All* (WCEFA, 1990) and with the recommendations of UNESCO's Medium-Term Strategy—1996-2001 (UNESCO, 1975).

General culture

Individuals will be faced with a growing diversity of physical objects, social situations and geographical and cultural environments. They will be exposed to a flow of discontinuous items of information, which are interpreted and analyzed partially in many different ways (Commission Européenne, 1995). Faced with this challenge, school systems must try to ensure that children and young people understand how the world works, while acquiring an independent ability to manage their personal lives in all their dimensions. As the White Paper points out, *general culture is back in force.* Following the same line of thought, there is a business elite which would like young people to be trained not as tools for the economy, but as complete human beings. They are therefore in favour of formal education which provides the foundations of a scientific and humanistic culture, and which trains the person's character, personality and social responsibility (ERT, 1995). One cannot help thinking of Comenius' utopian view of the school as a *workshop of men* (Denis, 1994, p. 61).

There are five challenges which emerge from the teachings of the author of *The workshop of wisdom* (Denis, 1994, p. 61 et seq.):

(a) ***Understanding the meaning of things:*** European schools have to provide young people with the necessary keys for understanding the world so that they can participate in the multiple search for meanings. We say 'meanings' because the modern trend towards specialization, which has been one of the keys of European development, has led as a corollary to unidimensional and univocal attitudes, which hold no promise for the future, not even in science. Interdisciplinary and intercultural approaches are the present keys to understanding reality.

(b) ***The meaning of things and Eurocentrism*** **:** The logical consequence of rationalism and positivism has been a tendency for European culture to think of itself as unique, as if all things can only acquire the meaning which we Europeans and Westerners give to them. The enormous influence which European civilization has had throughout the world is quite obvious. Even so, it has clearly not been easy to combine European culture with that of minorities (who are in less of a minority than they used to be), who have been living for decades in Europe. The European education systems, which are supposedly so keen on multicultural diversity, are reluctant to integrate the cultures of the children who are considered non-European on account of their parents' origins.

(c) From a pedagogic point of view, culture has to signify both *militant interculturalism and scientific hybridation.* European schools should develop one of the positive keys of European culture, namely a critical attitude and a spirit of tolerance, which allows everything to be brought into question, implying acceptance of others and what is different. An intercultural educational approach is also a key to democratic co-existence and solidarity in the classroom and in the school.

(d) ***Knowing how things work*** **:** Schools are at present based on deductive thought, on a logical and abstract order of concepts and disciplines, in which mathematics occupies a dominant position. As opposed to this 'standardization of knowledge', the White Paper proposes the development of a 'practical culture' integrated within general culture, that is, for schools to cultivate creativity, imagination and innovatory attitudes. The courses on the history of science and technology, which several countries are introducing in their curricula, serve this purpose.

(e) ***Learning to discern and to decide :*** This entails the acquisition of ethical, esthetic and scientific criteria, a knowledge of the history of the home culture (the memory of the past) and an intuition of the future (knowing how to read the signs of the times). In other words, developing a critical spirit is an essential part of schooling, an aspect which is highlighted in several national reports (Finland. Ministry of Education 1994, p. 65).

All this together amounts to general culture, which authors like Gaudin (1990, p. 534) see as essential intellectual equipment for surfing through globally interconnected data banks without getting lost and finding what one is looking for. In this sense, general culture provides a passport for moving on from the *spectator society to the education society* (Ibid., p. 527).

Work attitudes and aptitudes

While in the 1980s the European Commission helped to disseminate what we might call the 'economistic' approach, the White Paper tries to achieve a deeper understanding of relations between education, development and employment. It points out that the new industrial world requires professional training combining basic knowledge, technical know-how and social aptitudes. Basic professional training is identified with personality training. In that sense, personal education constitutes a pre-requisite for social and economic initiatives aimed at developing employment, solidarity and social cohesion. From this point of view, technical and professional education and training are raised to the rank of 'culture' (Gaudin, 1990, p. 547).

Holistic thought, curriculum and methods

Edgar Morin pointed out some years ago that *the global era requires situating everything in a global context. Knowledge of the world as a world is becoming both an intellectual and a vital necessity* (Morin, 1994). This will only be possible if we change our compartmentalized way of thinking, which is typical of the educational structure inherited from the Middle Ages. Transposing this proposal into organizational terms (through a traditional type of curriculum by subjects, or one of its thematic or globalizing variations) has given rise to an endemic polemic within education systems and among researchers, which is revived each time any significant new report is published. The results of some empirical research are pointing towards a 'return' to traditional disciplines and teaching methods, reversing *pedagogism,* the search for facility and irresponsible innovations (Alexander, Rose & Woodhead, 1992). Many teaching teams, however, when explaining the results of their 'work projects' in specialized reviews, show that systematic learning improves if subjects are not used as a starting point (Cuadernos de pedagogia, January 1996).

The available evidence indicates that there is no single answer as to the best organization and methods to help a child gradually to build up a holistic, multidimensional, systemic understanding of environments and contexts and not only of the texts of each subject or area of knowledge. With a view to the future, however, it should be possible to establish a consensus regarding the need to progress with the theory and, on the basis of successful experiments of all kinds (within and across disciplines), both within and outside the school system, to build organizational and methodological models using tools which have already proved their effectiveness in the teaching/learning process.

Research and experimentation must be applied in initial training and especially in in-service teacher training, since teachers cannot legitimately be expected to achieve methodological miracles in their classes, when all the training they were exposed to consisted of classroom teaching.

The new 'comprehensive' and compensatory vocation of schools

The decision to opt for general culture as a common curricular base for all implies simultaneously retrieving the deep motivations of the 'comprehensive school' movement and compensatory policies. In this respect, there is a widely held belief that, in the future, the labour market will tend to stabilize around four segments: (a) some 20 to 30 per cent would consist of professionals able to produce, analyze and interpret symbols (words, images, data); (b) some 25 to 30 per cent would only have to handle series and flows on a routine basis, regardless of whether data-bases or automobile parts are involved; (c) between 30 and 40 per cent would remain available to work in the extremely vast area of services and personal care; (d) and there would then be a variable percentage left over, which would no longer be the old 'industrial reserve army', but rather retired people without rights or those who are purely and simply 'excluded' (Commission Européenne, 1995).

Clearly the skills and attitudes required for each of these segments differ greatly and there is a spontaneous temptation to make the school system more responsible for training the segment consisting of tomorrow's professionals. In this respect, the policy of the European Commission's White Paper is, nevertheless, unequivocal: *the school system must apply the principle of equal opportunity to the new situation.*

In practice, equal opportunity would mean educational policies combining a new version of *comprehensive education* with diversified care for certain groups and individuals, especially in the segments faced with social exclusion. Experience has shown that such policies do not necessarily imply a particular choice of curriculum or methodology and that therefore past polemics on this subject can be avoided (Forquin, 1992).

Quality and efficiency: the need to renovate school organization and culture

One of the consequences of technological change is the need to restructure all types of organizations, starting with business enterprises. Reorganization affects entire systems, some very close to education, such as social security and health. Most analysts agree that the European education systems hardly stand out as enthusiastic renovators of their administrative machinery, despite the fact that an endless stream of research has indicated that the factors most likely to enable one school to obtain better results than another are not those connected with material conditions or even with the training of individual teachers, but aspects which may be considered to be related to school organization and culture.

In the light of this tendency for organizations to change, many see as anachronistic a political-administrative and technical system which, in the image and likeness of other State institutions and major enterprises of the industrial era, determines, supervises and finances a large number of schools, whose degree of autonomy, whether great or small, is invariably delegated or conceded from the top down. Administrative decentraliza-tion may make systems smaller, but it will not necessarily render them less hierarchical and compartmentalized. In some countries, even those with a decentralized tradition, schools are no more than the branches of an external organization, enjoying even less exchanges of information and relations with other schools and institutions than have been achieved by the branches of banks or the district offices of major service companies, which, thanks to their computing networks, can carry out small operations with clients in other branches.

The size of the machinery is such that there can be no single corporate culture. Yet the vertical structure has so far prevented the emergence of corporate identities at the level of individual schools. In the absence of an institutional culture able to rally all its supporters, education systems and many individual schools have for decades been cauldrons of tensions which tend to cancel each other out, producing as a result an 'institutional culture and image' little given to dynamism or innovation, which, as we said earlier, is a fundamental drawback in a cultural environment marked by the desire to innovate.

The European Commission's White Paper (1995), which considers *debates of principle* as out of date, proposes introducing greater flexibility in present structures, which *are still too rigid* in order to meet the *requirements of cognitive society.* Behind the euphemism of flexibility lies the substantive issue. The question is then: Is it enough just to add a dose of flexibility to the management of existing education systems or should a sustained effort be launched to reinvent and reconstruct their structures, management and culture?

IV. Society's View of Teachers and Schools

In view of the requirements arising from the educational challenges outlined in the first two chapters, we have to be concerned with the preparation and morale of teachers and the organization of schools, if we are to move in the direction which current changes appear to suggest.

Families, businessmen and politicians level severe though different criticisms at the way the education system operates and especially at school results. Many of the criticisms refer to the lack of preparation, motivation or responsiveness of teachers to society's requirements. *Teachers,* on the other hand, feel demoralized and suffer the effects of hostility or social indifference towards a type of work which, though offering a few compensations, implies a considerable effort in the present social circumstances. The direct customers, that is, the *youngsters,* criticize their teachers' teaching methods, standards and procedures, mentality, character and capability. Thus *the climate of dissatisfaction has been affecting the school environment as a whole* for some years already, with similar expressions being used to describe the situation in reports published at different times and in different countries.

This chapter looks at the situation of teachers in relation to educational change and social change, from three points of view:

- the view of teachers from the outside, which has become the view commonly held in the international media;
- the opinions held by the teachers themselves regarding their own malaise and that of the education system; and
- the view which emerges from the data, facts and thoughts produced by international research.

A. Teachers and schools seen from the outside

A substantial quantity of international studies and reports have appeared in the last decade concerning the situation of teachers, either in OECD countries or those of the European Union (OECD, 1990; Neave, 1992; Ghilardi, 1993; EURYDICE, 1995; Archer & Peck, undated). These studies have taken a serious look at a set of basic themes which, through congresses and conferences, have shaped the prevailing social image of teachers and schools.

The social image of school malaise

It is almost commonplace to comment on the inadequacy of schools before the magnitude of the tasks implied by present educational challenges. From that starting point, some studies of schools and teachers tend to concentrate on a few indicators and to ignore others, giving a pessimistic interpretation of my disturbing symptom. This is the most frequent type of image to emerge from publications of all kinds concerning teachers in Western Europe, which are very much influenced by the intellectual output of the United States.

- Concerns are expressed regarding several aspects touching on the composition of the teaching body, such as: (a) trends in the numbers of teachers; (b) ageing; (c) feminization, and (d) the unattractiveness of the profession among the more qualified young people.
- At the same time as these concerns are expressed, greater skills are called for in the more qualified sector of the labour market, based on the fear that it might become more difficult to recruit teachers for some subjects, for some educational levels or for particular countries, towns or districts.
- A completely opposite concern is the possibility of a surplus of teachers, on the grounds that school enrolments are declining and that in some countries a large number of qualified young people wishing to be teachers are jobless.
- There might be the danger of a double standard arising in the 'teaching market', with a higher or lower status depending on factors such as subjects, levels or school locations.
- Although initial and in-service teacher training is generally considered to be a desirable remedy, the insistence on the need to change the status of such training and to improve its quality, content, duration and/or intensity is symptomatic of the poor opinion held of the professional capability of present-day teachers.
- Education systems are facing difficulties (both quantitative and qualitative) with the renewal of their human resources precisely when new blood is most needed to meet the challenges arising from the general change in society, starting with the cultural change in new students.
- Teaching staff suffer feelings of dissatisfaction, one symptom of which may be the stress which is believed seriously to affect between 25 and 33 per cent of teachers in the most developed countries, according to an international survey (OIT-UNESCO, 1994, § 84).
- As an explanation of or a backdrop to this dissatis-faction, some experts highlight the gradual break-down of the traditional consensus regarding the purposes and functions of education and

more specifically the role of teachers (Neave, 1992, p. 3 ff.).

— Teachers are going through a crisis of identity, the most visible sign of which is the debate on the teaching profession and professionalism, which has arisen frequently in congresses and conferences in recent years.
— Although the more specialized studies of teachers relate the problem to the structure of the education system and the way it is organized, in less sophisticated discussions on ' education more emphasis is placed on the personal aspect of both the problem and the solution. Schools would be more efficient if they had 'better' teachers.

Effects and fears brought about by demographic changes

Demographic trends have become a threat to the education system, not only because they reflect in themselves the drastic decline in the birth rate in all European countries, but also because the population factor is combined with the gradual introduction of neo-liberal policies of cutting State expenditure. A certain fear has spread of massive teacher redundancies, an aspect which in itself is sufficient to generate considerable disquiet among teaching staff. Another fear has been the possibility of a cutback on new recruitments, which would accelerate the ageing process among teachers already occurring in several countries. Lastly, the effect of demographic changes combined with the financial worries of the welfare state might tend to maintain or even raise *student/teacher ratios,* a sensitive issue which is related to the so-called school working conditions. Nowadays, having too many students in class complicates the teacher's work even more than it used to, because of the varied socio-cultural backgrounds of the students.

It is easy to understand the anxiety of teachers potentially affected by one or other of these risks—even imaginary. But this does not mean that the different facets of the diagnosis are consistent, and even less that the diagnosis is applicable in all countries as a means of undertaking the desired changes.

Statistics : All the statistical series available[1] on Western European countries from 1975 to the academic year 1991/92 show clearly that these fears are fortunately groundless. *In primary education alone,* the number of pupils has clearly fallen in general, though the size of the fall, its timing and rate have varied from country to country. For Western European countries as a whole, in the period 1975-92, i.e. covering seventeen years, the drop in the number of pupils may be estimated at between 25 and 30 per cent. It might be feared that the number of primary school-teachers might have fallen as well. This is not the case. Up to 1990, only in the United Kingdom was the drop in the number of pupils partially reflected in a decline among teachers. It appears that in Germany as well there are fewer teachers now than in 1975. It should be added, however, that despite the incorporation of the new *Lander,* there appear to be 600,000 fewer children in German schools in 1992 than in 1975. In all countries taken together, the number of teachers has not fallen and in some cases has even risen. It may be asserted that the pupil/teacher ratio in 1975 varied between 13:1 in Denmark to 36:1 in Portugal, ten years on, this ratio had been reduced by four or five points in all countries. This trend appears to have continued until now, although the ratio cannot diminish indefinitely. The United Kingdom started with a ratio of 23:1 in 1975; by 1985 this had fallen to 21:1 and by 1992 to 19.5:1. In some countries, if the total number of primary school children is divided by the total number of teachers, we obtain a single figure result, a ratio which would have appeared utopian only a few years ago.

The fall in the ratios in *secondary education* is equally spectacular (Ghilardi, 1993). Although real ratios may still be high in some schools in metropolitan areas, and in private schools, there does not appear to be any reason to draw pessimistic conclusions regarding population trends. The OECD's report is quite categorical in this respect: *The general assumption of a declining profession, with fewer teachers and a declining job satisfaction and status, is hardly borne out by the facts* (OECD- 1990, p. 22). In order to discover the roots of the current malaise among teachers, it is not worth looking at either the demographic trends or probably at the pupil/teacher ratios.

Recruitment difficulties versus jobless teachers

A number of countries have had difficulties recruiting teachers to work in some subjects and in some geographical areas. In other countries there has been a chronic problem of jobless teachers or frustrated applicants to the profession. Both types of problem have appeared simultaneously in a few cases, though in relation to particular levels, subjects or regions.

While, generally speaking, teacher statistics are not easy to interpret, in this particular respect it has not been possible to analyze and compare significant series of data supporting one or other interpretation about the failure of teacher supply and demand to adjust. Some countries have quantified unfilled vacancies, have made estimates of future needs and have developed strategies for recruiting future teachers among young people, and even for stimulating adult professionals to discover the delights of teaching. Countries with chronic surpluses have, on the other hand, adopted different strategies in an effort either to make teacher training more diversified, so that trainees can move to another occupation, or to lower the age of admission to school for very young children, as a means of increasing the number of pupils and indirectly absorbing the recruitment of teachers.

Several reports (OECD, 1990; Ghilardi, 1993) seem to indicate that the discrepancies are an effect of demographic change and of labour market trends in general, much more than of the greater or lesser attractions of the job of teaching. These real problems have given rise to persistent concerns, which have strengthened the fear that in the near future, and if nothing changes, it will no longer be possible to find sufficient suitable candidates to replace retirement losses or gaps in particular subjects, schools or geographical areas. Jobless young graduates, however, have difficulty sympathizing with such concerns. To the extent that structural unemployment persists and grows in post-industrial societies, even in countries which have taken in millions of foreign workers for decades, the problem needs to be seen in qualitative terms. Will the education system be able to recruit the best professionals or will it have to be content with those who cannot find any other kind of job?

The root of the problem : *Will education systems be able to hold on to their best professionals and to attract the most qualified young people to teaching?* This double question touches on the heart of the problem: the fact that teaching is unattractive.

It is worth taking a closer look at this challenge, which has several aspects. On the one hand, primary and sometimes lower secondary school-teachers are recruited among young people who have studied in *ad hoc* training centres. Who then opts for training schools, even in countries where teacher training has been raised to university status as a means of enhancing the teaching profession in the eyes of young people? The facts (incidentally fragmentary and taken from different accounts) are nowhere encouraging. In the order of priorities of future teachers, primary school is reportedly practically never at the top of the list and frequently, in a given class of forty students, the great majority are preparing to be teachers because they were not accepted for three or four other options which they thought more interesting. There is clearly little sense of 'vocation'.

In countries where *upper secondary school-teachers* are recruited among students graduating in different subjects, the pattern appears similar. Those who go in for teacher training or apply to be secondary school-teachers appear to be mainly graduates who have no other job possibilities. Once again, there are few 'vocations'.

Lastly, this 'negative career selection' effect is also apparent among students of *teacher training faculties,* which are the natural breeding grounds for future teacher trainers, policy-makers and inspectors. Everywhere, many of the students are working primary school-teachers, with very different motivations. For those entering the career directly from the end of secondary education, the pattern again appears to be the same: most students opt for teacher training as a last chance to attend university. We repeat that these conclusions are based on partial data and the reiterated testimony of lecturers in teacher training faculties and colleges in a number of countries. In any event, it should be taken as an alarm signal which cannot be ignored.

Ageing : It is a fact that in many countries primary school-teachers are nowadays much older than twenty years ago, partly because many of them have not changed. It is also a fact that in countries which expanded their secondary education later, the teachers tend to be younger. Generally speaking, the average age of European teachers is greater than ten years ago. It might also be said that twenty years ago teachers were too young, because the baby boom and policies aimed at expanding and generalizing primary and secondary education led to the mass recruitments of teachers, mostly young, who have now become 'old'. It is also likely that, in other sectors of public administrations in some countries, there has been a similar ageing process—just as in European society as a whole. If we bear in mind that most European teachers are civil servants, and therefore appointed for life, ageing hardly comes as a surprise. On the other hand, over the next twenty years the average age of computer programmers will also increase!

Ageing does not appear to be a particularly educational problem. It should be remembered that new blood is not synonymous with wisdom, nor is maturity necessarily a sign of rigidity (OECD, 1990; Ghilardi, 1993). It so happens that ageing has been given a symbolic significance in the argument that teaching is a declining profession, lacking in dynamism and unattractive. If, on the other hand, there was the possibility of large-scale recruitment in education, thousands of young graduates who are now out of work would fill the classrooms with new blood. Even so, the basic problems of education, of which the teaching malaise and ageing are symptomatic, would still persist.

The feminization of the teaching profession

The growing feminization of the teaching profession constitutes in all respects a crucial issue for the future. It is therefore worth taking a careful look at the facts in an effort to identify future tendencies. There appears to be a firm historical tendency to consider that the proportion of women at all educational levels is inversely related to the 'status' of each level, by which is meant social prestige and pay (Duru-Bellat & Van Zanten, 1992, p. 147). Let us look at this in a little more detail.

Women hold a virtual monopoly in pre-school education: In 1991/92, Ireland, with 75 per cent of women, Belgium with 78 per cent and France with 79 per cent were the only exceptions to the majority figure of over 90 per cent of women in pre-primary education (Commission Européenne, 1995). If the statistics are to be trusted, the trends apparently differ somewhat between countries when the figures for 1986/87 are compared with those for 1991/92. While in Denmark the proportion of women teachers fell from 96 to 90 per cent, in Germany it rose from 91 to 96 per cent and in Italy from 95 to 99 per cent. The most spectacular change would be in France, where the figure fell from 96 per cent to only 79 per cent in just five years. As the sources of the statistics are different (OECD for the first year and the European Commission for the second), it is possible that one of the technical problems pointed out in the introduction regarding statistics may have intervened.

About 75 per cent of primary school-teachers are women: The upward trend at this level appears to be confirmed. In several countries the proportion is rising at the rate of one percentage point a year. In others, the annual rise is only half a point. In France, the figure has risen by seven points in the five years under consideration. Only in Denmark, which already had one of the lowest percentages of women at this level (59 per cent), the figure has fallen by two. In Greece, the percentage of women in primary education has remained stable—at only 48 per cent, the lowest in the European Union.

From lower secondary education onwards men and women teachers are more evenly balanced: It is at this crucial point that it may be worth taking a closer look at the trend. In view of the precarious and heterogeneous nature of the available statistical series, it would be unwise to make any premature categorical statements just yet, but there are some interesting pointers in the statistical summary given by the European Commission (1995, p. 106). Although there is no breakdown between lower and upper secondary education in terms of distribution by sex, it would appear that the proportion of women is increasing in secondary education as a whole. Since the number of women among university teachers is also increasing, there is reason to believe that teaching is increasingly becoming a female profession.

Interpretation: Teaching was the first intellectual type of professional field which was opened up to women in Europe and as a job it continues to be more compatible than others with women's role in family life. Moreover, since teaching is part of the public sector in most countries, there is less pay discrimination than in other areas (Duru-Bellat & Van Zanten, 1992).

Apart from these sociological explanations, there are other less frequently heard considerations. The argument that feminization is a symptom of decline does not look at the other side of the coin; for instance, the disproportionate number of men in posts of responsibility, even in pre-school education, where it is not unusual for the only man in the establishment to be the principal. On the other hand, the likely increase in the number of women in secondary education appears to indicate that women are better prepared than men to compete in entrance tests for teaching jobs. Despite the supposedly unattractive nature of the profession, it should not be forgotten that between ten and twenty people apply for every vacant post. It would be interesting to analyze the trend of recruitment by sex in recent years in countries using the public examination system, as this is perhaps another key to the increase in the proportion of women.

A comparison of these two trends and others of equal interest might shed more light on the matter. On the one hand, it is clear that the school system displays contradictory signals with regard to women and relations between the sexes, an issue which, as we have seen, is not restricted to education. On the other hand, there is the *hidden curriculum,* that is, what schools do as a matter of daily routine. Sometimes old habits reappear in a post-modern guise. Thus, the culture of aggressive management, which is more typical of men than women, can influence the distribution of roles in the school. This may be so in a patriarchal type of school. In both cases, even though the majority of workers are women, and even though the rights of women are defended in class, the message that comes across—that is, the *hidden curriculum*—is one of male dominance. This could be one of the manifestations of not-always-fruitful co-existence between pre- and post-modern values in the school system.

The feminization of school and the femininity of education: It could be said that education and schools have been and continue to be women's entrance door to human history. Mixed schools have contributed enormously in this respect, although there are still disparities in higher education and vocational training. In compulsory schooling, on the other hand, there is one factor which was unknown until a short while ago and has still been little studied, namely the better average performance of girls (Commission Européenne, 1995a) and the resulting feeling of insecurity among boys. Schools can and should do much more to re-educate understanding, feelings and behaviour between the sexes. In this respect, why is the feminization of the teaching profession generally perceived as an indication that education is a second-class option rather than as a sign of the irresistible ascension of women and of the feminine aspect of human society? Might we not consider that it would be worth incorporating more femininity in teaching and in school management?

This is a relatively unexplored field, on which the action-research of teaching teams, backed up by psychologists, anthropologists and sociologists, should have more to say. The psychologists who insist on the need for both masculine and feminine figures in early education might find ways of avoiding the almost total preponderance of mother figures precisely in the infant stages of schooling. Anthropologists, on the other hand, could find a deeper meaning to feminization, in the light of new research into matriarchal and patriarchal cultures and their relationship with current cultural developments. Sociologists could look at the real causes of feminization in education and the male counterparts in the army and religion. It would also be helpful if educationists started a social debate regarding some established ideas, such as how to take advantage of the feminization of the school system.

In any event, it would be worth reconsidering whether there is any real justification in continuing to treat feminization as a symptom of educational decline.

B. The teachers' view of schools and of their work

We have just seen how a certain psychological climate can affect the interpretation of statistical data, which in turn aggravates the pessimistic outlook on the school. If this is the case with statistics, it will be even more true when it comes to complex aspects such as 'working conditions' and their implications for teachers' personalities and behaviour.

Working conditions: the school environment as seen by teachers

The expression 'working conditions' is taken to refer to all the rules, rights, resources and circumstances surrounding teachers' lives, including their contracts, salaries, teacher/student ratios, workload, teaching resources, and the system of teacher support, supervision and evaluation. Clearly working conditions vary between schools, regions and countries. One astute observer has noted, however, that teachers earning \$ 2,000 a month and working in well-equipped schools in a European country complain about job conditions just as bitterly as those who earn \$ 100 and work in makeshift buildings in a developing country. It is as if in teachers' minds worldwide 'working conditions' were synonymous with 'poor working conditions' for teachers. For this reason, in this section we refer not so much to the objective working conditions of European teachers, but to their attitude towards them. It is more than likely that the collective appreciation by teachers and other players of their unsatisfactory working conditions affects school life as much or more than real working conditions. It would be interesting to carry out some comparative studies between countries with very different 'working conditions', in order to measure to what extent teachers' health and behaviour are affected by real working conditions and by the way they experience them subjectively.

At an international conference on *The teaching profession in Europe*[2] at which a large number of teachers actively participated, one of the working groups made a detailed analysis of *occupational and material conditions which in many countries have deteriorated compared with other professions*. We have selected some items from the impressive list, which coincide with the issues raised in the ILO-UNESCO Joint Committee:

Rigidity of education systems and school organization; instability of education policies and fragmentation of responsibilities; impatience of political authorities to see reform results; uncertainty and increased job constraints and increased stress (physical and psychological) among teachers; pay stagnation compared with professions requiring a similar level of qualifications; pay uniformity ('no real reward for work quality); lack of or very limited career prospects; stagnation or degradation of buildings, installations and equipment; too few further training opportunities; lack of long-term recruitment policy; poor guidance for teachers and students; unfavourable conditions for team work; too little time for out-of-school activities and increased workload owing to proliferation of subjects; added responsibilities without increased resources; loss of job satisfaction and low morale; less social consideration; lack of clear role and status, etc.

In the minds of these qualified teachers, working conditions cover practically the whole of the *school environment,* including structures, organization, old and new professional duties (teaching and management), social expectations, etc. There is a continuous link between real-life events and the 'symbolic' burden, which is no less real, and which weaves a psycho-social thread underlying what in today's jargon we would call 'school culture'. The 'school malaise syndrome' has reached a European dimension, because it has continued to feed over the years on meetings and documents which refer to this malaise and to working conditions practically in the same terms. It is as if the school environment was an accumulation of difficulties, a kind of straightjacket immobilizing and conditioning the educational activity of every teacher, not to mention the capacity for change and innovation of the system as a whole. This was not the case with the participants at the aforementioned meeting, who displayed considerable experience and ability not only in describing the problems, but also, and even more so, when it came to proposing strategies and practical measures for changing the school environment. The scenario described in such detail, however, indicated that many European teachers feel as if they were no more than *the employees of a weighty administrative machinery* (OECD, 1990, p. 120), which blocks all creativity and imagination.

It is often thought that when teachers talk about working conditions, this is really a euphemism for a pay claim. The militant movements in recent years in practically all countries help to give this impression, which, like many other negative attitudes, has detracted from the image of the profession. Studies of teacher satisfaction and dissatisfaction have shown, however, that only a very small proportion of teachers at all levels mention low pay as a cause of dissatisfaction. Curiously enough, it is among those who earn most, namely the university teachers, that the proportion is greatest, at 6.5 per cent, of those quoting low pay as the first cause of dissatisfaction, while among primary and secondary school-teachers, this is given as the first reason by only 2.5 and 1.6 per cent respectively (Zubieta & Susinos, 1992, p. 279). Adding support to this argument, it was pointed out at the Netherlands conference mentioned earlier (para. 63) that those tempted to quit teaching are not the lowest rated teachers or those who earn the least, but quite the opposite.

The effects of working conditions on the personality and behaviour of teachers

Some analyses of the 'teaching malaise' suggest that it may be considered as a way for teachers to call society's attention to their 'working conditions', that is, to what the daily classroom and school routine means to them, the difficulties they meet with when teaching children and especially the latter's learning problems. Rather than a complaint on some particular aspect or other, 'working conditions' appear to be a criticism of a structure which many teachers feel is neither functional nor satisfactory and which may hold the keys of health problems and especially the abnormally high stress among teachers, as mentioned in the survey referred to earlier (ILO-UNESCO, 1994).

Detailed studies have been made about what is sometimes referred to generically as stress or mental health problems, resulting from working conditions. Some of the studies have managed to identify a rising scale of twelve types of symptoms of the teaching malaise:

- feelings of confusion and dissatisfaction when faced with the real problems of teaching practice;
- transfer requests as a form of escaping from situations of conflict;
- development of inhibition patterns;
- an explicit wish to quit teaching;
- absenteeism from work;
- fatigue derived from tension;
- stress;
- anxiety as a feature;
- self-depreciation and guilt feelings at the inability to achieve success in teaching;
- reactive neuroses;
- depressions;
- a permanent state of anxiety related by cause and effect to various symptoms of mental illness (Esteve, Franco & Vera, 1995, p. 47).

Some local studies have quantified the percentages of teachers at each step of the scale. Obviously this cannot be done on an international level. These are clearly serious symptoms of important problems. Studies and experiments are now being conducted, such as deliberately introducing *stress as a preventive technique in early teacher training* (Esteve, 1995). In view of the proliferation of this type of study, it may be worth looking into each of the particular conditions and to try to peer inside the 'schools' black box'.

Working conditions in private schools

To complete the arguments about working conditions as perceived by the teachers and its effects on their behaviour, we should say something about the difference between public and private schools. To start with, the notion of private school covers a variety of situations (as to the origins and the relative importance in each national tradition) in different European countries, so that it is not possible to generalize with regard to the social origin of students, or the working conditions of teachers, or operating conditions, or the results obtained compared with public education. In quantitative terms, for instance, the great majority of legally private schools are financed everywhere from public funds (EURYDICE, 1993b). Working conditions are similar to those in public establishments and, if there is any difference, timetables, working hours and especially pay tend to be rather worse for teachers in the private sector.

As far as the subjective experience of teachers is concerned, there are no comparable data, even though some local studies and national surveys have been made (Zubieta & Susinos, 1992), which appear to indicate that there is no significant correlation between conventional working conditions (pay, working hours, etc.) and the degree of teachers' satisfaction or identification with their school and their work. Without wishing to insinuate any kind of generalization, these studies do reveal an apparent paradox. The private school-teachers surveyed tended to teach several hours a week more than their public education counterparts, earned about 15% less and in some cases used some of their summer vacations to attend courses, and yet when indicating their degree of satisfaction and positive identification with their schools, private school teachers gave higher ratings.

No general conclusion can be drawn from these data, nor can they be used as an argument in the public/private education debate, since the data reflect the micro-structure and culture of the school system rather than the external authority responsible for organizing and financing it. As the researchers themselves noted, the feelings and views expressed by teachers running against their own interests are only surprising from a mechanistic view of educational quality and teaching. Without having to be militant altruists and while still fighting to achieve better pay and shorter working hours, teachers can find *satisfaction in other ways;* for instance, if there is a clear educational policy, a stable teaching team, a coherent educational culture and management and support for teachers' work by efficient managers. Probably in countries with centralized systems, where the ideal is for all schools to be the same, the features which are popular among the teachers surveyed are probably more easily found in private schools than in public establishments. This should not lead one to the conclusion, however, that this is due to the private or public character of the school. As we shall see below, as part of a general tendency to make schools more independent, some European countries are undertaking an explicit policy of promoting the individual identity of each school.

C. The content of the schools' black box

While it is still possible to improve the material conditions of schools and the working conditions of teachers, even in the wealthiest countries, there is no denying that European schools nowadays have decent buildings, with libraries, basic laboratories and often computer equipment. It also seems that teachers' pay improved in real terms in practically all European countries between 1986 and 1991 (CMOPE, 1991). Despite this, however, the working conditions that did not improve are the 'environmental' and 'psychological' conditions (Vaniscotte, 1994), in other words, conditions which may be directly changed by organized teachers in schools.

It is therefore worth taking the analysis inside the school, and looking at some of the information provided by an abundant intellectual national and international output.

The schools' capacity for change

In recent years more has been discovered about the teaching/ learning process and about teacher/pupil relations. It is also known that the performance of individual schools and teachers has a significant effect on learning results. This has been shown by research carried out in several countries (Escudero Muñoz, 1991; Ghilardi, 1993; OECD, 1989), and more specifically by the results of work projects undertaken by the teachers themselves, as we said when we referred to action-research. A number of international bodies have done pioneering work in this field, such as the OECD-CERI's '*International school improvement project* (ISIP)' (Van Velzen, 1988; Hopkins & Bollen, 1988; OECD, 1989), and similar work has been sponsored by the World Bank in developing countries. A fair amount is known nowadays about why some schools facilitate more and better learning than others. This has broken a trend which has persisted for several decades, during which educational policies and research underestimated the management of the teaching/learning process and the methods and techniques developed by teachers in the classroom (EURYDICE, 1994; Tedesco, 1995).

Until a few decades ago, it was believed that educational results were determined by the social environment and that schools fulfilled a mere reproductive function. Recently, on the other hand, the pendulum of opinion has swung over towards the professional training of individual teachers and improving working conditions in schools, that is, towards considering the parts and components of what is referred to as the black box of education. The approach of wanting to improve schools only by means of better buildings, more computers, better salaries, lower ratios, and more qualified and younger teachers appears to have been exhausted.

With regard to schools, educational opinion is now rediscovering, after an accumulation of evidence over the past twenty years, that the key lies not with individual teachers, nor with buildings, nor laboratories, but with *school procedures, methods and management,* that is to say, with *organized activity in the black box.* With all the caution that would seem appropriate in the light of recent educational history with regard to any dogma or magic recipe, one has to observe that a series of studies undertaken by institutions or experts in the last decade all agree that differing school performance may be attributed to *variations in structure and educational practice* (EURYDICE, 1994; OECD, 1989a; 1989b; 1990).

What we should point out now is that behind all these variables there is the organized human factor, in other words, the *teams of teachers.* This research 'feat' has been achieved thanks to many teaching teams which have carried out new experiments in ways of teaching and learning and of managing time and space, resources and relations with the environment (OECD, 1989a, p. 148). *These teams have made it possible to appreciate differences between schools.* Although innovation and experimentation have not been quantified, in all community programmes we can find interesting examples of transnational co-operation between teams of teachers involved in innovating and researching. In specialized reviews published in all countries, we always find a section permanently set aside for significant school experiments.

There is no possibility of measuring the degree of innovatory capacity of any particular system or sector, and even less to compare two systems, such as health and education, to find out which innovates best. It makes even less sense to try to compare situations in twenty very different countries. This being the case, only a negative outlook by and on the education system, *a defensive 'institutional culture' established by educationalists,* can explain the generally shared view regarding the education system's and even more so the teachers' particular reluctance to change and resistance to reform. Judging by the information currently available on innovations, there are objective facts on which an optimistic outlook could be based, much more favourable to change than the pessimistic approach which has gone on long enough.

The complex attitudes of teachers in relation to change

Rediscovering the importance of teaching processes may have another effect, namely, breaking the chain of mutual accusations between the authorities and teachers and replacing it with a common assumption of responsibili-ties. Innovating teachers do not ask the authorities for more money, but rather for administrative facilities and incentives to innovate. Educational authorities aware of innovation, on the other hand, do not ask teachers either to undertake more retraining courses or to be present physically in school for all their working hours, but rather to organize and manage their schools differently.

When the idea emerges that they may be the main agents of change, many teachers are seized with uncertainty and doubts regarding their psychological, methodological or professional preparedness. This insecurity may lie at the root of some of the teaching malaise. Many teachers, especially in secondary education, talk about the *Monday syndrome,* a certain anxiety related to returning to the classroom. When they are asked why, they tend to reply in terms of what we have referred to generally as 'working conditions' (Zubieta & Susinos, 1992; Esteve, Franco & Vera, 1995; Ghilardi, 1993). Some admit that they do not know how to cope with difficult students, while others more shyly confess to problems with motivating or teaching their classes in general. *'Every new class is less well prepared',* or *'this group is a disaster',* are comments frequently heard among colleagues. Some are not sure that their knowledge or their methods are up to date and feel that the courses offered do not meet their needs or expectations and therefore do not dispel their anxiety. In discussions among themselves, teachers normally avoid these subjects, taking it for granted, as A. Prost says, that the problem lies not with them, but with the children: *The major assumption in all discussions about education nowadays is that its difficulties come from the students and not from the teachers (...). In other words, nothing can be done without a massive development of research into teaching methods, even if teaching cannot provide the whole answer.* Some of the teachers who distribute streams of bad marks may arouse the suspicion that the 'fault' may lie with them, even though at meetings with colleagues and at evaluation meetings they are constantly referring to the need to be strict with the students.

According to several studies, when the teachers are formally interviewed in the course of a survey, most of them reply (up to 91%) that their greatest satisfaction lies with the students and that education is a vocation and not merely a job, while most assert that they would go in for teaching again if they had the choice. Similar replies and percentages emerge from surveys in the United States and in European countries (Ghilardi, 1993; Zubieta & Surinos, 1992; OECD, 1990).

In the face of somewhat conflicting feelings and opinions, several authors have made a bold attempt to classify teachers according to their attitudes to current changes (Esteve, Franco & Vera, 1995, p. 43), which may shed some light on the very varied subjective outlook of teachers. The first category includes *those who accept educational change* as an inevitable consequence of social change, agreeing that they themselves have to change their practices and giving critical support to reforms from above. The second category are the *passive* teachers—those who are inhibited because they are not strong enough to overcome their fear of the unknown. These include many who are disillusioned after earlier attempts at change. The third category of teachers oscillates between recognizing the need for change and denying its viability in practice. The fourth and last category is *afraid of change,* because reforms would uncover their shortcomings or because they cannot bear uncertainty or doubt. In the local sample given in the above-mentioned study, the positive category accounted for 34 per cent of the total, the fearful category 28 per cent, the inhibited or passive category 22 per cent and those torn between opposite tendencies 15 per cent. It would be absurd to extrapolate these figures on a national and even less a European level, although they do provide a useful indication, since this distribution of basic attitudes is reflected in other surveys and studies (Zubieta & Susinos, 1992).

Many teachers, like many other citizens, do not understand what is happening in the world. While in other professions this does not have adverse implications for work, in education it presents a serious difficulty. The complete separation between the cultural climate in schools and the culture experienced by children and adolescents outside school and which they bring with them into the classroom is neither healthy nor productive. Schools are still very unidimensional, since they do not welcome cultural diversity. Is it not true to say that administrative rules impose a type of school culture (an ethos, teaching routines enclosed in rigid time and space constraints, a form of management and co-existence), which is out of phase with the lives and real culture of both students and teachers?

D. Conclusion

To sum up this chapter on the situation of teachers, we may reiterate the following points:

- The first consideration is the need to improve the critical attitudes to schools and teachers, in order to create a body of opinion which, though critical, is prepared to help change and improve a system which sees itself in an optimistic light.
- One positive message to emerge from all these discussions concerning internal and external views of schools and teachers is that what needs to be changed, namely the school environment and the internal functioning of schools, is in principle within reach of today's teachers. Change is not easy, but the teachers are able to intervene much more in this type of change than in decisions to build new buildings or to pass laws giving them a professional status and increasing their salaries. This is an important fact, which could lead to a new approach to the demands made by society, administra-tions and teachers and to relations between them.
- Changing school-teaching is within reach of the teachers, though not taken individually, but only in so far as collectively they constitute the backbone and heart of the school system.

V. Changes and Reforms in European Education Systems

Change and reform are not the same thing. In the educational debate, they are sometimes used with contrasted meanings. In simple terms, reforms may be said to be attempted changes undertaken by governments. Changes are taken to mean transforma-tions in the practices of teaching staff and school organization promoted by the educational players themselves. An attempt is made below to identify the links which may be established between these two processes, with regard to teaching practice.

In the last decade most countries have undertaken greater or lesser reforms, to which not only governments but also parliaments have contributed. In practically all the bills calling for these reforms, the most significant argument used is the need for education systems to prepare individuals for the challenges raised by structural changes. It would therefore seem worth taking a look at the reforms of the education system in the light of the above comments, with special emphasis on the role played in them by teachers. For the sake of clarity, we distinguish different types of reform applied in European countries, although some countries are introducing all types of reform simultaneously as well as changing their policies specifically related to teachers.

A. General educational reforms

This category of reforms includes those which, within the educational tradition of each country, reorganize the formal structure of cycles, stages and educational procedures, and/or modify general curricular guidelines or specific programmes in some subjects or cycles on the basis of new legislation. Curriculum-oriented reforms spread the general cultural contents over the ten years which European children usually spend in school. Many countries have undertaken total or partial reforms of their curricula in recent years, with the aim of adapting the content of education to requirements arising from the drastic changes described above, and deliberately to establish a cultural basis for the human resources required by the new economic situation.

Reform processes and their limitations

Much has been written, in all languages, regarding the lack of credibility and ineffectiveness of this type of reform. Some argue (Gimeno, 1992) that major *reforms* usually fail to achieve *changes* in school practices and culture. The scepticism or even outright rejection of the reforms on the part of teachers is pointed out, as well as the reluctance of families and the passive attitude of students. The final reason why they are ineffective is said to be the fact that one reform merely paves the way for the next.

The reason why many of those involved fail to identify with reform processes lies in the way they are approached and in the strategy and methodology used to design and implement them. The starting point is usually a diagnosis identifying supply weaknesses in the face of future educational challenges and a proposal for priorities and strategies for altering educational structures. Once this initiative has been launched, it is followed by a period of consultations and public discussion, which naturally includes teachers' unions and other organizations, but which turns into a complex process of political negotiation, usually also involving political parties, trade unions, local authorities, churches and employers. Teachers and students alike are then forced to stand by and watch these negotiations, until such time as an act is passed, signalling the start of an equally long period of adjustment and gradual implemen-tation, which can last anything from ten to fifteen years.

Some authors draw attention to the distortion which the initial purpose suffers during the whole political negotiation of each and every detail. With the pragmatic approach adopted in all reforms, the problems raised in political negotiations and the long period of time required for implementation, there is bound to be a certain 'dilution' of the initial reformist impulse. After a few years, the systems revert to their inertia, having incorporated the key ideas of the reform to a greater or lesser extent. A militant minority of teachers will maintain the flame of research and experimentation alive, which will be rekindled in the next wave of reforms.

Teachers and reforms of teaching methods

Changing curricula and restructuring a system's architecture imply a small revolution in the lives of teachers. Some have to move from one cycle or stage to another. As an undesired but no less significant effect, in some cases children or teachers have to change schools or even towns, since structural reforms imply 'concentrations' or 'relocations'. Any reform of the curriculum implies that all teachers will have to be 'retrained' as regards their knowledge of contents and methods, so that practically all teaching reforms entail reforming the policy and structures of initial and in-service teacher training.

As far as teachers' attitudes to official reforms are concerned, there is a widespread view among teaching staff that educational reforms are promoted by governments as a result of external diagnoses and proposals, in which 'their' (the teachers') world is seen through the eyes of 'others' (experts or politicians), even when the teachers have been invited to participate in the preparation and in the implementation of the reforms. Many are prepared to accept that changes have to be made in school organization and educational practice, but that such changes should not come from above. A certain percentage of teachers will support, with a degree of criticism, the reforms undertaken by the ministries, and will seize the opportunity to introduce innovations and educational experiments based on their own experience. For other teachers, adapting to frequent reforms is one of the working conditions which causes stress and professional insecurity, while many others are inhibited or survive in a sea of contradictions. Some teachers consider that society's criticism of the school system is unjustified and that educational reforms amount tc a denial of their professional status or, at best, a set of bureaucratic measures which, because they have been designed from above, are bound to be ineffective.

Reforms and changes from below

There has been a great deal of criticism of government-initiated reforms. It is said that general educational reforms are ineffective and costly and that it would be more productive to stimulate teachers who are competent and motivated to undertake work projects in some schools or areas as a means of generalizing new attitudes and practices.

The reforms mentioned so far have not been the only changes, however, taking place in European education systems. We have already alluded to the tendency for education to come closer to economics, which has taken the form of endless experiments of linkage between schools and businesses. These types of experiment are sponsored by governments, especially since they have become a *leitmotiv* of several European Union programmes. On the other hand, as an effect of the more significant changes occurring at present, all over Europe there are teams of teachers working with their students in the most varied fields, such as ecology, values education and education for democracy, for peace, for cultural identity, for computing and telematics, etc.

The antagonism between reforms and teacher-led changes seems neither necessary nor of benefit to anyone. Whether the desired structural changes are implemented or not, every reform process brings together and co-ordinates a minority of researchers and teachers, who can provide a significant leavening element for the development of changes in a country's education. A common challenge to general reforms and innovating experiments is the difficulty of assimilating in practice the different kinds of scientific and technical advances produced by educational research. In this respect, the conditions are now right for co-operation between several disciplines (epistemology, psychology, systems theory, computing, telematics) in both their theoretical and their practical aspects.

In other words, the most productive climate is probably one favouring synthesis, given that reforms and changes in all countries are converging around a set of central themes. When a connection is established between initiatives coming from below and reforms and policies from above, then a clear impulse is given to educational change, for the greater satisfaction of both teachers and students (Cuadernos de pedagogia, 1996a, 1996b). The innovators can take advantage of the impulse and climate of official reforms to achieve a greater impact and to spread the example to more schools and teachers, considering that proposed reform policies usually coincide with the feelings of the more innovative and creative teachers, as well as with the guidelines issued by international organizations. It would therefore be worth stimulating and encouraging those teachers who adopt a critical but constructive attitude to reform.

B. Institutional reforms

Practically all educational reforms are accompanied by some type of institutional reform. The policies followed by several countries in recent years have focused on administrative and territorial decentralization, improvement in system management and greater independence for educational establishments. There is a clear link between these reforms and the general movement sparked off by the new scientific, technical and organizational paradigms, which call for a review of the administrative and management structures of State machinery and of education systems as part of the latter.

Decentralization and concentration of responsibility in educational administrations

The historic configurations of education systems and the diverse political and administrative traditions of European countries have given rise to a variety of ways of sharing out educational, administrative and financial responsibilities in the field of education and training (EURYDICE, 1990, 1993 and 1995b), which have been used as models by many countries all over the world.

Two main groups stand out: countries whose systems are directed and administered by the national government; and countries with either regionally or locally based independent educational administrations. It is often said that these two groups of countries are travelling the same path in opposite directions. In fact, some countries with a centralized tradition have been transferring some or all responsibilities to regional and local administrations, while other countries with a very decentralized educational management are moving in the opposite way, trying to institute a centralized authority able to intervene in matters which are vital for public education. Then there are countries where the basic emphasis is placed on autonomous provinces, regions or cantons, leaving the existing distribution of responsibilities as it is. This general picture does not take account of specific situations, which are much more complex.

The degree of 'power' wielded over the curriculum at every stage, from the ministry downwards to the teacher in the classroom, lies at the heart of policies for reallocating educational responsibilities geographically, alongside such topics as budgets and the so-called 'working conditions' of teachers, starting with the recruitment system. Mere administrative centralization or decentralization may either not have much effect on the lives of schools and teachers or may have apparently contradictory effects.

- Decentralization may be very important in the case of regions and communities which subordinate educational responsibilities to clearly differentiated linguistic and cultural policies. Another possible effect of decentralization is that teachers who used to be able to work in any part of the country find their inter-regional mobility restricted, precisely at the time when the free movement of workers is being achieved in the European Union.

- The independence of individual schools is not directly related to the degree of centralization or decentralization of the educational administration, but rather to other factors, such as a country's political tradition or culture. In fact, countries with a long-standing tradition of local educational administration argue that the independence of schools is a point in favour of instituting more centralization (United Kingdom, White Paper, 1992). On the other hand, the decentralization occurring in a number of regional and local administrations may merely repeat the previous pattern of national centralization, in a more mitigated form, without leaving schools any more real autonomy than under the centralized system (Pedró, 1993). There do not appear to be any comparative studies available on teachers' views of this dual situation.

Quality and efficient management: evaluation

One of the main concerns recently has been for countries to achieve a better return on resources invested in the education system. In the early 1980s, many American businessmen and some intellectuals and politicians sharply criticized the inefficiency of that country's education system, which they blamed for *endangering the nation.* The idea then began to spread in Europe of applying management and efficiency to education systems. More recently, this aim has been more directly linked to the problem of *quality.* Although this type of reform does not assume any specific profile, it usually takes the form of administrative and financial rationalization, including the decentralization measures mentioned earlier; with regard to quality, there is a tendency to strengthen the management aspect of schools, much affected by a loss of authority and efficiency, which has been attributed to poor training of teachers in management and to opposition between parents and teachers on management bodies.

Evaluation

Probably the clearest manifestation of the paradigm of educational efficiency and effectiveness is the introduction of external systems for monitoring and assessing student performance, the results of educational establishments and the operation of the education system as whole (Tiana, 1996).

From the beginning, European systems have always incorporated a body or organ of inspection, which has been a key component of the structure and operation of the education system so far. Its function was traditionally to ensure compliance with the standards and procedures established for schools, teaching staff and students, on the assumption that conformity with standards was the best guarantee that the purposes of schools would be met. External supervision and monitoring of educational processes went hand in hand with full responsibility on the part of teachers for student evaluation, subject to the latter having to sit external examinations as part of a selection process for entry to the next stage upwards.

The evaluation procedures which are emerging at present are different. It is no longer a question of evaluating processes, but of knowing the results of what is going on inside the *black box*. The International Association for the Evaluation of Educational Achievement (IEA) and OECD have been developing concepts and procedures for the new evaluation strategies. Both bodies have accumulated a considerable store of data and analysis, which are disseminated in books, reviews and meetings of all kinds. The INES project (international education indicators), which was launched a few years ago, carries considerable influence with the new evaluation policies and strategies in all countries (OECD-CERI, 1994). The identification, preparation and application of quantitative and qualitative indicators of educational performance amount to a substantial change in the general approach to information concerning education systems. Everything is being evaluated, including the evaluation processes themselves (Escudero Muñoz, 1991, p. 436).

Practically all European countries have introduced some evaluation body and/or scheme in recent years, for purposes of educational diagnosis and improvement. Governments and societies want to know the results of students' learning, either through more detailed analysis of teachers' evaluations and marks, or through surveys and/or national examinations at specific ages. They also want to know the results achieved by individual schools, in order to provide support for those that need it, but also to keep the client-payers (the families) duly informed and, from another point of view, to introduce a process of emulation or competition between educational establishments. There is also a wish to know whether programmes are adequate, whether the curriculum works, and whether the reforms are producing the desired results. The study of intended changes is an objective much appreciated by evaluators.

Although there are seldom plans for direct teacher evaluation, *according to the new evaluation reasoning, priority is now being given to the professional performance and training of teachers* (Tiana, 1996). In effect, the teachers are to a large extent responsible for what their students learn. Therefore, if results are evaluated in terms of learning, this amounts to indirectly evaluating the teachers' performance. But it is through the evaluation of the schools where they teach that teachers feel themselves most directly evaluated. They are jointly responsible with the authorities and the legislation in force for school organization and culture. For this reason, any evaluation of schools amounts to an evaluation of teachers, as well as an evaluation of the structure and operation of the education system as a whole. As a substantial element of school activity, the teaching process, for which teachers are personally responsible, is one of the causes (or indicators, as appropriate) of student performance. One recommendation of the OECD report (1990, p. 133) referred to the need to attach *high priority to research into the teaching process itself, linking it practically and as, far as possible with the teachers' routine dealings with their students.* We are now aware that a school's organization and culture are factors which contribute fundamentally to the effectiveness of a teacher's didactic activity. There are 'significant shortcomings', however, in the indicators used to measure the efficiency of individual teachers' methods (Ghilardi, 1993, p. 43). Since evaluations have more difficulty 'measuring' quantitative rather than qualitative results and indicators, not much progress has been made with the 'measurement' of teachers' performances. Since the merit of individual teachers cannot be measured, moreover, the idea of *linking part of pay to 'merit'* does not appear to have made much headway, except perhaps in university teaching, where indirect indicators are used, such as publications or studies, rather than the academic performances of students. There is, however, a fear that the 'evaluative fashion' may culminate in monitoring teachers to introduce pay differentials within groups of teachers.

A positive view of efficient management

As with other subjects, the new talk about quality, efficiency and evaluation is generating as much or more concern as the measures introduced to give it effect. Among supporters of public education (whether teachers, trade unionists or experts), there is a fear that the economic jargon may be hiding a neo-liberal paradigm, with all its consequences, such as competition, economic liberalism, privatization, duality of the education system with schools for the rich and schools for the poor, etc.

Beyond these fears, many sources indicate a need to identify the real challenges of 'total quality management' in education (Xavier, 1994). Summing up the conclusions of an international discussion on education, a United Nations body said as much without any euphemisms: *The educational function of the future cannot be exercised by a routine, hierarchical structure, where teachers are civil servants, in a society which is indifferent to its financial needs* (ECLA, 1992, p. 119). This statement can probably be applied in a somewhat different form to European education, which has also come in for some severe criticism: *The system is organized as if all the students, all teachers and all schools were identical and interchangeable... This completely standardized educational myth has now been burst as under* (Robert, Y. 1990, p. 68).

It would seem inevitable that culture and the logic of supply and demand, diversification and competition should be brought into the discussion about improving the administrative machinery of education, a necessity on which all agree. Teachers who complain at the cumbersome nature of educational bureaucracy should welcome with enthusiasm the idea of improving management, if this idea were not associated with real or unfounded images and fears. Introducing efficient management methods does not imply privatization, commercialization or abandoning the cultural function of schooling. The debate should have only one starting point, namely *how can all available resources be better managed to achieve the purpose of the system, that is, to ensure equal opportunities for all and equal obligations to learn more, better and with greater enthusiasm.* There is no single approach. Teachers now have an opportunity to climb out of their defensive trenches and to try to open up new ways forward. Should teachers not be keen for 'their' schools to be 'learning organizations', which is one of the ideals of the new management paradigms?

School independence

In view of the considerable historical diversity, there are many different forms and degrees of dependence or independence in European schools (EURYDICE, 1990, 1990, 1993 and 1995). Although there is no automatic correlation between school independence and the type of centralized or decentralized, administration involved, it is worth noting that the management and teachers in primary schools in Denmark and in the United Kingdom have always enjoyed a degree of independence, which has allowed them to design and manage their *curriculum* in the fullest sense of the term, including programmes, organization and methods. Only the community and the local authorities intervene, so that the schools' autonomy also expresses itself in its ability to co-ordinate and negotiate in that respect. In countries with a centralizing tradition, on the other hand, the ideal is for the same lesson to be given at the same time in equivalent classes throughout the country's education system.

These two extremes have been coming closer together. The schools and teachers in some countries have been losing part of their independence and having to learn to manage new types of relations and dependencies, while in other countries they have been called upon to assume certain responsibilities beyond merely complying with general instructions, established programmes, timetables and working hours laid down at the beginning of the school year.

A general tendency has been to invite or oblige each establishment to draw up a 'school plan'. Under this or a similar heading, the schools have to assume certain educational responsibilities, which they may manage with a degree of discretion, in accordance with the consensus established between the team of teachers, the principal and/or the school management board, subject to the approval of the relevant administrative office. This school plan includes different items, such as:

- Preparing and managing a plan of out-of-school activities, such as exchanges with other educational establishments and/or businesses, outings, visits to museums, sports, theatre, etc. This degree of independence is practically general.

- Management of resource budgets allocated by the supervisory administration for expenditure arising from the above activities or for current expenses in general.
- In some countries there always was and in others there is beginning to be some capacity for financial management, including the search for additional resources, through the sale of services, business sponsorship, European Union funds, etc.
- Planning and organizing different educational activities for groups of students or individuals within the diversification margins allowed under the new curricular policies.
- Freedom (in varying degrees) to establish links and co-operation agreements with associations, institutions or enterprises within the educational area.
- In several countries the central and/or regional authorities are content with prescribing curricular guidelines, without entering into specific contents. The schools are then responsible for curriculum design and for managing the teaching aspect. The degree of independence may depend, for instance, on whether the general regulation imposes flexible or rigid time schedules.
- Independence may imply not only *the dismantling of central regulation and local 'devolution' of the power of decision over curriculum design, but also allowing schools to acquire their own identity and image* (Finland, Ministry of Education, 1994).

An EURYDICE study (EURYDICE, 1990) on the administration and evaluation of schools in the European Union arrived at the following conclusions:

- Schools tend to be the core of the administration of education systems;
- Parents and other local community representatives are increasingly influencing school objectives and targets, as well as monitoring their operation and results;
- School management must be an essential element of strategies for promoting the development of school organization, the improvement of school efficiency and the achievement of a better standard of operation;
- The increasing independence of schools and the concern for efficiency and quality have given rise to greater interest in matters

related to school evaluation (summary in Vaniscotte, 1994, p. 25).

A few years ago, a CERI report, produced as a result of an international study highlighted the beneficial effects of transferring responsibilities to schools and of team work by teachers in the following terms:

Greater participation in decisions reduces the impression of helplessness and isolation which is often felt by teachers who are nothing more than the employees of a weighty administrative machinery. By taking part in decision-making, they may gain greater trust in those involved in administering the school (...). Teachers have access to information from other sources than the principal... There are fewer conflicts (...). Teachers have less of a tendency to think in terms of 'them' as opposed to 'us'(...). Decision-making encourages teachers to take an interest in more general educational problems, while facilitating exchanges with teachers in other disciplines, other classes and other regions, and encourages them to consider different solutions and to state and defend their opinions (OECD-CERI, 1990, p. 120).

C. Specific policies regarding the teaching profession

The most common diagnosis regarding the teaching profession tends to point towards a similar type of policy and strategy in all countries, revolving around three objectives:

- Attracting a sufficient number of able and motivated young people to the profession (recruitment and/or initial training);
- Improving the motivation and professional competence of working teachers (continuous training);
- Giving teachers incentives in order to enhance their self-esteem and their social image.

Recruitment and initial training policies

Specific measures: As already mentioned in Chapter III, many measures have already been suggested either to make good quantitative shortages or to tackle the problem of quality, such as: campaigns to promote the image of the profession and status of teachers, especially in sectors with recruitment problems; cash incentives for practical work during training; removing age limits and encouraging adults with experience in other fields to think of taking up a teaching career; setting up information and guidance services in universities; adapting the content and methods of initial training, etc. To deal with the surplus problem, either due to lack of access for young people, or to redundancies following school closures, certain palliative measures and retraining facilities have been suggested. While some of these measures are actually applied, most do not go beyond the recommendation stage, being unable to overcome the tangle of administrative obstacles.

Initial training as an instrument of recruitment policy, professionalization and enhancement: A significant aspect of policy as regards teachers has been the emphasis on changing initial training. This topic alone has accounted for a considerable share of the literature devoted to teachers (Escudero Muñoz, 1991, p. 125 ff) and has been a central theme of meetings and conferences. The main strategy has consisted in raising the status of establishments providing initial teacher training. This has meant extending the training period and making it more academic. Training establishments (teacher-training colleges and others) have often been raised to the status of higher education institutions or in some countries placed fully on a par with universities.

The initial enthusiasm did wane somewhat. It was probably realized that neither extending courses, nor turning old teacher-training colleges into universities automatically implied transferring the knowledge produced by university research to teacher training. The instructors of trainee teachers may be as far removed as ever from the results of research, including those produced in 'neighbouring' faculties of psychology or pedagogy. The watertight departments of universities do not make matters any easier. Moreover, raising colleges to the status of higher education institutions does not appear to have made the profession any more attractive either.

Both the experts and those directly involved agree that there are no clear ideas where the objective of professiona-lization is concerned and that the administrative environment neither of education systems nor of the universities themselves makes it any easier to incorporate teacher training simultaneously in universities and in teaching practice.

In-service training policy

As in other areas, in-service training arose as a means of making up for shortcomings in initial training and has since been developed as a tool for extending knowledge, improving teaching skills, and analyzing and changing the professional attitudes of teachers (EURYDICE, 1995, p. 8). Until recently, in-service training meant short courses on the contents of a subject or on teaching methods, or in some cases on aspects of management. Nowadays strategies have diversified and training colleges and instructors have multiplied. Continuous training is not compulsory in any country, although in some it is a requirement for advancement in the career. The replacement of teachers undergoing training is dealt with on a case-by-case basis, as is the payment of salaries during training, which is nowhere guaranteed by law. The lack of any administrative regulation leads experts to believe that in-service training of European teachers is still not well established as a sector (EURYDICE, 1995, p. 25).

One significant development is worth noting for its effect on the role of teachers in educational change. While traditional training courses may be either more academic or more practical in nature, they are by definition detached from the life and practice of individual schools, since they are intended for a variety of teachers from different establishments. The report of the Holmes Group (1986), which was so influential in Europe, pointed out among its eight 'commandments' that *schools had to be a place of learning not only for students, but also for teachers* (commented in Vaniscotte, 1994, p. 74). While many European countries have been inclined to follow the suggestions of the Holmes report enthusiastically, and even more so those.of the Carnegie report on the hierarchical professionalization of the teaching profession and the need to give university status to teacher training, they proved less eager in this respect, while the experts agree that there is only a weak link between continuous training and innovation in schools (Vaniscotte, 1994, p. 82).

Things are changing, however (EURYDICE, 1995). Under the heading of *interactive and reflexive strategy,* activities are currently being programmed to train the human resources of educational establishments (Netherlands Conference, 1991). Continuous training Is looked upon as a collective practical exercise. The group involved may consist of all the teachers of a particular school, or professionals from different schools, who analyze the different types of educational practice with which they are familiar. According to some studies, *a great majority of teachers feel that training can be based on class practice* (Vaniscotte, 1994, p. 86).

International research on strategies for introducing change in schools by modifying the capabilities of individual teachers or the collective attitudes of teaching teams (Escudero Muñoz, 1991, p. 97 ff.) has already brought to light data and ideas on which further work needs to be done. This is one of the potential linkages between action-research groups in education and more dynamic businesses, which are trying to improve not only the personal skills of their staff, but also equipment and the enterprise as a whole. This approach (Senge, 1990 and 1995) has already been noticeable for some years among European and American educational researchers. To sum up, the idea and the central challenge of initial and in-service teacher training revolve around the objective of converting schools into institutions which learn.

D. Conclusion

To sum up the changes and reforms of European education systems, we may note that:

- Times of change are marked by uncertainty. As far as changes in education are concerned, public policy and society's requirements oscillate between a desire to solve problems inherited from the past and the search for a new scenario to face future challenges. Even when research has revealed some of the keys of educational renewal, traditional policies continue to be pursued out of inertia. In the case of teachers and their role in educational change, some reforms still insist on concentrating the problem on individual teachers, and therefore on promoting measures to improve their skills, their professional status and their working conditions, thereby underestimating the importance of the organization and culture of the institutions where individuals perform.
- The second point to consider is the need to identify the functions of schools. The changes required of education systems do not imply simply improvements, but an upheaval

similar to that experienced by the industrial system in recent decades. Since the Faure report, *Learning to be,* and until the first thoughts and recommendations were produced by the *International Commission on Education for the Twenty-first Century,* chaired by Jacques Delors, the number of requests directed at education has been impressive. The Commission's thinking is summed up in the phrase: *education, which must be for all and lifelong, must teach people to know, to do, to live together and to be. Who is capable of doing all that?* The role of teachers in educational change is therefore linked to a new educational pact, which consists in setting out in practical terms the minimum expected of each school and then reviewing who can work on the remaining challenges or educational purposes which schools and teachers are unable to pursue, either for historic reasons or because society does not provide them with the explicit mandate or with sufficient resources to do so.

VI. Teachers and Educational Change : A Possible Strategy

In this fifth and last chapter, we shall try, on the basis of the elements we analyzed in earlier chapters, to postulate an *open strategy hypothesis,* offering teachers a role as protagonists in educational change.

This working hypothesis, which is submitted for the consideration and discussion of meeting participants, is intended as a *synthesis* of :

- the main line of international educational thinking;
- the recommendations of some international organizations;
- the basic intentions of some educational reforms;
- the results of educational research and action-research on organization, strategies and working methods which differentiate some schools from others;
- some of the views of significant professional organizations in European education.

The first four chapters reviewed a variety of arguments,

hypotheses, criticisms, experience and recommendations. At the end of each chapter, some comments were given summarizing questions related to the role which teachers play and could play in the required educational change. All that remains, therefore, is to took in more detail at the central aspects of the role of teachers in educational change.

A. Teachers and the educational enterprise

The breakdown of consensus regarding the purposes of schooling is not due to opposing views. There are, needless to say, differing attitudes and opinions, but these could all agree on the need for a *'return to the school'*. The focus on schooling is basic to the theme of the forty-fifth session of the International Conference on Education, as we shall see below.

The direction of change: the central role of schooling

The assumption in this proposal, which is by no means always taken into account, is that isolated teachers cannot assume the sum of responsibilities implied by the educational consequences of current changes, even if the education system and schools hold a monopoly of teaching.

We may recall some results of international research, which indicate fairly unequivocally that *schools can really improve and we are now understanding better and better how and why they are improving* (Vaniscotte, 1994, p. 290). We may also bear in mind the low correlation between the educational performance of students and some key variables, such as the academic standard of teachers, student/teacher ratios and, nowadays, the socio-economic circumstances of parents. On the other hand, there is a clear correlation between academic performance and some organizati-onal processes and cultural dynamics (OECD, 1990, p. 79 ff; EURYDICE, 1994, p. 63 ff.; Xavier, 1994, p. 301 ff). From these studies, we may deduce the quality criteria and characteristics which appear to affect good results in school. In this respect and despite the time which has elapsed since the book first appeared, the ten characteristics of good schools listed at the end of the OECD's book on the quality of education still remain applicable (OECD, 1989, p. 154).

The characteristics include: really sharing educational views, objectives and plans; giving students positive expectations regarding their learning capabilities; having a co-operative working plan based on self-analysis but subject to external monitoring, evaluation and support; a favourable learning climate; and an undertaking by all to devote their best efforts and as much time as possible to teaching; a continuous stream of transparent information to all those involved with the results of learning; and, lastly, strong, dynamic and democratic management.

These factors of success are in principle within reach of a school's teaching staff, so that the latter should be allowed a greater degree of independence with their decisions. *No individual teacher can introduce them in his classes, nor can any ministerial decree impose them on the whole of the system.* Even though school plans are formally complied with, they may still exist only on paper. Passive compliance with changes in curricula can detract from the spirit of curricular reforms. Teachers are well aware of the fact that a reform can be made to have no effect at all if they do not want it to. At the same time, the determination of an individual teacher or even a school principal is not sufficient, if there is not some sort of team effort to give coherence to a working project and supply the necessary management capability. *All policies and strategies begin and end in the school. This is where all official acts meet with success or failure.*

Teachers as the driving force of school change

Sectoral changes or local teaching experiments just as much as general reforms boil down in the end to the same effect, namely that a school or part of a school, that is, a team of professionals, usually referred to under the common heading of 'teachers', decides to incorporate changes in its teaching practices, its organization and/or, its outside relations. This common sense statement is the basis of the strategy towards which the experts' opinions and recommendations, as well as national reforms and policies affecting teachers, are pointing. *The key is to make teachers the real driving force of educational change and to convince them that this is what they are.*

This approach is very different from the strategy which consists in wanting teachers to adopt and implement plans and programmes developed outside the school, however satisfactory they may be. This point may be explained as follows:

- Strategies for change based on the professionalization of 'teaching staff' (for instance, through training) have proved inadequate because they assume that teachers are the *only* problem.
- Traditional reformist strategies (consisting in planning changes in which teachers and students are subsequently requested to participate) have also proved ineffective because they assume that the 'teaching body' as such is not mature enough and that it needs to be spoonfed.
- It is no use either thinking that, since teachers are part of the school problem, they cannot assume respon-sibility for the change. The problem is that there are no other agents of change which can take on the task. There simply can be no change *against or without* teachers.
- Changes will only be effective if they are discovered by teachers, understood by them and/or accepted with conviction and, better still, with enthusiasm. Without belittling the importance of other players and factors, improvements in schools will happen as teachers can, know how to and want.

It is more than likely that if schools are given greater responsibility in educational change, teachers who are already innovating and who at times are merely tolerated would become leaders in their schools, thus creating a favourable climate of change. All the other players, including students, parents and other community representatives, who often quarrel over trifles in the present framework of limited responsibilities allowed to schools in most countries, would find an environment more propitious to overcoming minor conflicts, and would be able to concentrate their efforts on managing the school business, which would in that case be entirely their own, as is already the case in some European countries.

The task of changing schools in accordance with the guidelines of the European Commission's White Paper (1995) could provide the driving idea for European teachers, as advocated by the European Teachers' Association (Association Européenne des Enseignants, 1989): *Schools must be given the mission of becoming once again, with a new sense of purpose and in a new context, the liberating force they were at the end of the nineteenth century.*

It is worth recalling the thread of the argument put forward by the OECD experts: *The question is whether all the parties concerned have properly understood the sequence of cause and effect: a healthy society and a sound economy depend on a sound education system, which itself depends on a dynamic, motivated and competent body of teachers* (OECD, 1990, p. 10).

The school as an enterprise

Schools, which may be termed 'critical communities', are becoming significant' protagonists (...) as units of planning action and educational change (...). The collegiality paradigm is beginning to predominate over a model based on individual preparation, planning and classroom-centred action (Santos Guerra, 1995, p. 109).

There are more and more statements of this kind, describing schools in the same terms as those used in business manuals, although the next step, which would consist in saying that the school really is an enterprise, is rarely taken. As we saw in earlier chapters, the fear of words plays a non-negligible part in current tensions in the school system. Managing is not the same as following routine administrative guidelines, and 'educational establishment' or 'school' may be euphemisms to describe passive subsidiaries of school administrations, which take practically all the decisions, leaving teachers with just a few liberties (and obligations). In fact, in many schools the 'school plan' is seen as yet another imposition by the educational authorities, part of the *paper school* syndrome due to the huge quantity of forms and reports received and sent out.

The independence of individual schools is therefore part of a move towards emancipating schools from the condition of obedient subsidiaries of a distant power, rather like railway stations or the old local post offices. Every school is potentially, and has in fact become in a number of European education systems, *an independent enterprise belonging to a network which is the education system.* As an enterprise, it is very much *sui generis,* like other human organizations or enterprises, whose purpose is not to earn money, but to learn and to teach how to see, to hear, to live and to coexist—in the best manner possible. While, as an enterprise, it also belongs to a network or a system, it must, like the production units or teams in other types of efficient enterprises, be allowed a degree of initiative and independent management precisely to fulfil the objectives it has been set. At the same time as it accepts external indicators and monitoring criteria, the school-enterprise would share the culture and policies of the *education system macro-enterprise,* which is not always the case in schools in centralized systems. The link between all units in the system, their *raison d'être,* is not a collection of laws and standards, but the common task of organizing on a daily basis the means of arousing wonder and the desire to learn, while managing the work of individuals and the use of space and time for this purpose in order to ensure that all teach and learn.

There are many lessons which can be drawn for the education system from current developments in the business world. For instance:

- Laws do not change a real situation. What happens in every class and every school depends on the attitude, conscience and values of individual teachers and individual teams. Laws and outside ideas, however, can and should influence teachers' attitudes and objectives.
- The process of change can begin before the plan has been finalized. Although processes of change are systemic, they cannot be uniform or synchronized. In fact, every change is gradual and varied, depending on the collective potential of each organization in its local context.
- Standards should smooth the path towards diversified change.
- Heeding user requirements is not so much a post-modern fashion as a reminder of traditional educational doctrines.
- Management and quality control are not neo-liberal slogans, but part of a responsibility owed to millions of persons.
- The achievements of an educational enterprise are not the sum of individual efforts, but the product of a common task, in which all individuals assume their responsibilities.

  If not only OECD and World Bank documents, but also the writings of some educationalists, sociologists and educational administrators are analyzed from this point of view, it is possible to detect links and unsuspected affinities, but also a critical detachment from the economic world, which is still the inescapable reference, for better or for worse, of current educational changes.

Collective professionalism of the educational enterprise

The educational function in general and the functions derived from promoting educational change in particular take on a different meaning when considered from the point of view of a collective role. If it is assumed that all the professional components of education have to be attributed to every individual teacher, then teachers, who are no supermen or superwomen, will feel overwhelmed by the impressive list of knowledge, attitudes, values and skills expected of them. If such qualities are attributed instead to a school, or more specifically to a team or teams of teachers, then we are approaching a more realistic situation, with a resulting relaxation of tension and malaise.

We may take any list of the professional attributes of teachers, according to the best educationalists (Paquay, 1994; Pérez, 1995; Schön, 1987; OECD, 1990; Escudero Muñoz, 1991). Beyond differences of teacher 'paradigms' or 'models', all agree that a teacher must be *'a cultivated master or mistress, a technician, a practical craftsman, a reflective practitioner, a social actor and a person related to others and developing personally'*. To achieve this, teachers would need to:

- acquire a set of general theoretical knowledge far greater than that required of other professionals at present more highly rated;
- acquire specific knowledge related to a special subject or area, as appropriate;
- develop thorough knowledge of methods of dealing and working with people, and teaching methods in particular;
- develop the necessary practical know-how to fulfil a series of functions, which can now be identified thanks to studies of the 'teacher workstation', such as planning a class, explaining, keeping order, evaluating, managing group relations, managing projects, working in a team, drafting, handling electronic and computer equipment, communicating with parents, mastering administrative skills, etc,:
- possess the qualities of a lucid, critical social actor, of a complete personality, of a citizen of Europe and of the world;
- be able to cope with the social and cultural diversity of students;
- be able to manage a process of change while maintaining continuity.

This list may appear impressive, but this and much more appears in the analyses of components of the teaching profession, which translate school activities into the skills required. May be the problem lies in wanting to assign the sum total of all these functions and skills to each individual teacher. It is as if every worker in an enterprise had to master all the knowledge and know-how that the enterprise requires, at the same time as being constantly adaptable in order to remain efficient and competitive in the production and sale of goods and services. If it is truly believed that every teacher has to assume all the functions of the education system and of the school system within the classroom and that therefore each one has to master this whole list of skills and qualities, then change will continue to be an unattainable utopia.

School as a learning enterprise: Schools have to develop extensive professional capabilities if they want not only to adapt to change but to take an active part in it. The collective professionalism of a school is therefore more complex than that of any other organization of that size. It is also, however, more stimulating, because although it has to be very efficient, the school-enterprise does not need to compete.

Most schools do not possess this collective capability. Nor will they acquire it by the stroke of a magic wand. They will have to learn it and build it. The abilities which make up collective capability involve the rudiments of planning and strategic and participative management, group work, relations with the environment, and creating a culture and a climate propitious to learning. All these abilities may be acquired in an organized process of self-analysis and exchange, with constant informal communication among all those involved. Businesses that learn have accumulated a wealth of experience, which teachers would do well to consult. On the other hand, the experience accumulated as schools undergo change should prove very useful for the learning of business enterprises.

Collective learning is not the sum of individually acquired learning and knowledge. It is a question of learning together what has to be done together. Organizations that do not want to learn usually work below the standard of efficiency of their best members, while organizations wishing to learn as such usually stimulate the less efficient among their members without holding back the more dynamic.

Placing themselves in a condition of wanting to learn (more exactly to learn to teach) constitutes a crucial challenge of today's European schools as they prepare for the immediate future.

B. Roles and functions in the school system

The common professionalism of educators: Not only 'teachers' work in schools; there are a number of new and old professions which also contribute to the common task, such as principals, documentary assistants, guidance counsellors, tutors for external relations, religious advisors, social workers and psychologists. Obviously, there are still schools that have only one or two teachers. But even these schools in a number of countries are beginning to benefit from co-ordination and collegiate management schemes, which give them access to support services comparable to those of larger schools. Linking schools and local administrative bodies, many countries have introduced educational support facilities and teaching resource units, particularly in the field of new technologies. It is clear, too, that most of these other jobs are carried out by teachers on special detachment or working part-time alongside their actual teaching duties. Equally, there is no doubt that schools are increasingly incorporating not only teaching activities, but many other activities related to education, including administrative, technical and supervisory tasks.

Nevertheless, all professionals related to the school system should share a common outlook and common knowledge and attitudes. In the school-enterprise, roles and functions will need to be differentiated by levels and areas of activity, while watertight compartments should be broken down. Although any teacher so inclined should be able to aspire to the top position, all future teachers should not be forced to acquire managerial skills. While all departments should be imbued with intercultural values and attitudes, there is still room for specialists in minority cultures and languages, who would be responsible for informing and exchanging views with their colleagues.

The figure of the principal: It emerges from research that *the principal is a key figure* as a means of ensuring efficient management of the school. In this respect, one should not fall into the temptation of taking businesses as the only reference, since even though schools may be businesses, they are not any type of business. In the educational field, there are empirical data and evidence which indicate what it means to head a school in the light of the challenges and objectives mentioned earlier.

A stable basic team : Another key appears to be a fairly small **team,** which will be responsible together with the principal for the educational and not only administrative management of each school. A stable minimum team is essential to run a school efficiently, especially when changes need to be introduced. This *core team* (consisting of teachers, counsellors and members of the local community) will create and sustain a school's outlook and 'identity'. While being part of the neighbouring social fabric, the team will transcend the local community and will establish a diversified network of relations which the school needs to find its place in today's world.

The principal and the members of the team would probably be expected to have the professional profiles normally attributed to teachers. This core team will be the engine of change in the school and will therefore organize continuous training activities, as a means of forging a shared outlook on education and an open workplan, in which the school's other teachers and professionals will be invited to participate.

The specialists: The other professionals, including course or subject teachers, should possess essential common qualities, without having to fulfil unrealistic expectations. If they are well managed, however, they can be more productive than in a traditional school. They will all be able to take part in more or less formal training activities aimed at improving the running of the school and more especially teaching-learning methods.

In addition, each professional will be assigned specific responsibilities and will have both the right (which is practically nowhere officially recognized) and the duty to undergo suitable in-service training within his or her specialization.

There are two types of specialists which are worth mentioning in particular, as they are connected with some special concerns of the forty-fifth session of the ICE. They are the teachers who are responsible for everything connected with the introduction of NITs in schools and those dealing with children who have special difficulties.

Educational management of NIT: Some years ago computers were introduced in a great many European schools. As either learning or working tools, they have become part of the school scene and have lost the magic aura which always surrounded 'audio-visuals'.

Initiation of teachers and students to computers: Not all children by any means are yet being initiated to computing. European children often have their first contact with computers outside school and become very familiar with keyboards and programmes through personal exchange networks, which are becoming a source of interesting and significant learning for children.

Some countries have been introducing computing in general secondary education, although even among adolescents and young people learning mostly occurs outside school, on the informal circuit and on the huge quantity of courses ubiquitously available. Most teachers starting to use computers appear to have acquired their training outside the education system, although it is worth noting that in some countries the relevant ministries have made significant efforts to introduce computing facilities in schools.

In telematics, the picture is very similar. Many young people are already surfing the Internet and other networks, while the more mature teachers feel a certain panic. In some education systems, experiments are being conducted to set up internal communication or information networks allowing schools to connect up with data banks or ministerial departments or to communicate with other schools. Similar initiatives on a trans-national scale have been started within the framework of European programmes.

Comments on some national experiments: Although more than ten years have passed since computers were first introduced as learning tools in schools, it is still not easy to find general reports or comparative studies which tell us what is happening with computing in schools. There are some specific studies and *ad hoc* reports in educational reviews (*Le Monde de l'éducation,* 1994), which express ideas and opinions about teachers' feelings regarding computing, telematics and 'multi-media', but little systematic information. According to some of these reports, multimedia computers may well end up in the cupboard, like video-recorders, or else they may help to extinguish the few embers of wonder left alive in children by television.

OECD has commissioned experts to evaluate the development and results of some *national schemes for introducing computers in schools as tools in the teaching-learning process* (OECD/CERI, 1991).

Although the data are not overly significant and the comments refer to the case study of a single country, there are some ideas which may be of general use:

- It is important that the operation should be entirely designed with educational aims in view. This will determine the type and number of computers and other peripherals in each school, as well as the balanced investments made in equipment, programmes and staff.
- Diversification in the production of programmes is a positive factor. In the case under study, there were three types of programmes (software): prototype programmes prepared by the educational team directing the programme from the ministry of education, programmes made up by teams of teachers (and students) on their own initiative or stimulated by competitions launched with the project, and lastly programmes produced by specialized firms under ministry instructions or on their own initiative.
- Aspects identified as very positive by the evaluators include support teams available in teachers' quarters, voluntary participation by schools and teaching teams, and training support for the teachers involved.
- Although the idea that computing should be integrated in every school when new curricula are introduced with educational reforms had not been developed in practice at the time of the evaluation, it has been a strategic factor in ensuring the consistency of the programme.
- Lastly, a high degree of satisfaction was shown by teachers and students taking part in the project. This is due to a noticeable enhancement of the teaching/learning process.

Topics for discussion: In discussions, some have suggested that schools should not be content with introducing new technologies in their classes, but could intervene creatively in the networks that are replacing schools and local libraries as sources of information. It is not enough to criticize the chaos and poor quality prevailing among products running on the information superhighways. An effort should be made instead to circulate the products of the thousands of European schools and teachers who are creating educational programmes with a high added value, but which at present never leave the school circuit. If schools were opened up to and instituted exchanges with these networks, according to others, that could serve as a stimulus to awaken curiosity and an interest in learning among many children who are not keen on textbooks but are very active in front of a screen.

The subject of NIT raises the topic of connections between schools and the education system as a whole and 'the outside'. Those who make up the 'education system' face the challenge of overcoming the notion of a closed system and seeing themselves as part of a set of open networks, which include local socialization networks as well as the complex global web of information networks, as pointed out by Coombs (1985). This open approach would enable schools better to fulfil their functions as catalysts and their socializing role in providing links with the local environment and community, which becomes all the more necessary as the globalization process moves ahead. The role of schools should be crucial not only as regards the production and dissemination of knowledge, but also for rebuilding ethical and aesthetic values, which have suffered the effects of post-modern cultural fragmentation. If schools fail in their educational duty towards young people with regard to society's new challenges, then the State will have to be called in to take protective ethical measures (as is occurring in the case of Internet), just as it is being urged to intervene less in the economy.

Managing NIT: *in schools.* In order to move in this direction, however, it is not enough to have a competent, motivated and efficient team working in a ministerial building. Every school must become involved. In view of the nature of present-day teaching staff, it is hardly realistic to expect all teachers to join in the same way in the dynamics of NIT. There are enough teachers available to deal with the matter in each school or in the schools of particular districts or areas. The teacher or teachers responsible for NIT should not be mere computer 'buffs', who are often reduced to tinkering on behalf of their less 'computer-minded' colleagues. This kind of job could be seen to with the help of external technicians, who could in addition bring to schools the cultural climate and style of this world which is so alien, but with which the students are already familiar. The teachers responsible for NIT should manage the whole process of interactions between NIT and the schools. They should therefore be able to encourage and help all the others to learn and should find ways of introducing computing and telematics in schools as well as introducing the schools to the new world of telecommunications.

Managing diversity in education: The European Union is very prone to tension between the emerging *global culture, traditional European national and regional cultures and cultures imported* to Europe by immigrants and refugees, especially from former colonies. Thousands of European schools take in children who, like the best Europeans of the Middle Ages, are the bearers of 'three cultures'. European schools are, however, by tradition monocultural. It is still considered normal for White Papers on education to refer only to the 'indigenous' religion and culture of individual countries, even though in practice the schools make an effort to welcome and to respect 'imported' cultures. We come up against expressions of exclusion and intolerance both inside and outside school, and, more often still, with the indifference of schools in relation to cultural diversity. Although this diversity is present in many schools, it is not always reflected in class organization and methods, and even less in out-of-school aspects, such as weekly days of rest, holidays, eating habits, and cultural and religious symbols.

On this general subject, the European Commission, at the initiative of the European Parliament, has for some years been running a few specific small programmes, designed for the intercultural treatment of immigrants and ethnic minorities in general. Since 1989, a special operation has been opened for gypsy children. Unfortunately, the LEONARDO and SOCRATES programmes are not too explicit in this respect, even though practical actions have continued.

All countries with significant immigrant populations have for years maintained bilateral agreements with countries of emigration, taking the form of the appointment of native teachers to teach children their mother-tongue. In recent years, some schools have made significant progress in their educational approach to cultural diversity. As a result, a significant store of knowledge and know-how has been accumulated, which should be now be made available to schools. All details on the subject are accessible through the EURYDICE databases.

Clearly all the teachers cannot be expected to have the same amount of information, the same sensitivity or the same motivation in this respect. Moreover, as in other social sectors, there may among European teachers be left-overs of xenophobia, in varying degrees of intensity and awareness, which are transmitted either through the *hidden curriculum,* or even at times through the open curriculum. *It is important that schools should collectively adopt the intercultural approach advocated* in the Commission's White Paper (1995). The intercultural policy of a school, especially where there is a great cultural diversity, should be reflected in a school's educational plan and should take the form of activities, projects and constant attention to successes and failures. Intercultural policy in schools should therefore be managed and organized by specifically appointed teachers or teams, who would not be in charge only of minorities, as is all too often the case at present with minority language teachers.

C. Conclusion and final recommendation

The strategy suggested is intended as a synthesis of different recommendations and proposals which do not always appear to be reconcilable. Clearly the working hypothesis will have an impact in areas which are not strictly educational. For instance, the diversification of functions and roles in schools will affect teachers' working conditions and, in practical terms, their salaries. This is an issue which has made no progress for years, even though salary differentials have been finding more or less transparent expression in every education system. We believe that the debate should be clarified and made more open. It is no good continuing to look for artificial arguments to defend apparent uniformity among people doing different things, with different dedication and responsibilities, but who are all supposed to be considered as 'teachers' and therefore officially to earn the same salaries. The business aspect of schools, diversity of professional roles, and evaluation and monitoring by indicators are issues which need to be debated, since there is no *one best way.* What we must not do is to try to side-step the debate in the name of acquired rights, which it would be wrong to ignore or to underestimate, but which it would be senseless to defend with spurious arguments.

We believe that UNESCO and its regional bodies, the ILO, the European Union and OECD could come up with some joint effort, bringing in professional teacher organizations, with a view to comparing the advances already made, but not yet socialized or assumed by education systems, and in order to give a new impetus to reform, opening up different options for education systems, schools and teachers within the context of a changing world. One practical aim of any joint project could be to improve statistical information in some crucial aspects for educational change, and to prepare really comparable reports on the same subjects.

For many teachers, global change can be just a threat or an illusion, and educational change an unrealizable dream. Both may provide a great opportunity for the development of education and for the personal satisfaction of all concerned. There is no doubt that children and young people would be the sure winners in this change of outlook. It is very likely, moreover, that by dealing with the problems of education in educational terms, solutions will be found to other types of problems affecting education systems.

Reference

1. The Reader is referred to the comments on educational statistics in the introduction.
2. Organized at the initiative of the European Commission and the Netherlands Chairman of the European Council, the conference was held in Noordwijkerhout, Netherlands, in October 1991. The quotation is taken from the final report of the conference.

Bibliography

Albertini, Jean-Marie. 1992. *La pédagogie n'est plus ce qu'elle sera.* Paris, Seuil.

Alexander, R.; Rose, J.; Woodhead, C. 1992. *Curriculum organization and classroom practice in primary schools: a discussion paper.* London, Department of Education.

Alvarez Junco, Josá. 1995. Tiempo de incertidumbres? El pais (Madrid), 25 January.

Archer, E.G., Peck, B.T. no date. *The teaching profession in Europe.* Glasgow, Jordanhill College of Education.

ATEE-AEDE. 1989. Etre un enseignant européene. Brussels, Association Européenne des Enseignants.

Boillot, H.; Le Du, M.. 1993. *La pédagogie du vide.* Paris, PUF.

Calvino, Italo. 1989. *Seis própuestas para el proximo milenio.* Madrid, Ed. Siruela

Castells, Manuel, *La nueva Revolución Rusa.* Madrid, Ed. Sistema,

Castells, Manuel. 1994. *Flujos, redes e identidades: una teoria critica de la sociedad informacional.* Paper presented at the International Congress 'Nuevas perspectivas criticas en educación', University of Barcelona, July.

CEPAL-UNESCO. 1992. *Educación y conocimiento. Eje de la transformacion productiva con equidad.* Santiago de Chile, Libros de la CEPAL.

Conferénce internationale de l 'éducation. 1975. *Recommandation* n 69 *aux ministres de l 'éducation concernant l évolution du róle des maitres et les incidences de cette évolution sur la formation professionnelle préalable et en cours d'emploi. Paris,*

UNESCO.

CMOPE. Confédération Mondiale des Organisations de la Profession Enseignante. 1991. *Les enseignants: salaires, retraites, temps de travail, négociations. Atelier européen de la CMOPE,* April 1991. Sofia, Bulgaria.

Collège de France. 1985. Propositions pour *l'*enseignement de *l'*avenir. *Le monde de l 'éducation* (Paris), n° 116, mai.

Commission Européenne. 1993. *Croissance, compétitivité, emploi: les défis et les pistes pour entrer dons le XXIe. siècle.* Luxembourg. (Livre Blanc.)

Commission Européenne. 1995a. *Les chiffres-clé de l 'éducation dans l 'Union Européenne, 94. Luxembourg, OPOCE.* [This publication has served as one of the statistical references for this study. It is sometimes compared with OECD and UNESCO figures, especially to take account of Eastern European countries, which may not have been or may not be members of the European Union.

Commission Européenne. 1995. *Enseigner et apprendre: vers la societé cognitive.* Joint document by DG XXII and DG V. (Livre blanc.)

Council of Europe. 1993. *Education and social change.* CDCC Project, Final Conference Report.

Council of Europe. 1995. *Education reforms in Central and Eastern Europe. Symposium.* Prague.

Coutin, André; Vadrot, Claude-Marie. 1991. *La raison des jeunes.* Paris, Robert Laffont.

Cuadernos de pedagogia. 1996, *Proyectos de trabajo. Otra manera de saber. Barcelona,* January, n°. 243. (Several articles.)

Cuadernos de pedagogia. 1996. Autoevaluación institucional? Barcelona, February, n°. 244.

Dalin, P.; Rust, V. 1983. *Can schools learn*? Oxford, NFER-Nelson.

Denis, Marcelle. 1994. *Comenius.* Paris, PUF.

Duru-Bellat, M.; van Zanten, Henriot. 1992. *Sociologie de l'école.* Paris, A. Colin.

Eraut, M.. 1985. Knowledge creation and knowledge use in professional contexts. *Studies in higher education* (Abingdon, U. K.), vol. 10, no. 2, p. 117-33.

ERT-European Round Table/Table Ronde des Industriels Européens. 1989. *Education and European competence: an ERT study on education and training in Europe.* Brussels, ERT.

ERT-European Round Table/Table Ronde des Industriels Européens. 1995. Une *éducation européenne. Vers une societé qui apprend* Brussels, ERT.

Escudero Muñoz, J.M., 1989. La escuela como organización y el cambio educativo. *In: Martin Moreno, comp. Organizaciones educativas* Huelva, p. 7-36.

Escudero Muñoz, J. M., ed. 1991. *Los desafios de las reformas escolares: cambio educativo y educacion para el cambio.* Sevilla, Arquetipo Ediciones.

Esteve, J. M.; Franco, S.; Vera, J. 1995. *Los profesores ante el cambio social.* Barcelona, Anthropos.

EURYDICE. Unité Portuguaise et Unité Danoise. 1990. *Structures de 1 'administration et évaluation des écoles primaires et secondaires dans les douze Etats membres de la Communauté Européenne.* Bruxelles.

EURYDICE. 1993a. *Les compétences administratives et financiéres en matiére d'éducation et de formation dans les Etats membres de la Communauté Européenne.* Bruxelles.

EURYDICE. 1993b. *Enseignement privé-enseignement non public: formes et statuts dans les Etats membres de la Communauté Européenne.* Brussels.

EURYDICE. 1994. *La lutte contre 1 échec scolaire: un défi pour la construction européenne.* Brussels.

EURYDICE. 1995a. *La fomation continue des enseignants dans l 'Union Europénne et dans les pays de I 'AELElEEE.* Brussels.

EURYDICE. 1995b. *Structures des systèmes d'enseignement et de formation dans l'Union Européenne. Brussels.* (A second edition is accessible on Internet on the European Commission's 'Europa' server.)

EURYDICE. 1995c. *Calendrier et rythmes scolaires dans l `Union Européenne.* Brussels.

Faure, E., et al. 1972. *Learning to be.* Paris, UNESCO.

Finland. Ministry of Education. 1994. *Developments in education* 1992-94. Helsinki.

Forquin, Jean-Claude. 1992. *École et culture: le point de vue des sociologues britanniques.* Bruxelles, De Boeck Université.

Fullan, M. 1991. *The new meaning of educational change.* London, Cassell Education.

Gaudin, Thierry, ed. 1990. *2100: récit du prochain siécle.* Paris, Editions Payot.

Gaudin, Thierry. 1995. *Les métamorphoses du futur.* Paris, Economica.

Ghilardi, Franco. 1993. *Crisis y perspectivas de la profesión docente.* Barcelona, Gedisa. (Original Italian version by Editori Riuniti, Rome, 1990.)

Gimeno, J. 1992. Reformas educativas: utopia, retórica, práctica. *Cuadernos de pedagogia* (Barcelona), n°. 209, p.62 et seq.

Goble, Norman M.; Porter, James F. 1977. *The changing role of the teacher: international perspectives.* Paris, UNESCO. (IBE Studies and surveys in comparative education.)

Godet, Michel. 1991. *L 'avenir autrement.* Paris, Armand Colin,

Groupe de Lisbonne. 1995. *Limites á la compétitivité. Pour un nouveau contrast mondial.* Paris, Edit. La découverte.

Hage, Jerald; Powers, Charles. 1992. *Post-industrial lives: roles and relationships in the 21st century.* London, Sage Publications.

Hopkins, D.; Bollen R. 1988. *La pratique de l 'autoanalyse de l' établissement scolaire.* Paris, OCDE-IS IP/Economica.

Houssaye, J. 1992. *Les valeurs á l'école.* Paris, PUF.

Huntington, Samuel. 1993. *The clash of civilizations.* (An article published in journals in several countries.)

IRDAC. Industrial Research and Development Advisory Committee of the Commission of the European Communities. No date. Les déficits en qualifications en Europe. *Avis de l'IRDAC* (Brussels).

Katz, R.L.. 1988. *The information society: an international perspective.* New York, Praeger.

Kemmis, S.. 1995. Sociedad y cambio social : implicaciones en el curriculum y en la investigación educativa. *In: Teoria critica e investigación-acción.* Valladolid, Universidad de Valladolid.

Le Métais, Joanna. 1992. *The conservative values and education policy 1979-1990.* Uxbridge, U.K., Brunel University. (Ph.D. degree thesis.)

Les méthodes d'enseignement du futur. 1994. *Le monde de l' éducation* (Paris), n° 220, novembre, p.40 ff.

Morin, Edgar. 1986. *La Méthode:* Tome III-*'La connaissance de la connaissance* '. Paris, Seuil.

Morin, Edgar. 1994. El desafio de la globalidad. *Cuadernos americanos* (Mexico), n°. 43, Jan-Feb.

Najmanovich, Denise. 1994. De 'el tiempo' y las temporalidades. *In:* Bleichmar, ed. *Temporalidad, determinación, azar: lo reversible y lo irreversible.* Buenos Aires, Paidós.

Neave, Guy. 1992. *The teaching nation: prospects for teachers in the European Community.* Oxford, Pergamon Press.

OCDE. 1989a. *Les écoles et la qualité: un rapport international.* Paris.

OCDE. 1989b. *L 'éducation et l' éonomie dans une société en mutation.* Paris.

OCDE. 1990. *L 'enseignant aujourd'hui: fonctions, statut,* politiques & Paris.

OECD. 1993. *Education at a glance: OECD indicators.* Paris.

OECD-CERL 1991. *International Seminar on 'Policies and strategies for integrating computers in general education'. The Spanish Atenea Project. The issues for the international community.* Paris, CERI-NTI, 291-302.

OECD-CERI. 1992. *Schools and Business: a new partnership.* Paris.

OECD-CERI 1994. *Making education count: developing and using international indicators.* Paris.

OIT-UNESCO. 1994. *Informe del Comité mixto de expertos sobre la aplicación de la Recomendación relativa a la situación del personal docente. Sexta reunión ordinaria. CEART/VT* Geneva, ILO.

Paquay, Léopold. 1994. Vers un référentiel des compétences professionnelles de *l'*enseignant. In: *Recherche et formation* (Paris, INRP), n° 15, June.

Pedró, Francesc. 1993. Estado y educación en Europa y los Estados Unidos. *Revista Iberoamericana de educación* (Madrid), n°. 1, Jan.-April, p.59 ff.

Pérez Goméz, A. 1995. La formación del profesor como intelectual. *In: Teoria critica e investigación-acción. Valladolid,* Universidad de Valladolid.

Pisani, Edgard. 1995. Las autopistas de la informació. *El pais* (Madrid), 22 mayo.

Prost, Antoine. 1985. *Éloge des pédagogues.* Paris, Seuil.

Prost, Antoine. 1990. L'école entre *l'*état, *l*a famille et *l'*enseignant. *In: PROJET 2001: L'horizon de l école* (Paris), n° 223, p.8 ff.

Puelles, Manuel de. 1993. Estado y educación en las sociedades Europeas. *Revista Iberoamericana de Educación* (Madrid), n° 1, Jan. -April, p. 3 5 ff.

Ramonet, I. 1993. Temps nouveaux. Le monde dioplomatique, n° 470, May.

Robert, Y. 1990. Gérer les personnels et rénover le système éducatif. PROJET 2001: L 'horizon de l'école (Paris), n° 223, p.67 ff.

Santos Guerra, M. 1995. Teoria critica y proyecto educativo de centro. *In: Teoria critica e investigación-acción.* Valladolid, Universidad de Valladolid.

Schön, D.A.. 1987. *Educating the reflective practitioner.* San Francisco, Jossey-Bass.

Senge Peter. 1990. *The fifth discipline: the art and practice of learning organization.* New York, Currency.

Tedesco, J.C. 1995. *El nuevo pacto educativo: educación, competitividad y ciudadania en la sociedad* Madrid, Grupo Anayo.

Tertrais, Yves. 1995. Le réseau d'institutions de formation: une experience européenne. *Recherche et formation* (Paris, INRP), n° 18.

Tiana, Alejandro. 1995. La evaluación de los sistemas educativos. *Revista Iberoamericana de educación* (Madrid), n° 10, Jan-April.

Touraine, Alain. 1995. Pensando os movimentos sociais neste final de século XX. Cadernos do CEAS (Rio de Janeiro), Jan-Feb.

United Kingdom-White Paper. 1992. *Choice and diversity: a new framework for schools.* London, HMSO. (Cmd 2021.).

UNESCO. 1995. *Estrategia a medio plazo: 1996-2001.* Paris, UNESCO. (Draft document 28 C/4.)

Universidad de Valladolid. 1995. *Teoria critica e investigación-acción.* Valladolid, Departamento de didáctica y organización escolar.

Vaniscotte, Francine. 1994. *Étude synthetique des publications relatives á la profession* d'enseignant. Bruxelles, EURYDICE.

Van Velzen, W. G., ed. 1988. *Parvenir â une amélioration effective du, foncionnement de l' école.* Paris, OCDE-ISIP, Economica.,

Villar Angulo, L. M.. 1991. *Los profesores y el cambio educativo: teorias subjetivas y reflexión sobre la práctica. In: Escudero Muñoz,* J.M., ed., op. cit., p.97 ff.

Waterman, Peter. 1994. Global, civil, soiidario. *Nueva sociedad* (Madrid), n° 132, July-August

1994. (English original: *Institute for Social Studies. Working paper series,* n° 130, 1993. The Hague.)

WCEFA. 1990. *World Declaration on Education for All and Framework of Action to Meet* Basic Learning Needs. New York, Inter-Agency Commission on WCEFA.

Xavier, Carlos A., ed. 1994. *Gestáo escolar: desafios e tendências.* Brasilia, IDEA.

Zubieta, J.C.; Susinos, T.. 1992. Las satisafacciones e insatisfacciones de los enseñantes. Madrid, CIDE-MEC.

* Reference paper prepared for the European Consultation to the UNESCO's 45th Session of the International Conference on Education, 1996.

Courtesy : International Bureau of Education, UNESCO, Geneva, Switzerland.

PART—III

Overview of OECD Work on Teachers, Their Pay and Conditions, Teaching Quality and the Continuing Professional Development of Teachers

I. Organisation for Economic Cooperation and Development

1. Introduction

The Organisation for Economic Cooperation and Development, as its name suggests, is primarily concerned with the economic policies of its 27 Member countries, which include most of the world's developed nations. Education did not figure among the original concerns and purposes of the OECD but the economic focus of the organisation was tempered by a concern for the social dimension and purposes of economic growth and an awareness of the importance of human capital which implied an educational role. Over the last 35 years the educational activities of OECD have developed within two principal programmes, the Education Committee (EDC) and the Centre for Educational Research and Innovation (CERI). During that time OECD has developed a distinctive role. In the words of it Secretary-General:

In relating education to other sectors of policy, economic, social and environmental, the OECD has developed an approach to its work that distinguishes it from other international organisations. Education is seen as a major partner of such policies, with which it interacts, both contributing and responding to them. By relating education to the socio-economic realities within which it operates, the organisation has, I believe, rightly emphasised the role which education plays in the total polity. (Jean-Claude Paye, quoted in Papadopoulos, 1994).

Given its expertise in the economics of education, and considering that teacher costs represent such a high proportion of the total costs of education, it is not surprising that OECD has always been concerned with teacher-related issues of supply and demand, status, conditions of work and remuneration. The early work of CERI and the EDC in these areas are examined in section 2.

OECD carries out reviews of the education systems of Member countries, at their request, Some twenty such reviews have been conducted since 1990. These reviews give the organisation's secretariat an unrivalled insight into the concerns of Member governments. The quality and training of teachers have figured prominently in these reviews. Section 3 looks at a sample of country reviews, focusing on the interchange of information and themes between national Ministries of Education and EDC.

Sections 4 and 5 examine three recent OECD reports on quality in teaching and professional development. As the problems of teacher supply diminished in the late 1970s, governments became more concerned with quality issues and OECD was encouraged to carry out comparative studies of teaching quality. The two resulting reports are the subject of section 4. More recent work has focused on the need for teacher education and training to be related to other educational policies in the context of more systemic approaches to reform. Over the last decade, OECD has produced a series of authoritative reports on curriculum and assessment which, together with its work on teachers, form the basis of the current study of Teachers and Curriculum Reform in Basic Schooling. This study, and particularly the unpublished report on teachers' professional development, is the subject of section 5.

OECD has continued to develop its statistical database in response to policy makers' needs for reliable comparative data. These concerns led in the 1980s to the development of indicators of educational systems, published since 1992 as Education at a Glance. Section 6 looks at the picture these indicators give of the condition of teachers in the 1990s.

The OECD is thus well placed to contribute to the theme of UNESCO's 45th International Conference: the changing context within which teachers carry out their tasks has been at the centre of OECD's educational work since its inception. The recent decision by the Education Ministers to make lifelong learning the theme of OECD's next five-year mandate reinforces this approach to educational systems through the perspective of the social and economic contexts within which today's pupils will lead their lives. The strong focus on teachers which has been a feature of OECD's work reflects the awareness that they will be the principal agents in developing new approaches.

II. The Development of OECD's Work on Teachers 1960-1990

Questions of teacher supply and demand were the main concern of OECD throughout the 1960s, reflecting the preoccupations of the Member countries at that time. A survey carried out by OECD in the late 1960s showed that while countries had succeeded in vastly increasing their teaching forces in response to demographically-led demand over the previous decade, this had been largely at the expense of recruitment standards within the profession:

By the mid-sixties, in spite of some improvement, there were still, in many countries, 10-15 per cent uncertificated teachers in primary education; in secondary education....up to a third of the teaching in some subjects, particularly in science, mathematics and technology, was in the hands of improperly qualified teachers. (Papdopoulos, p. 77)

The consequences of recruitment policies implemented in this period are still working their way through the educational systems of OECD countries. In particular, the young teachers recruited then still constitute the bulk of the teaching force and as a result the average age of teachers in all but a few of these countries is high. The recruitment policies adopted then were partly responsible for the low professional status of teachers and the consequent feminisation of the profession. As governments became less concerned with the problem of "getting bodies in front of classes" and more concerned for the quality of education, the focus of their policies shifted to the professional development of teachers.

Between 1970 and 1975 OECD carried out a number of detailed analytical studies bringing together the results of research and experience in Member countries with a focus on innovatory practice. The OECD's Paris Conference in November 1974 brought these studies together in four sets of issues: the changing context of the professional activity of teaching; changes in working conditions and needs for teachers; new standards for teacher education; and the consequences for costs and planning. The Conference helped to set the agenda for teacher policies and to identify priorities, for both government action and research, over the following decade. In particular, the improvement of both initial and in-service training became priorities for governments. OECD took this work forward, focusing particularly on the organisation, contents, methods and requirements of in-service education. It reviewed practice and policy in Member countries, looking especially closely at school-focused in-service courses (INSET). Its report, In-Service Education and the Training of Teachers: a Condition for Change (1982), concluded that:

the traditional INSET strategy, whereby individual teachers attend courses provided by outside agencies, is valuable but too limited and ... should be deliberately extended to encourage teachers and school staffs to plan their own INSET programmes in the light of their self-identified needs. (OECD 1982, p.29)

The new concern for quality in education was reiterated at the 1984 meeting of the OECD Ministers of Education and as a result, a study programme specifically concerned with teachers and teaching was set up under the auspices of the Working Party on the Condition of Teaching. The centrality of the teacher in achieving high quality education was recognised by the international conference organised jointly by the OECD and the Italian government in Rome in 1986 (Quality in Education: The Vital Role of Teachers) at which the first findings of the study group were presented. The final results of their work were published in The Teacher Today (OECD, 1990), which accurately portrays the issues and pressures—both political and economic—which combined to "push the teaching profession squarely under the spotlight of education debate and policy" (p.7). It is worth recalling that there were damaging strikes over teachers' pay and conditions in at least nine of the (then) 24 Member countries of the OECD during the 1980s.

The report identifies four major factors which characterise the condition of the teaching profession at the end of the 1980s:

There is a profound dissatisfaction *within the teaching body in many countries and the experience during the 1980s of a sharp deterioration in industrial relations between teachers and their employing authorities in some. Teachers feel acutely the pressing demand for* accountability *and the subjection of public services, including education, to the intense glare of outside scrutiny, and this is in turn related to the sheer scale of the resources needed to maintain the teaching forces in OECD countries. The emergence of the pursuit of* quality *as a general priority of educational policy has been a hallmark of recent years and with that has come the growing perception of the key role of teachers, both positive and negative, in realising that broad ambition. Finally, there are growing expression of concern in a number of countries that, following an era of managing a decline of student enrolments and a general surplus of teaching resources, problems of teacher* supply *are re-emerging, especially in key subjects of the curriculum. (OECD 1990, p.7)*

The report describes the new political context in which the pursuit of quality would be conducted in the 1990s. Teachers would have to accept that enhanced professional status could only be achieved as part of a new definition of their role in which they would be more accountable to parents and the community both for their effectiveness as teachers and their efficient use of resources. Governments should recognise that:

rigidly bureaucratic top-down forms of accountability that claim to promote professionalism may well actually undermine the necessary act of professional judgement, serving neither teachers nor students well. (OECD 1990, p.11)

The description of the condition of teachers across a broad range of Member countries, which was based on national statistics and specially commissioned national papers, is still recognisable as accurate in the mid-1990s. The impact of declining birth rates and consequent over-supply of teachers is shown to be uneven across countries but, in general, teaching forces did not shrink in line with these trends because governments took the opportunity to improve pupil: teacher ratios. The feminisation of teaching forces is also shown to be very varied, applying to all educational levels in a few countries such as Finland, but generally related to the primary-secondary divide and the level and prestige of educational institutions. The ageing of the teaching force and the under-representation of women in leadership costs are more universal trends.

Building on the statistically-based analysis of the actual condition of the teaching forces, the report explores aspects of teacher professionalism, emphasising the heterogeneity among teachers (in qualifications remuneration, conditions of work and status) in most countries, and relates this to policy issues such as improving the attractiveness of teaching and diversifying the sources of recruitment of teachers. Three factors are picked out as especially influential in determining teachers' professional status: the sheer size and cost to the public purse of the teaching force; the massive expansion of higher education which means that graduate status and advanced knowledge is increasingly widespread in many occupations; and perceived feminisation, although the report acknowledges that the direction of causality here is difficult to establish: is it a "normal market mechanism" that status and pay decline as women come to occupy a higher proportion of posts, or is it that society systematically undervalues women's work ? This chapter concludes with a review of the teacher supply situation in OECD countries and an analysis of the factors affecting both demand, which is in part policy-driven and supply, which is determined by both salary and other considerations. Much of this discussion is still relevant to the current debate.

The report concludes with a review of teacher education and teacher assessment in the United States and a brief summary of the changing tasks and roles of the teacher which foreshadowed the direction of future OECD work.

III. Country reviews

While OECD is able to draw on statistics and specially prepared papers from its Member countries, it has also developed considerable knowledge and expertise within its own secretariat. Much of this has accumulated through bilateral and multilateral discussions with officials and experts in these countries and through cooperative ventures with other international organisations. The periodic Reviews of National Policies for Education which OECD carries out at Member countries' invitation are a rich source of information and comparison of developments. Each review is intended to provide an overall assessment of the functioning of a country's education and training system but country authorities also identify the policy fields which they consider important and expert reviewers are chosen by the OECD to reflect these aspects. The focus of the reviews thus usually reflects both the preoccupations of the governments involved and OECD'overarching concerns. These in turn are determined mainly by the periodically renewed mandates which the Education Ministers of Member countries collectively decide. Over thirty years the condition and training of teachers have figured prominently among the aspects chosen for review.

Not all Member countries have been prepared to submit themselves to such scrutiny while others have been reviewed twice or even three times. The issue is complicated by the fact that in federal political systems such as the United States, Germany, Canada and Australia education is a local or State matter and the federal authorities have limited scope for legislation or control. Reviews of Sweden, Finalnd, Denmark, Switzerland, Ireland, Netherlands, Norway, Austria, Hungary, Poland, France, Belgium, Mexico, Greece and Korea have been published since 1990. Reflecting the OECD's wider concerns, each study provides a description of the education system and an analysis by a team of independent external examiners of the functioning of the system in terms of its efficiency and its relation to the economy and society. A brief summary of four of these reviews—Ireland, Sweden, France and the Czech Republic— in which teachers and their training or teacher supply were among the main aspects for examination will give the flavour of this activity.

The Review of Irish Education published in 1991 focused particularly closely on the condition of teaching and teachers, to which the examiners were invited to pay special attention, and the specific problems of teacher supply and training. The three external examiners were academics from Australia, Scotland and the United States. The Review is in three parts: The Examiners' Report, the Record of the Review Meeting and a Summary of the Background Report (which is always prepared by the country authorities). Each of the three parts covers the same ground in more or less the same order, beginning with a description of the education system, reviewing the policy issues and problems before focusing on the organisation and functioning of schools and analysing the deficiencies of the curriculum and the changing values underpinning it. The chapters on the supply and quality of teachers and their training and career prospects follow.

Having acknowledged the traditional, comparatively high, quality of teachers in Ireland, the examiners' report analyses the combined effects of the decline of the birth rate and the raising of the pupil teacher ratio (as part of economic austerity measures) on teacher supply and the future of the training institutions. Its major recommenda-tions are the appointment of more specialised teachers of disadvantaged pupils (selective lowering of the PTR) and the merger of monotechnic teacher training institutions with university departments of education in order to safeguard an expansion and rationalisation of in-service provision. The following chapter looks at the organisation of pre-service education and training, comparing the advantages and disadvantages of concurrent and consecutive courses, and assessing induction procedures and in-service training, and concluding with the need for research to stimulate innovation in teaching.

The Review of French Education, published in 1995, also gave prominence to teacher-related issues within a wider review of the decentralisation reforms of the 1980s. The OECD examiners assess the strength and weaknesses of the State role, and call for actions by four constituencies: society as a whole; the education system; new partners in the system; and the community of education specialists. The review is also concerned with important reform initiatives which have focused on other issues of broad comparative interest, including: under-achievement and marginalisation; consistent quality with diversity; and education and employment. To combat failure at school, the French authorities established education priority areas in which schools receive special financial assistance to support a more flexible organisation of the education programme and new partnerships with parents and the community. The OECD examiners identify advantages and disadvantages with the approach, and plead for even more active, integrated urban policies.

To overcome the great divide between primary and secondary teachers and to strengthen the links between theory and practice in teacher training, the French authorities established new teacher training institutions (*Institute universitair de formation des maitres*—IUFMs) in place of the separate primary *ecoles normales* and university-based teacher training. The OECD examiner recommend a stronger role for the IUFM in school reform strategies, and argue for a more structured programme of continuing education for teachers through teachers' centres serving groups of schools. With the transition to large-scale participation in secondary education, about one-fourth of the age cohort were leaving the education system without any qualification. To address the problem, the French authorities have undertaken a number of efforts to redress the balance in favour of vocational training and apprenticeships. The OECD examiners identify a number of specific steps that might be taken to enhance further the quality, status and competitiveness of vocational training within the education system.

Teacher-related concerns are less prominent in the Swedish Review, published in 1995. Since the early 1980s, Sweden has been giving increased emphasis to decentralisation, management by objectives and national and local assessment and evaluation. Freedom, quality, internationalisation and a growing focus on learning outcomes characterise the new context of education in Sweden. The review reveals and considers the sea change in education policies and priorities which took place in the early 1990s. The examiners note that the big step in deregulation, combined with a more autonomous system of education and other innovation processes at the workplace, have to be assessed and developed in the wider educational community. The issues examined include the policy-making process and its potential impact on school management and performance; the future of adult education which is accorded less direct policy attention in the new framework; and higher education, where a range of reforms enhancing autonomy and choice have been introduced.

The Background Report includes a brief account of the reforms and rationalisation of the teacher training system which were carried out in the late 1980s and useful diagrams of the system as it now is. The examiners link their comments on these reforms with the Government proposals to increase the academic content both of secondary schooling and teacher training. They report common concern amongst those interviewed that the two sets of reforms follow too closely and unease with the government's views on the separation of academic content from children's social development in education. They also comment on the lack of innovation in curriculum and pedagogy which they consider relates to the way teachers and school leaders are trained. Teachers and school leaders will have to assume very different roles in the future under the government's decentralisation proposals but at present they are not prepared for these broader responsibilities in their pre-service education and there appears to be no focused effort to provide preparation through in-service programmes. They conclude that there are serious questions about whether professional educators have the knowledge and skills needed to respond to the reform agenda proposed by the government.

The OECD has devoted a considerable proportion of its time to Eastern Europe since 1990 and the Review of School Education Policy in the Czech Republic (1996) is a good example of its work in this region. One of the seven chapters of the Examiners' Report concerns "Reinforcing Quality in the Teaching Force". Education is crucial to enabling these countries to make a successful transition to democratic, pluralistic, advanced-market economy status. The examiners found that while many Czech teachers were highly qualified, they were not necessarily well prepared for these challenges. They need to have

> *the capacity and motivation to become more pro-active, to become more engaged in teaching and in communication with their peers, parents and the community at large, to exercise greater initiative and to acquire and apply new techniques in teaching." (OECD 1996d. p.29)*

They argue for a large professional role for teachers which will require changes in pre-service and in-service training.

The Review includes a detailed analysis of the educational manpower needs and planning policies of the Czech Republic. It concludes that the country is likely to have a substantial surplus of teachers, especially at upper secondary level, unless measures are taken quickly; and that Czech teachers are underpaid. Overall, it asks for a strategic view of teachers policies which would entail a strong role for the Ministry of Education

> *in building a consensus on the crucial role of teachers, establishing the overall goals and ensuring co-ordination and coherence among a set of teacher policies covering pay, carrier paths, recruitment, initial teacher preparation, and in-service education. (OECD 1996d, p.37).*

It also identifies three priorities: an expansion of in-service provision within a more flexible framework, targeted on the needs of schools adapting to challenges in an economy and society in transition and the needs linked to the development of new career profiles and new responsibilities for teachers; improved teacher pay; and the development of a coordinating framework for policies on recruitment, retention, redeployment and retirement of teachers.

While most other country reviews give less substantial attention to teachers, nearly all refer to teacher-related issues, and many include descriptions of the teacher training system in the country concerned. The accumulation of country background papers in itself constitutes a very substantial database of facts about education systems and trends in policy developments. The review meetings at which Ministers of Education and their officials discuss the examiners' findings face-to-face with them, with members of the OECD secretariat and representatives from other Member countries is a unique opportunity for bringing this collective experience and knowledge to bear on an individual, national system. At the same time, these confrontations allow the secretariat to modify its evolving, "state-of-the-art" interpretations of developments in education. It is from this position of accumulated knowledge of its Members' systems that OECD is able to identify developments which are sufficiently important to enough countries to warrant specific study. The quality of teaching emerged in this way as a major concern among OECD countries articulated in Schools and Quality: An International Report (OECD, 1989). Education Ministers declared at their meeting in Paris in 1990 that "*expert, motivated, flexible teaching staff are the most vital component of high quality provision*". Eleven countries agreed to provide experts to participate in a study of how to promote good teaching in primary and secondary schools.

IV. Identifying and Promoting Good Teaching

Over the last six years, OECD has carried out two major studies of quality in teaching which reflect the concern felt in most countries that the increasing difficulty and complexity of teachers' tasks have not been matched by higher standards of preparation to perform these tasks. These studies have resulted in two reports, one published as Quality in Teaching (OECD), 1994) and the other. Active Learning for Students and Teachers, which was presented to the Governing Board to CERI in autumn 1995.

Researchers from the eleven countries which participated in the first study met twice in Paris in 1992 to plan the design of the study. They decided on three distinct kinds of inquiry: case studies of policies to improve the quality of teaching; seminars for teachers to discuss the definition of quality and what affects it; and descriptions of new developments in initial teacher education. Teachers and schools were selected for study on the basis of outstanding reputation and evidence of effectiveness in achieving positive outcomes for students. The study began with a definition of teacher quality that encompassed five dimensions:

- *knowledge of substantive curriculum areas and content;*
- *pedagogic skill, including the acquisition and ability to use a repertoire of teaching strategies;*
- *reflection and the ability to be self-critical, the hallmark of teacher professionalism;*
- *empathy and the commitment to the acknowledgment of the dignity of others;*
- *managerial competence, as teachers assume a range of management responsibilities within and outside the classroom. (OECD 1994 a, p. 14)*

This "ideal profile" of the individual teacher has to be set within school, community and country contexts. Values and public expectations of teachers vary across cultures, as do the qualities of individuals recruited to teach, and the circumstances in which teaching occurs define to a considerable degree the scope for effective use of the dimensions of teacher quality.

The report reviews the policies employed in Member countries to promote teacher quality which is increasingly seen as the most important factor in raising student achievement levels. Traditionally policies have focused on teacher education and qualifications but more recently the range of policies has been broadened to include some or all of the following approaches:

— upgraded, more effective pre-service education;
— upgraded, more effective in-service education;
— teacher appraisal or evaluation;
— alternative paths to teaching posts;
— alternative careers in teaching;
— economic and social benefits to enter teaching;
— economic and social benefits to remain in teaching.

These policies interact with the local context of schooling so that the effectiveness of the policies varies from school to school. The report points out that although polices set directions and provide a framework they do not determine outcomes which depend rather on successful implementation of the policies. The multiplicity of policies that impinge on schools which was revealed by the country studies suggests that there is a real danger of policies piling up and paralysing schools and teachers.

The design of the study was influenced by the research on school effectiveness and school improvement and by previous OECD work which suggested that qualitative approaches, such as in-depth, school-based case studies and seminar/focus-group activities are the most appropriate for examining the impact of policy initiatives. Eighteen separate studies were conducted in 1993 in the eleven participating countries (Australia, Austria, Finland, France, Italy, Japan, New Zealand, Norway, Sweden, United Kingdom and Unites States). Chapter 3 of the report provides a useful summary of the samples and procedures in each country 4 attempts to convey the dynamic character of teacher quality that emerged from the country studies by selecting snapshots of good teachers at work, concluding that:

> *the country studies depict the world of teachers as increasingly complex and changing. A tenacious commitment to helping students learn makes good teachers keep trying to improve, even when the work is difficult and demoralising. They must keep up with changing conceptions of their subject matter, and continually add to their repertory of instructional methods. Creating the necessary rapport with students is a fresh challenge with each new class, especially when there are more students who come from other countries or who lack family support. Simply growing older requires learning new ways to relate to students. Increasingly, teachers are diversifying their pedagogical strategies to incorporate pupil-centered and small-group techniques, which are more consistent with contemporary theories of human learning and also more appealing to students who prefer interactive learning. Computers and other digitised-information technologies are also becoming more important tools for teaching and learning, finally changing the ancient method of chalk and talk. The complex interactions of personalities and pedagogies make classroom dynamics increasingly*

unpredictable, and teachers must be adept at improvisation. As there is more to think about, reflection has come to be an expected part of teacher's work, and good teachers may even become somewhat obsessed, working on weekends and waking in the night with ideas for their classrooms. Exchanging ideas and support with colleagues has become increasingly vital. In addition to informal exchanges, teachers participate in formal conferences and workshops, contributing to the professional knowledge base. Collaboration among teachers is also increasingly being required, as teachers in many schools are given additional responsibility for planning curriculum and instruction, managing resources, and organising their own professional development programmes. (OECD 1994 a, p. 70)

Analysing the school-level conditions that influence the quality of teaching, the report identifies five key characteris-tics of the contexts of those schools that exhibit unusually high levels of teacher quality:

— *a clear vision or moral purpose;*
— *a commitment to collaborative teacher development;*
— *an investment in high-quality teachers on the part of the school (recruitment, staff development, resourcing of collaborative activities, risk-taking and leadership);*
— *an infrastructure within the school supportive of high-quality teaching and learning;*
— *a symbiotic relationship between the school, its district authority and community (OECD 1994a, p. 112).*

The dilemma posed to policy-makers by the case studies is how to translate these characteristics into an enduring and widely supported policy framework, so that all schools can be improved. The final chapter discusses the policy implications of the study's findings and ends with a conundrum:

Relying on central policy to sustain and improve teacher quality implies greater consistency of practice but a slower rate of change. In contrast, relying on individual teachers and schools allows continuous change and experimentation, but also permits some schools and teachers to lag behind. The big challenge is to improve the terms to this trade-off by channelling together the different sources of teacher quality. (OECD 1994a, p. 117)

In 1993, the Governing Board of CERI authorised a further study to follow up certain issues raised in the study of Quality in Teaching. Drawing on samples of innovative teaching in eight countries, this study focused more sharply on the methods used to promote active learning by pupils. The OECD's interest in this issue arose from its analysis of the human resource implications of current economic trends. In particular, the emergence of a "learning economy", in which continual learning is an increasingly important part of work, has profound implications for basic schooling. Teachers also have to keep their own practice abreast of new knowledge and changing conditions and therefore need themselves to be "active learners". The study looked at how a sample of innovative teachers involved their pupils in more active forms of learning, and how the teachers themselves learned through their own work.

After an overview of theories about active learning, the report arrives at an operational definition:

active learning is defined in one sense to mean that the learner uses opportunities to decide about aspects of the learning process. A second definition of active learning connects it to mental activity in another sense: it refers to the extent to which the learner is challenged to use his or her mental abilities while learning. Thus active learning on the one hand has to do with decisions about learning and on the other hand making active use of thinking. (OECD 1995c, p.16)

The report argues that there has been an accumulation of findings that certain forms of cooperative, small group learning promote pupils' achievement. Based on that evidence, the researchers produced a classroom observation protocol to record practices that were thought to represent effective forms of independence and cooperative learning. The protocol was applied in 74 selected classroom in 28 schools, and in one programme for pupils sponsored by a major corporation. Teachers were also interviewed, both about the experience of pupils in their classroom and about their own experiences as active learners. The main findings are that:

— *students are rarely given much choice about what they are to learn (even in classrooms selected to exemplify active learning), but they are sometimes given considerable choice about the method, pace and sequence of learning.*

— *in the observed classroom students are often found to be working in small groups, and this practice also appears to be consistent with self-regulated learning by students as individuals.*

— *active learning methods often include the production of a document, display or other tangible result that can be immediately appreciated, and sometimes even use, by other people. (OECD 1995c, p. 165)*

The report was presented to the Governing Board of CERI in 1995 but has not yet been published. The work on the professional development of teachers is being taken forward within a major study of Teachers and Curriculum Reform in Basic Schooling which will be discussed below. The concern of policy makers in most OECD countries is now focused on how quality practices can be generalized and made permanent within education systems hence the focus of this new study on "systemic reform".

V. Teachers as the Key to Successful Educational Reform

Since early 1994, CERI has been conducting a wide-ranging study of reforms of basic schooling, supported by seventeen of its Member countries. The study has been partly financed by the U.S. Government which drew on the study in preparation for the implementation of the bi-partisan Goals 2000 educational legislation. The study included working groups, with overlapping country representation, on curriculum, assessment, teachers' professional development and equity. The working groups each produced reports which were brought together under the overall theme of "systemic reform". The term is used to convey the growing awareness in OECD countries that changing one element of an education system has (often unexpected) knock-on effects on the rest of the system and that it is more effective to aim at changing the system as a whole coherently so that, for example, the professional development of teachers is seen as closely related to changes in curriculum and assessment.

The report of the overall study will be published in 1997 and will include the report on teachers' professional development. One of the early conclusions of the study was the successful implementation of innovative proposals depends on involving teachers at each stage in the development of new approaches. Reforms have in the past failed wholly or in part, because the passing of legislation was seen as the culminating point of the process whereas in fact the reforms failed to be successfully integrated into teachers' classroom practice. A very large number of Member countries have embarked on major reforms of their educational systems in the last decade and the study was able to draw on their experiences.

The report focused on in-service development rather than the initial preparation of new teachers in recognition of the fact that it is largely the existing corps of teachers who will be called upon to implement the reforms. In all OECD countries, turnover in the teaching profession is low and new teachers cannot be expected to alter significantly the culture of schools. In any case, policies in most countries are increasingly focused on the school and teachers are viewed as a team, led by a head with collective responsibilities for developing curriculum, pedagogical and assessment policies in dialogue with parents, pupils and the local community. School-focused professional development is the key to successful team work and to individual self-development.

The report draws on specific submissions made by several OECD countries which are giving a high priority to the professional development of teachers within their reforms. It also draws on the reports from other working groups on curriculum and assessment and on the record of the discussions held at six conferences which were held during the period March 1994 – May 1996. The focus is on policies for professional development. It begins with an analysis of the changing culture within which teaching and learning occurs.

The prevalent culture of teaching and learning is attuned to a relatively static society, in which the necessary knowledge, competencies, and values are predefined and stored in curricula, tests and textbooks. A few dozens of years ago the job structure was still stable and the demands for employees were relatively invariant.

Only in a few positions in culture, politics, business and in social pressure groups was there a call for dynamic qualities such as independent thinking initiative, ability to cooperate, to seek responsibility, to define problems to reflect anticipate thinking, etc. School was expected to prepare young people to fulfill satisfactorily the tasks which other people had set for them. As a consequence there was a strong demand for diligence, sense of duty and discipline.

The main characteristics of this culture are as follows:

***A predominance of systemic knowledge:** High priority is given to well-established facts, allowing schools to maintain a close relationship with the results of academic knowledge production. Low priority is given to open and controversial areas of knowledge and to personal experience and involvement.*

***Specialization:** Knowledge is compartmentalised in subject-matter fields which more or less correspond to the academic disciplines. This facilitates an orientation towards established standards of quality and gives teaching and learning a clear and predictable structure. On the other hand, complex, real-life situations tend to be disregarded because they cross the disciplinary boundaries.*

***A transmission-mode of teaching:** This mode facilitates the retention of the systemic character of knowledge and its reconstruction by the student. However, it tends to discourage the generation and reflective handling of knowledge.*

***A prevalence of top-down communication:** This facilitates the external control of predefined knowledge structures, provides stable frame conditions, and facilitates the maintenance of control in the classroom. However, it discourages initiatives as well as self-control, cooperation among students (or teachers), and networking across school boundaries.*

For the last two decades the limitations of this interpretation of educational tasks have been criticized with increasing intensity. The criticism comes from different sources. The following examples may illustrates this: One is the increasing importance of so-called 'key qualifications' such as the ability to cooperate and work in teams, the ability to communicate in one's mother tongue and in at least one other language, the ability to identify and solve problems, media literacy, techniques for lifelong learning etc. These abilities appear to become more and more threshold conditions for participation in work and in society. The convention is that schools fail to achieve these qualifications. (OECD 1996a, p.4)

Students also find it increasingly difficult to connect their school experience with a positive vision of a future for themselves partly because of the lack of jobs which connect with academic studies and partly because of the complexity of outside pressures on young people and the alternative sources of knowledge about the world which the mass media offer. The question facing policy-makers is therefore:

How can schools become more effective at fostering the development of studies as automous, self-regulating, and self-evaluating learners and at enabling them to construct their own futures? (OECD 1996a, p. 5)

The culture of schools will need to change radically to meet these challenges, retaining the strengths of the old system (to satisfy the demand for standards) while complementing them with more dynamic pedagogical and curricular approaches which open up new ways of accessing knowledge and learning how to learn. Teachers will be central to this change. This is recognised in the policy statements of many countries; for example The Irish White Paper on Education (1995) states that:

The capacity of the education system to cope with and lead change is critically dependent on developing the necessary attitudinal and professional competence of the teaching profession. (p. 125)

The report identifies the central policy issues for countries seeking a more dynamic and integrated approach to professional development:

A profession that has to cope with increasingly complex situations cannot "be told what to do" *but has to develop an inherent interest in continuous development.*

Professional development is not only an individual but more and more a cooperative endeavour involving partners inside and outside the profession.

Equity becomes more and more a pressing concern in many countries, not only because of considerations of social justice but also of the more pragmatic considerations of social and economic stability. As a result, teachers have to deal with the increasing heterogeneity of the student population.

More and more tasks have to be delegated to teachers and

schools, because beyond a certain complexity and variation of situations problems cannot be solved for the practitioners but can only be solved by them taking account of their specific practical situation.

Increasing autonomy necessarily is associated with increased demand for accountability. By what means can accountability be secured without crippling local initiatives?

Professional development is an urgent issue but its effects are critically interacting with policy initiatives in other areas, such as curriculum (e.g., the creation of space for local decision making with respect to educational aims) organisation (e.g., provisions for planning and reflection) and assessment (e.g. local responsibility for grading). (OECD 1996a, p. 6)

One of the aspects brought out most clearly in the report is the variety of national approaches to teacher accountability, despite a general trend to grant more autonomy to schools. The most common approaches include self-evaluation, peer evaluation and evaluation by inspection and by standardized tests. In German-speaking countries, teachers are subject to very little external evaluation and the emphasis is on input controls such as high standards of teacher preparation and selection. In more market-oriented countries like the US and UK the focus is an output criteria—published results as indicators of teacher performance, for example. The report argues that it is important to achieve the right balance.

between state-controlled, profession-controlled and consumerist accountability, which is adapted both to the extent of autonomy given to the school and to the resources and infrastructural support to use the autonomy constructively. Otherwise there is danger that the power is kept where it is while the blame is being decentralised. (OECD 1996a, p. 12)

There is a strong relationship between accountability and professional development. If teachers lose all control over accountability the danger is that they will retreat to a passive role of conforming to centrally-determined prescriptions. A strong element of professional self-government appears to be an indispensable core of any accountability concept which aims to promote schools with a dynamic culture of professional development.

The report examines the concept of teacher professionalism,

finding the traditional paradigm of "technical rationality" inadequate to meet the complexities of teachers' roles. An alternative conceptualisation is advanced based on "reflective rationality". Professionalism is defined by the ability to generate context-specific local knowledge in order to further develop the quality of service. This concept implies a new balance between individual autonomy and collegial, client-oriented cooperation. The isolation of most teachers within their classroom makes this difficult to achieve in traditionally organised schools.

Developing a new professionalism in schools will require action at three levels: the individual teacher, the school, and the responsible authority. Chapter 4 of the report examines a set of assumptions about the professional development of teachers which underlie current policies.

(a) The more complex a professional activity becomes the more policy interventions have to take into account the views of the practitioners and leave space for local adaptations. This assumption is based on the understanding that in complex modern societies many local practical problems cannot be solved for the institutions, by central regulations. Instead the problem-solving capacity of these institutions and of the persons working in them has to be improved. This policy implies that administrators listen to teachers, analyse ongoing developments, stimulate reflection and documentation, support communication and pinpoint policy measures to strengthen positive developments in the system.

(b) The closer in time, space and substance an intervention is with respect to actual teaching and learning activities the more influence it has. The effective utilisation of external ideas in complex practical situations is primarily a matter of direct access to the right ideas at the right moment. This implies that the local know-how that is available within a teaching staff has a high potentiality for professional development. It is close in a spatial sense, it is accessible at the right time and the chances that it is relevant are high because the situational conditions are similar.

(c) Innovations move along the social network of personal acquaintance. Indirect contact suffices to spread simple, well-structured and routine information. Direct contact is much more effective where there is an element of uncertainty or when results

are unpredictable. This assumption implies that informal contacts have strong effects on the dissemination of innovation and of local professional knowledge. In a complex social system the task of administration is less to provide answers to problems than to provide contexts for communication, in which know-how and experiences can be exhcanged, practices demonstrated, and in which ideas can be disseminated through emerging personal relationships. To develop strategies to initiate and organise effective negotiation processes between subsystems in the society may become one of the important new tasks of central administrations. An important way to do this in education is to simulate communication among teachers, so that they exchange experiences, stimulate and correct each other. Prerequisites are sabbaticals, opportunities to meet inside school and structured contexts in which professional exchange may develop, if teams of teachers share responsibility for groups of students.

(d) Innovations in complex situations cannot be 'cloned'. An understandable dream of the policy maker is the multiplication of innovative developments which have already shown their potential. This dream is not realistic, not only because the contexts are never identical, but also because the personal relationship to an innovation and the 'fit' between personal values have an equal (if not greater) influence on its impact on practice than its 'objective' quality.

This principle implies that any substantial innovation must be 'acquired' by teachers in a very personal sense. This means that they must be able to transform it and to give it their individual 'colour' and thus make it their personal property (and not a copy of somebody else's developments). As a consequence, professional development initiatives need to leave space for this ownership to be developed. Very often the direct access to innovative practices (without the pressure to copy them), the experience that obstacles can be overcome, and the chance to exchange ideas, are more effective than offering tested materials or behavioural specifications.

(e) Challenges of complex situations demand the production of local professional knowledge in situ. Only a part of the knowledge that is needed in situations which are characterised by ambiguous and partially contradictory aims can be transmitted by courses, regulations and materials. A significant part must be produced by the practitioners themselves. An important strategic competence to

be developed is an experimental approach to practice and systematic reflection on action in order to further develop it.

(f) Cooperation develops only if it is needed. Cooperation between professionals cannot be mandated nor is it a result of good will. In fact, most teachers say that they dislike their isolation and would like to cooperate. Cooperation only develops if the professional tasks as perceived by the teachers demand cooperation. This has not been the case with respect to most traditional tasks of teachers. However, cooperation become an imperative if a dynamic culture of learning is being developed, and if teachers create links to the community, engage in interdisciplinary projects, etc.

This assumption is illustrated in a Danish Policy Document: it proposes a move away from the present school day week based on a strict division of lessons and subjects to planning models with periods of topic or project work. Such planning models "would all have this in common, that they would be so wide in scope that no single person could span them all at a sufficiently high academic level, no matter how good a teacher education they have received. This requires close cooperation within the group of teachers attached to a class, a cooperation which promotes coordination and the communal assumption of responsibility" (quoted in Danish Council for Educational Development in the Folkeskole 1992b, p.250)

(g) Innovations of complex professional practices demand a systemic approach. Constructive answers to new educational challenges can neither be sustained nor be transformed into a change of the educational culture of schools if they remain individual initiatives. (OECD 1996a, p 15)

The message for policy-makers is that policies should support the growth of local, school-level, development rather than attempting to mandate change in detailed central regulations. The aim should be to promote policy-active schools which feel responsible for the innovations which are necessary in order to carry out their own policies, to meet the particular challenges they face in their social context. The recent Irish White Paper on Education epitomises this approach:

...the strong message emerging consistently from all quarters is that the approach to professional and personal development should be decentralised, school-focused and conducive to high levels of

teacher participation in all aspects of the process. This is not to say that there is no role for programmes and courses external to the school, nor for actions initiated by national bodies (quoted in OECD 1996a, p. 19)

The report contains a useful survey of national policy approaches, drawing on official documents, as well as papers specifically produced for the study. The policies are grouped under the broad headings of curriculum, student assessment, quality assurance, infrastructures for professional development, and schools as professional development centres. They offer a rich source of illustrations and examplars of the great variety of educational reforms being undertaken in the developed countries. At the same time, common concerns and patterns can be distinguished, although the starting points for reform may be very different.

There is widespread concern to involve teachers in curriculum development and to leave space within the national curriculum for school level and classroom level interpretation. This is most clearly evident in those countries with a centralised tradition which are now moving to reduce the amount of centralised prescription, in some cases, such as Spain and Sweden, reducing the national curriculum to a 'core curriculum' to leave space for regional and school level elements. In Sweden this is being monitored in 100 reference schools which are documenting the development of a local curriculum in conjunction with the new national curriculum.

The introduction of new systems of student assessment stimulates demands for new types of professional development. This has been a particular feature of developments in the United States where the move away from over-reliance on standardised tests, which is judged to have had a malign influence on teaching and learning, has led to the introduction of 'portfolio assessment'. In many countries there are attempts to strengthen the formative function of assessment. This has been a particular feature in France where the diagnostic testing of all pupils at key stages is intended, not for the construction of league tables of schools but for informing teachers and schools of the relative strengths and weaknesses of their pupils. For this reason the tests are carried out at the beginning of school years, so that they constitute less a judgement on previous teaching and more a basis for planning the coming year's teaching. However, it is already clear that teachers need help in using these diagnostic tests effectively.

Student performance data can also be used as an output measure of schools' and teachers' effectiveness, or indeed of the effectiveness of the system as a whole. As in the French example this latter function, can with sensitive handling, be compatible with a fundamentally formative approach. Either way, it is likely that the development of quality assurance mechanism will be an important influence on the future shape of professional development. In some countries, most notably in England, the appraisal of individual teachers by fellow professionals, usually teachers in the same school, is official policy. This could be a powerful stimulus to individual development linked to school policies particularly in the context of a four-yearly school inspection report.

Providing the training expertise to meet the increasingly diverse demands for professional development is a problem in many countries. There is a general movement away from the traditional offering of university and research-based courses. Even more traditionally 'practice-focused' providers such as teachers' centres or teacher training colleges are having to adapt to school-focused needs. In many countries, notably the United States, teachers' associations have been stimulated by this challenge and have extended their interests beyond salary and conditions of work issues to active support for quality development in the profession.

However, the most exciting development in many countries is the emergence of schools themselves as professional development centres. Such an approach is highly cost-effective but it does require authorities to provide the necessary time, space, resources and organisational structures to enable teachers to plan and develop their work and to reflect on their experiences. School development plans, which usually have a professional development dimension, are current practice in most countries. In some, this has led to organisational changes. In Denmark, for example, the recent reform of the Folkeskole requires interdisciplinary work in teams and official documentation acknowledges that "*picking out good teachers to act as consultants or team leaders has become a major task for heads and advisers*" (OECD 1996a, p36). The emergence of networks of teachers using new technologies to communicate innovations and ideas to each other (as in the OECD supported Environmental Studies initiative, which was particularly strong in German-speaking countries) is also an encouraging development.

The report's provisional conclusions are the strategic interventions by central authorities to support professional development are more effective than detailed regulations, at least in the long run. These interventions should be aimed at identifying and supporting local initiatives and creating a framework within which institutions and individuals are stimulated to become involved in self-evaluation and innovation because problem-solving at school level cannot easily be effectuated by the centre. Support for networking between schools and clusters of schools may be the cheapest and most effective way of developing the problem-solving capacity of institutions.

VI. The Economic Condition of Teachers in the 1990s

The developing concern for issues of quality and teacher development coexists in the OECD's work programme with its continuing efforts to provide policy makers in its Member countries with basic indicators of educational development and analyses of costs. Much of this work relates to teachers since teachers' salaries are the major component of educational spending.

For the last decade, OECD has developed and published a series of indicators, which are regularly update, on the organisation and operation of education systems. Since 1992 these have been published as Education at a Glance. The latest edition, published in 1995, presents a set of 49 international indicators covering the 1991-2 educational year. They provide an essential statistical basis for OECD's (and other organisations') comparative educational studies. The indicators are grouped into three broad categories: Contexts of Education; Costs, Resources and School Processes; and Results of Education. Those relating to teachers are found mainly in the second part under the sub-heading Processes and Staff and especially in the section on Human Resources which comprises six indicators. These are included as Appendix 1. Most of them are presented in more than one way (tables, charts, graphs) and they are accompanied by useful explanatory texts.

The first three indicators concern the numbers of educational staff, teaching and non-teaching, as a percentage of the total labour force, how they are deployed and their workloads. In the 16 OECD countries surveyed teaching staff at all levels represent between 2 and 5 per cent of the total labour force. The range is substantial and does not seem to relate to student enrolments as a proportion of the labour force: Belgium, Turkey and New Zealand have almost identical proportions of their students in full-time education but whereas Belgium has a markedly higher percentage of teaching staff (4.8 compared with the country mean of 3.1), Turkey has only 2.2 and New Zealand 3.3. The breakdown of personnel between teaching and non-teaching also varies widely across countries, as does the proportion of teachers working in tertiary education. The pupil teacher ratio (PTR) is another factor which varies sharply across countries although there is a pattern of progressively declining PTRs as pupils get older, the 'bonus for age'.

Teaching time is another major factor in calculating teachers' work-loads as well as the costs of education. The number of teaching hours per year is roughly double in Tureky, the United States and the Netherlands compared to Sweden, across primary, lower secondary and upper secondary education.

The other three indicators relate to the education and training, remuneration, and key characteristics—age and gender—of the teaching forces. Taken together, these three indicators give a clear picture of the comparative status of teaching as a profession across countries, and of the comparative status of primary, lower secondary and upper secondary education within countries. The length of education and training, the starting, average, and maximum pay rates (converted to purchasing power parity at January 1992 and then related to the per capita gross domestic product of the country concerned) and the relative numbers of men and women at each phase are compared. The variations among countries in these aspects both reflect teachers' historical status and to some extent determine the future make-up of the profession.

The picture revealed by these indicators is one of surprising variations within a relatively uniform pattern. OECD countries are quite similar with respect to the duration of teacher education. To become a qualified teacher at early childhood, primary and lower secondary levels, education lasts from 15 to 17 years, with a range from 12 years for early childhood education in Italy to 20 for upper secondary in Germany. Germany requires the highest number of years of education for all types of teacher.

There are large salary differences across OECD countries, particularly with respect to maximum salaries in lower secondary education. There is also a wide range in the number of years it takes a teacher to reach the maximum salary from 8 for lower secondary teachers in New Zealand to 45 for primary teachers in Spain. Again, it is in Germany that starting salaries are highest but maximum salaries are higher in Austria. Relating salaries to per capita GDP gives a slightly different picture. Only in Sweden and the United States do starting salaries fall below per capita GDP, in a ratio of 0.8 and 0.9 respectively, and the mean across the 15 countries surveyed is 1.2. The ratio of maximum salaries to per capita GDP varies much more, from over 3.7 in Portugal to only 1.1 in Sweden. In general, the less developed countries within the OECD pay their teachers at much higher rates relative to per capita GDP than the more developed countries, which may well reflect the higher status of teachers within more rural societies. The difference between starting and maximum salaries is highest in Austria and the United Kingdom.

The teaching force is ageing in almost all countries, most teachers being in the age category of 40 to 49, but there is considerable variation in the percentage of teachers in the lowest age category, younger than 30. A large majority of teachers are female, especially at early childhood and primary education levels. In general, the percentage of male teachers grows with the age of pupils and reaches a broad parity with females at upper secondary level except in Portugal where it is still only 29 per cent.

These indicators are of considerable help to policy makers both in planning for initial and in-service training and in projecting costs. Teachers' salaries are the most significant instrument at the disposal of governments as they attempt to shape their teaching forces, but other factors—most notably the characteristics of the existing teachers and the costs of their education and training—have to be taken into account when calculating recruitment and retention policies. An unpublished study commissioned by OECD from two academic researchers at Stanford University (How Well Do Teachers Do in

OECD Countries and Why? A Comparison using OECD Indicators) develops a number of alternative ways of comparing teachers' incomes and estimates costs per pupil at different levels of education as a function of teachers' salaries and pupil-teacher ratios (PTRs). They argue that:

Policy makers should be interested in knowing...whether differences in expenditures per pupil at different levels of schooling in the various OECD countries are primarily the result of a choice nations make about the optimal number of pupils each teacher should be responsible for (pupil-teacher ratio or time required in classroom work) or, primarily the result of differences in the salaries teachers have been able to get from society. (Carnoy, p. 5)

They note that whereas demand for teachers grew sharply in the period 1965-1980 in line with the growth of pupil numbers, teacher employment did not decline nearly as rapidly as did pupil numbers in the subsequent period. As a result, much of the increase cost of schooling at primary and secondary levels went into lower PTRs. They conclude that:

teachers withstood the adjustments of the 1980s better than might have been expected had adjustments been implemented in the form recommended by financial institutions. (Carnoy, p.12)

Higher income countries generally have lower PTRs anyway, and as their income per capita grows countries tend to reduce them further. The analysis shows that it is the per capita GDP which is the most significant factor in achieving low PTRs (PTRs are negatively related to per capita GDP). Teacher's salaries grew only modestly in most countries through the 1985-1992 period and relative to manufacturing wages did no better than stay even. OECD and other data suggest that both parents and teachers give a high political priority to lowering PTRs. In some countries this political imperative outweights the bargaining strength of teachers' unions and the authors suggest that there is a trade-off between maintaining or lowering PTRs and raising teachers' salaries:

changing pupil-teacher ratio becomes a highly significant explainer of changing teacher salaries. Indeed, the larger the decline in primary PTR, the smaller the increase in primary teacher salaries. In an OECD country where the PTR fell 10 per cent more than in another country, teacher salary increased an average of 8 per cent less. However, this also means that teachers did not pay the full price of lower PTRs, since their salaries fell less than the decline in PTR...The conclusion that can be drawn from this exercise is that teacher salaries increases were related to changes in their conditions of work. Teachers apparently got lower salary increases in those countries where PTRs fell more. That this was the case suggests that teachers bear at least part of the cost of the trend toward lower PTRs. Since much of the reason for higher PTRs in the OECD in recent years has been the inability of governments to fire teachers even when the growth of the school-age population slows drastically, this means that governments are pushed to cut costs by reducing salary increases. However—and this is also important—teachers' salary increases do not decline as fully as PTRs decline.... [which]...reflects the degree of bargaining power teachers have in these various countries. (Carnoy, p. 31)

Reforms in teacher education have important economic dimensions which are often neglected in the research and policy debates. However, as Alan Wagner has noted:

costs and financing, and their relationship to effectiveness, are essential elements for informed choices among alternative options for teacher education (Wagner, p. 12)

Wagner's entry in the International Encylopaedia of Education on the Economics of Teacher Education draws on OECD and other sources in its analysis of the demand for and supply of teachers and the costs and financing of teacher education. He shows that the sheer magnitude of the overall teacher education effort has been a factor in governments' search for alternative approaches to recruitment and training. In particular, the methods of financing in-service education are being changed in the 1990s in several OECD countries.

The most recent trend is to provide clearer signals and incentives to providers of in-service education via criteria included in categorical funding mechanisms, as in Norway and the United Kingdom (England and Wales), and to introduce competition by allowing authorities at the appropriate levels in the countries concerned (schools, municipalities, regions) to purchase inservice training from a provider offering the best training at the lowest cost (as in Sweden, Denmark, and the United Kingdom). These financing methods are believed to promote efficiency in the sense that provision has been "steered" toward priority areas, new knowledge or techniques have been diffused widely in the schools, and budgeted costs per participant appear to have been reduced in various ways. (Wagner, p. 17)

This does not obviate the need for a strong pre-service base which should lay the foundations for later development: teachers are lifelong learners too. What most countries are seeking are cost-effective and in many cases more practical, school-based, ways of preparing teachers for their initial entry into the profession and more frequent and flexible approaches to professional development thereafter.

Conclusion

OECD's central concern is with policies for economic development. However, education has not been seen instrumentally, as primarily a means of promoting economic productivity, but as an intrinsic good for individuals which also contributes to the social well-being of the Member countries. Nonetheless, the mere fact of being located within an economic think-tank has coloured the approach to educational issues and has allowed OECD to develop a strong focus on the economics of education and on policy issues such as manpower planning. The major concern is to provide policy makers with informed advice and statistical information which will allow them to make useful comparisons and learn from the experience of other countries.

It is inevitable therefore that OECD's concerns over the years have reflected the problems and challenges facing its Member governments, but it has also attempted to look beyond the immediate issues and to offer a forum within which policy makers can discuss future developments. Thus, in the 1960s and early 1970s, when most countries were grappling with the rapid expansion of their educational systems as a consequence of demographic pressures, OECD provided a platform for policies which were concerned with the quality of teachers and their professional development. Country reviews have been essential as a two-way communica-tion between the OECD secretariat and national officials and Ministers which has helped on the one hand to update OECD's database and keep it in touch with developments in the real world of national educational systems and on the other to bring to bear on national issues its expertise and comparative perspectives.

As the problems of teacher supply receded and governments turned to developing policies to respond to demand for higher standards, OECD's work on teaching quality became more relevant. The profiles of the teaching forces developed by OECD showed that in-service rather than initial or pre-service education and training would be the key to raising standards within the teaching professions and this became the focus of its work in the 1980s and early 1990s. Identifying good practice is useful in itself but OECD is also able to disseminate it and to provide a policy context.

Most OECD countries carried out radical reforms of the educational systems during the period under review. As it became clear that the aims of the reforms were not being fully achieved governments became increasingly concerned with policy implementation. The most recent OECD studies have taken a systemic perspective, seeing reforms in the areas of organisation and management, curriculum and assessment, and teacher training as inter-related and needing to be treated symbiotically. Professional development of teachers is seen as the key to this and the process of decentralisation of responsibilities to school level has reinforced the need for such an approach. The 'policy-active school' requires teachers to operate more as a team and to identify their own professional development needs which are to some extent determined by national policies on curriculum and assessment and quality control, but also by the local context within which the school operates. National policies must leave room for schools and teachers to shape policies to their own aims, concentration on strategic interventions to promote networking and dissemination of good practice.

Decentralisation also implies accountability and this is not easy to reconcile with professional autonomy or the encouragement of innovation (and even a measure of risk-taking) by teachers faced with novel social and psychological problems among their pupils. One of the central features of school-level professional development should be the promotion of collective and individual accountability by teachers so that the responsibility is not removed to a bureaucracy which in the long term will reduce schools' ability to respond creatively to new challenges.

Meanwhile, as the demographic changes work their way through the educational systems, economic constraints on school budgets are growing. Teachers' remuneration and conditions of work continue to be the subject of much of OECD's work and data collection. The implications of an ageing teaching force facing the challenges of the 21st century are an important consideration. What those challenges will be should be clarified by the focus on lifelong learning. The Ministers of Education agreed that their commitment to lifelong learning for all will require additional financial resources but

because lifelong learning provides substantial economic and social returns to all partners individuals, families, employers and the society as a whole—the additional investment must be mobilised by all concerned. (OECD 1996c, p. 14)

The foundations for lifelong learning will have to be laid within formal educational structures and therefore parents and teachers will have to be convinced that they need to look beyond the here and now, the preparation of their pupils for the next step, whether in formal education or work, and instead to provide them with skills and values for life. This should be the focus for the professional development of teachers as we approach the 21st century.

Bibliography

Carnoy, M. and DeAngelis, K. (1995), "The Social Benefits of Education", mimeo, OECD, Paris.

OECD (1974), *The Teacher and Education Change: a New Role,* Paris.

OECD (1979), *Teacher Policies in a New Context,* Paris.

OECD (1982), *In-Service Education and Training of Teachers: a Condition for Educational Change*, Paris.

OECD (1990), *The Teacher Today*, Pairs.

OECD (1991a), *Environment, Schools and Active Learning*, Paris.

OECD (1991b), *Reviews of National Policies for Education—Ireland*, Paris.

OECD (1994a), *Quality in Education*, Paris.

OECD (1994b), *The Curriculum Redefined: Schooling for the 21st Century*, Paris.

OECD (1995a), *Education at a Glance, OECD Indicators*, Paris.

OECD (1995b), *Reviews of National Policies for Education—Sweden*, Paris.

OECD (1995c), *Active Learning for Students and Teachers*, unpublished report, Paris.

OECD (1996a), *Teachers and their Professional Development*, unpublished report, Paris.

OECD (1996b), *Reviews of National Policies for Education—France*, Paris.

OECD (1996c), *Lifelong Learning for all*, Paris.

OECD (1996d), *Review of School Education Policy in the Czech Republic*, Paris

Papadopoulos, G.S. (1994), *Education 1960-1990. The OECD Perspective*, OECD, Paris.

Wagner, A. (1995), "The economics of Teacher Education", *International Encylopaedia of Education.*

Appendix

Staff employed in education

Chart P 31:
Staff employed in education as a percentage of the total labour force (full-time equivalents) (1992)

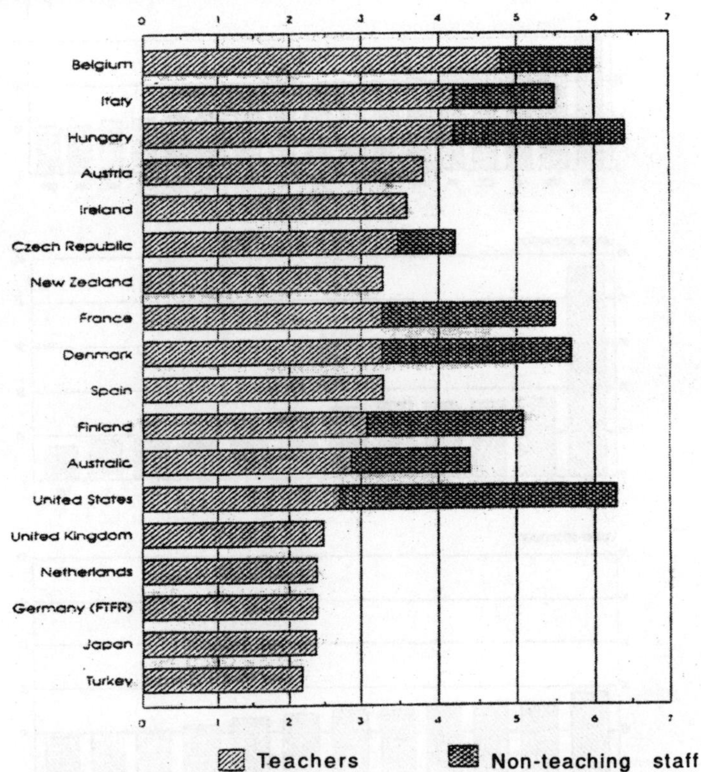

Countries are ranked in descending order by the percentage of teachers in the labour force

Fig. 1 :

Ratio of Students to teaching staff

Chart P 32:
Ratio of students to teaching staff, by level of education in public and private institutions (1992)

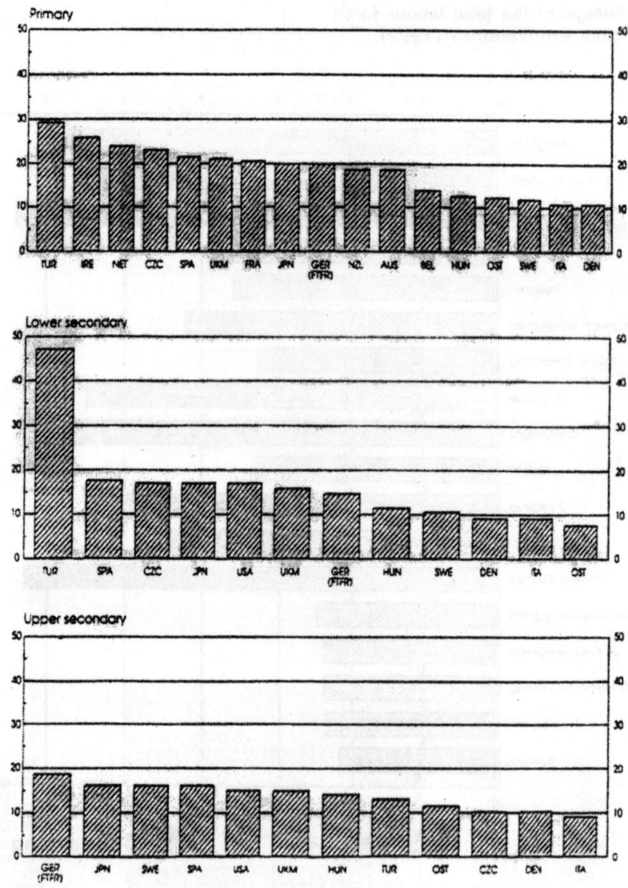

Countries are ranked in descending order by the ratio of students to teaching staff

Fig. 2 :

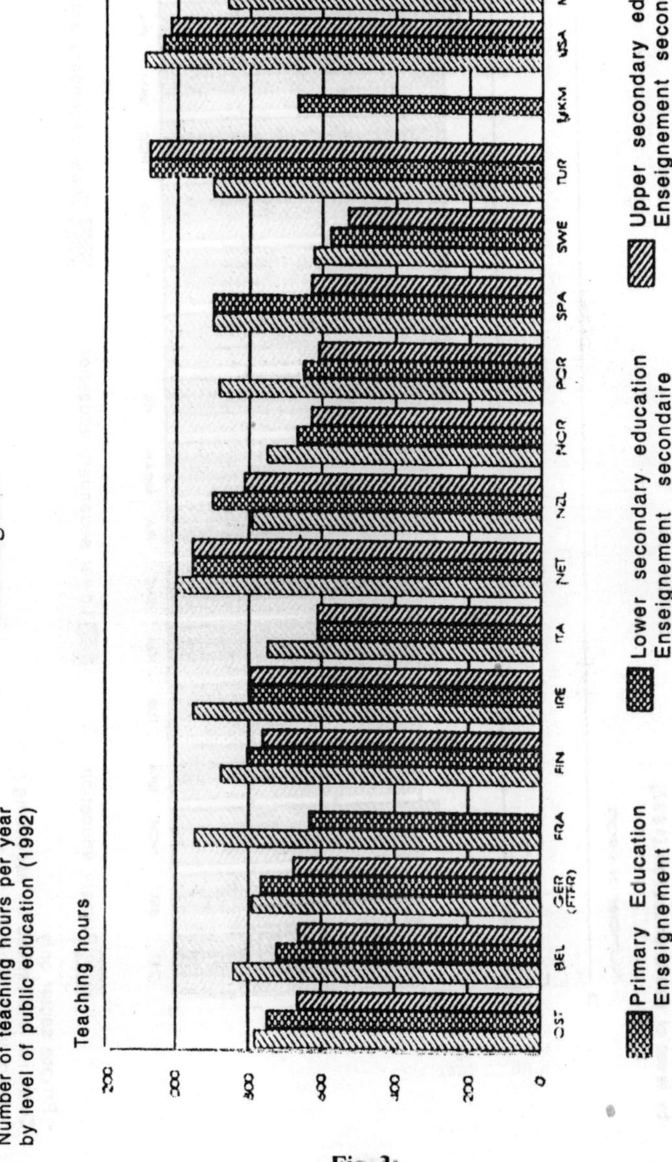
Teaching time
Chart P 33:
Number of teaching hours per year
by level of public education (1992)
Teaching hours
0
200
400
600
800
1000
1200
BEL
GER (FTFR)
FRA
FIN
IRE
ITA
NET
NZL
NOR
POR
SPA
SWE
TUR
UKM
USA
MEAN
Primary Education
Enseignement primaire
Lower secondary education
Enseignement secondaire 1er cycle
Upper secondary education
Enseignement secondaire 2e cycle
Countries are ranked by English alphabetical order

Fig. 3:

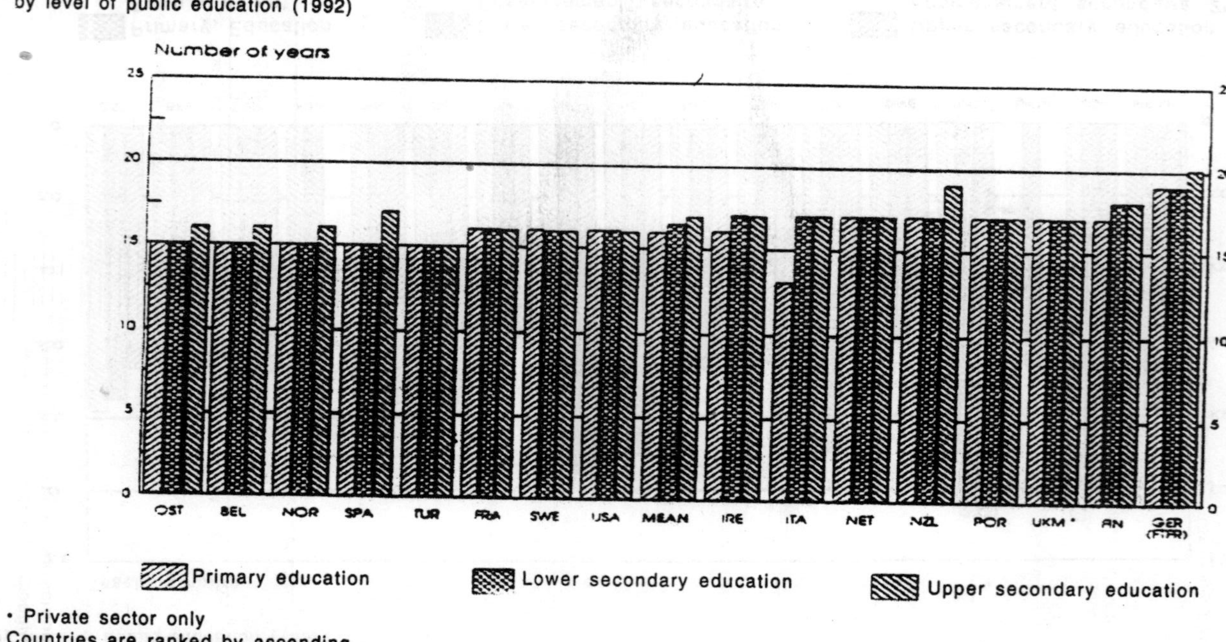
Chart P 34:
Total number of years of teacher education required for teachers, by level of public education (1992)
Teacher education
Number of years
0
5
10
15
20
25
OST
BEL
NOR
SPA
TUR
FRA
SWE
USA
MEAN
IRE
ITA
NET
NZL
POR
UKM *
FIN
GER (FTFR)
Primary education
Lower secondary education
Upper secondary education
* Private sector only
Countries are ranked by ascending order of years required to teach in upper secondary general education

Fig. 4:

Teacher compensation

Chart P 35(A):
Starting and maximum teacher salaries and GDP per capita for public primary and lower secondary education (1992)

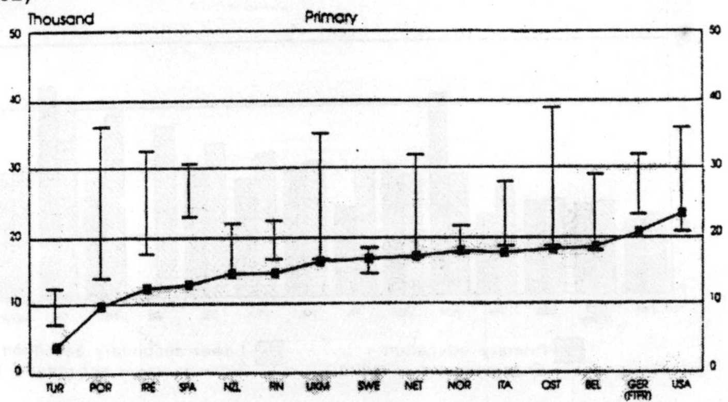

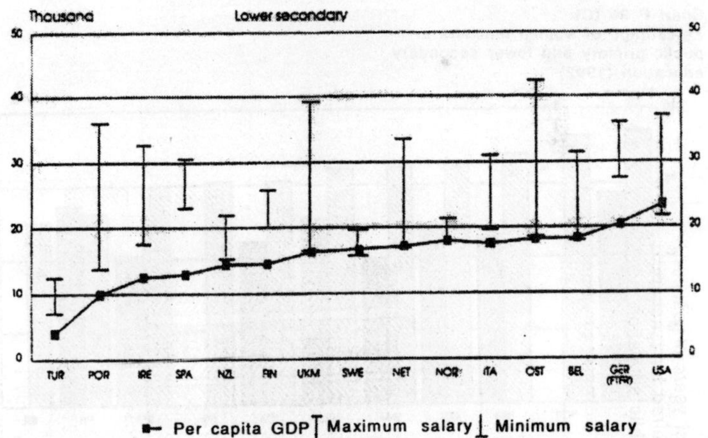

Per capita GDP Maximum salary Minimum salary

Countries are ranked from lowest to highest per capita GDP

Fig. 5:

Teacher characteristics

Chart P 36 (B):
Percentage of teachers under 40 years of age in public primary and lower secondary education (1992)

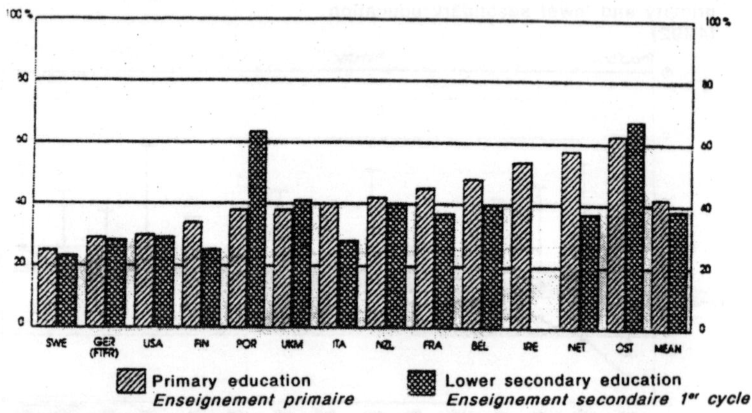

Consumes ranked from lowest to heighest percentage at primary education

Chart P 36 (C):
Percentage of women teachers in public primary and lower secondary education (1992)

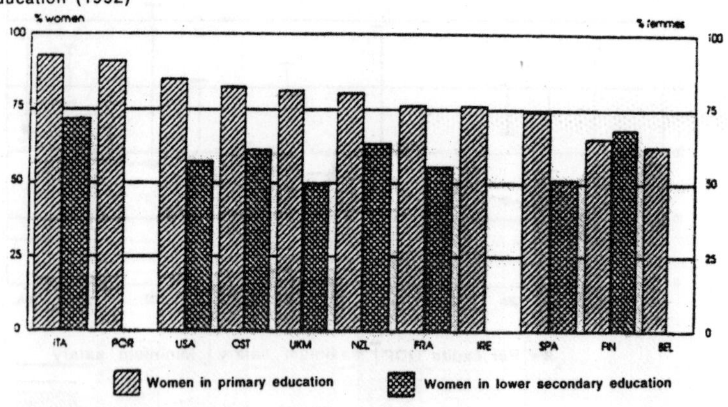

Countries ranked by heighest percentage of women in primary education

Fig. 6:

Educational R & D personnel

Chart P 41:
Personnel engaged in educational R & D (in full-time equivalent) as a percentage of total R & D personnel and of R & D personnel in the higher education sector (in various years)

Educational R & D personnel as a percentage of all R & D personnel

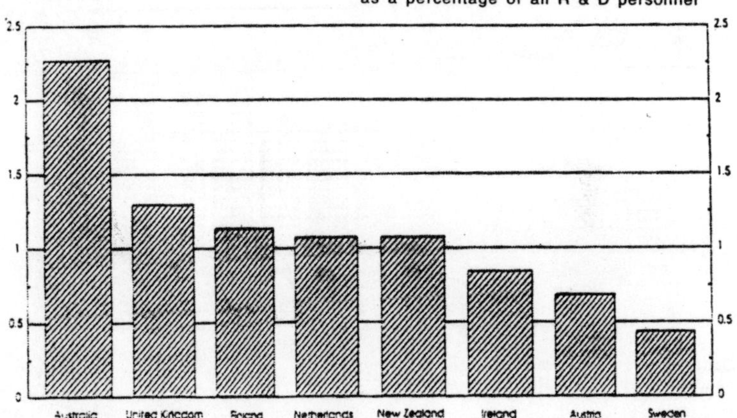

Educational R & D personnel in higher education as a percentage at all R & D personnel in higher education

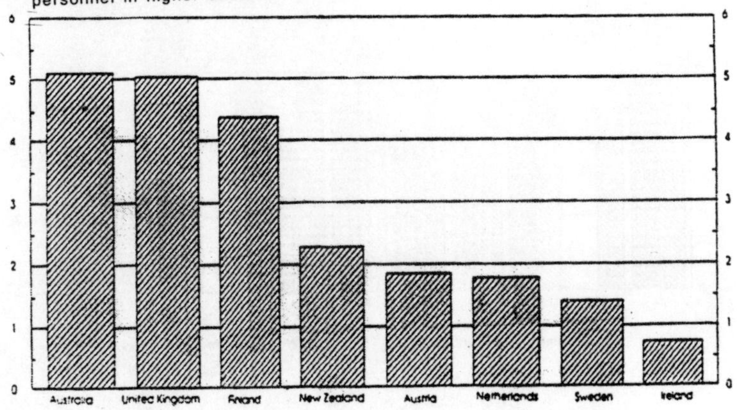

Fig. 7:

Courtesy: International Bureau of Education, UNESCO, Geneva, Switzerland.

PART—IV

Teacher Training in Europe

—***Professor Maurice Galton***
Consultant, Council of Europe

I. Teacher Training—the Enterprise

In the last decade most countries, not only those in Europe, have engaged in educational reform. Wherever this has taken place the reform of teacher education and training has been one of the key issues. Reasons for focusing on teacher training are not difficult to discover. Teacher training is a large enterprise. Throughout Europe more than half a million student teachers are to be found in up to a thousand institutions. Their training involves over fifty thousand teacher trainers (ATEE 1989). It is estimated that in-service training for teachers who have already received their initial certificate involves over five million individuals each year. In the 1960s and 1970s there tended to be a rapid turn around within the profession with a high degree of drop-out particularly of women. This is no longer so and the profession is now an ageing one. In the 1990s most teachers are over forty years old.

One of the problems confronting reformers is that there is much diversity across Europe. In different countries different institutions are charged with the initial training of teachers. This includes secondary schools, colleges of initial teacher education, institutes of higher vocational education and universities. There are different degrees of co-ordination between the practical work which is normally done in schools and the theoretical study of education which normally takes place in an institution of higher education. The length of courses also varies, some taking up to five years while in some cases one year is provided (for vocational training courses). The amount of course given over to practising teaching can vary from zero to over fifty per cent. However, most European countries now have a minimum of three years training for primary and four years for secondary. Some countries separate certification into to phases so that a new teacher must first pass the theoretical part of the course before later on gaining the practical qualification. In other countries, however, no qualification is given unless the student passes the practical work in schools. Thus, would be reformers in different countries across Europe find there is little consensus and because of this diversity the pattern of reform tends to see some countries moving in the direction which other countries are tending to move away from.

II. Teacher Training an Inefficient System

Despite these difficulties, however, the search for a solution to the problems of teacher training continues. There are a number of reasons for this. The period of the 1980s was characterised by a number of trends across the whole of Europe, not least among members of the CDCC, concerning the reform of teacher training. That decade, because of the extensive economic, political. Demographic and cultural changes taking place, demanded reform of the school system. Increasingly, in the 1990s, evidence from such innovations has demonstrated that instead of changing teaching methods in ways which were congruent with the objectives of the new programmes, teachers have tended to 'bolt on' new content and procedures to their existing practice. Another reason why teacher training has increasingly become the focus of European governments concerns the spiralling costs of education; the result of increasing pressures from a well-educated, intelligent public for high quality education for their children. In these circumstances, teachers as the most expensive resource within the education system have been required to become more accountable for what they do and for the result they achieve with pupils.

This attempt to create a more effective, flexible teaching workforce, however, has bad to face, what on the surface, appears a major weakness in the existing systems of training teachers. Research reveals that the novice teachers tends to model themselves on their school mentor with whom they gain their first school experiences. At the same time, these more experienced mentors tend to operate in a conservative manner when asked to change their own practice in response to school reform. Each new generation of entrants to the profession is, therefore, inducted into this conservative mode, despite the best efforts of the tutors in the training institutions. For the past thirty years, therefore, most countries have operated a model of teacher training whereby new entrants to the profession rapidly absorb the practices of existing, more experienced colleagues, while at the same time vast sums of money are devoted through in-service training in efforts to change the practice of these more experienced teachers. Attempts to break out of this cycle of training and retraining have been at the heart of most attempted reforms of teacher education within member states of the Council of Europe.

III. Key Issues

In the late Eighties, the Fifteenth Session of the Standing Conference of European Ministers of Education took steps to address the above issues at its meeting in Helsinki on the theme 'New challenges for teachers and their education' (CDCC, 1987). Ministers agreed that it was vitally important to attract better candidates into teaching and to help them to be more effective in meeting the needs of a changing educational system and, in particular, to equip their pupils to respond successfully to challenges of the twenty-first century. Among the themes which the ministers recommended that the CDCC should address were:

* the procedures used in different countries for the selection of candidates for teacher training;
* the selection and professional development of trainers providing basic teacher training;
* the need to train teachers to improve their methods of coping with children of widely varying abilities and backgrounds;
* the analysis of the selection procedures and the professional development of the trainers who provide basic teacher training;
* the creation of more relevant systems of appraisal of teachers and of their teaching;
* the development of induction programmes within schools for newly qualified teachers.

In addressing these issues more fundamental questions have been raised. The chief of these concerns the government's role in the control of schooling and teacher education. Many European governments, notably that of the United Kingdom, have sought to lay down in a very clear and concise fashion both the content of the initial training curriculum and the processes by which that content should be delivered. There are changing conceptions of pedagogy, partly because of the concern about basic standards of literacy and numeracy but also because of the influence of information technology. Throughout the 1980s the position and status of girls in school and women in teacher education has also grown in importance reflecting the wider issue of women in society (Galton and Moon, 1994). Another major concern has resulted from the expansion and democratising of education in the post-compulsory years. In many countries there has been a tendency to delay specialisation and to strive for greater equality of opportunities. Another particularly important issue in many countries has been the question of the status of vocational education where, in general, the standard required to gain entry into the profession has been much lower than for more academic subjects.

IV. Similarities and Differences in Initial Teacher Training

Mention has already been made of the wide diversity which exists across Europe with regard to teacher training. In order to investigate this matter the Association of Teachers in Education in Europe (ATEE, 1989) undertook a survey of practices within the different countries of the CDCC in order to identify the more successful practices as well as the common-alties and differences within each member state's training procedures. This work, carried out by Professor Friderich Buchbergar, is summarised in Galton and Moon (1994). Among the key findings of the survey was the wide diversity of practice, although there were some common elements:

* most countries have linked the need for improved qualifications with the notion of professionalisation of teachers;
* most systems, however, follow a static conception of initial teacher education and disregard the need for the continuous professional development of teachers following their training.
* In most countries, the emphasis given to different elements

within the educational system (primary/secondary/vocational etc) largely dictates the nature of the training programmes and determines whether the "historic European schism between primary and secondary schools and the teachers in them" is maintained (Judge, 1992).

Most courses contain a number of common course components, including studies in education sciences, academic/subject studies, studies in subject matter methodo-logies and a period of teaching practice. There are major differences in the lengths of courses, for example, training for teachers in vocational, commercial and technical schools in many countries is often very limited compared to the concur-rent models used for training teachers in primary and secondary schools, which usually last between three and five years.

There is also a wide diversity is the way in which these elements and themes are implemented. For example, primary teacher training can take place at post secondary school (Austrian Paedagogische Akademie), in colleges of education (Danish Staats Seminarium), in institutions of higher vocational education (the Netherlands), at universities (UK. Germany). Most teachers training for primary education follow a concurrent programme in which these various components are studied in parallel to each other. For teachers of subjects in secondary schools, however, the most usual route is a consecutive model in which the student studies their subject to degree level and then takes a further year of professional studies (eg the Post-graduate Certificate of Education route in England and Wales).

Another important difference is the distinction which can be made between one phased and two phased models of training. In one phased models the completion of the training provides the teacher with a qualified status and allows them to take up appointments in schools. In other countries, however, the training is only a first phase and then has to be followed with a period in schools in which a local school board or a local pedagogical institute, separate from the university, assess the competence of the prospective teachers.

Within these divergent systems, however, the balance between subject study, teaching practice and educational stu-dies varies considerably. For example, the amount of teaching practice varies from almost zero to more than 60 per cent.

As mentioned earlier, this wide diversity tends to result in different countries moving in different directions when engaged in reform. This can be illustrated by considering the case of recent reform in the United Kingdom and France respectively. Formerly, in the United Kingdom teacher training was very diverse. There appeared to be as many different programmes as there were institutions. Over the last fifteen years, however, first through the Council of Accreditation for Teacher Education (CATE) and now through the Teacher Training Agency (TTA) greater uniformity has been imposed. Now all primary and secondary training takes place in universities. Provision for nursery training (the rising five year olds) takes place in Further Education Colleges. At the moment no special training is required for vocational teaching although there are voluntary courses available in some universities.

At least sixty-six per cent of all primary school and secondary school teacher training must take place in the schools themselves. Training institutions are now regularly inspected and rated 'good', 'satisfactory' and 'unsatisfactory'. This rating determines the quota of students allocated to the institution. An unsatisfactory rating can lead eventually to closure. Currently courses consist of either four year Bachelor of Education (BEd) or three year Bachelor of Arts/ Bachelor of Science (BA/BSc) courses followed by a one year Postgraduate Certificate of Education (the PGCE). The award of these qualifications automatically gives Qualified Teacher Status (QTS). Recently there have been moves to institute a three year BEd course for primary teachers.

The curriculum is determined by the Teacher Training Agency. The number of hours to be offered per subject and the amount of time to be spent in schools is strictly controlled. A student teacher is only certified for QTS if they have reached a satisfactory standard on a number for specified competences. Currently, in an effort to expand the numbers of teachers and to create greater diversity, the government has also licensed a number of alternative routes. These include the licensed teachers scheme, for experienced, well qualified individuals who have had previously successful careers but who wish to train "on the job". There are also several distance learning PGCE courses and, more recently, the School-Centred Initial Teacher

Training (SCITT) scheme has been introduced. Under SCITT the whole of the training can be done in school with no reference whatsoever to a teacher training institution.

In contrast teacher training in France has replaced its equivalent of the SCITT model. Previously in France students took academic subject courses in college and were then attached to a school for training. At the end of one year's probation these new students took an examination which then licensed them to teach. This system, therefore, has some resemblance to the recently instituted SCITT courses now being developed in the United Kingdom. However, in the late 1980s concern was increasingly expressed about the quality of this training and particularly the lack of any theoretical underpinning of the school practice. Since 1991, therefore, all primary and secondary training, including vocational secondary, takes place at an Institut Universitaire de Formation de Maitres (IUFM). These are regional institutes and closely linked to universities. The courses last two years. In the first year the balance is made up of sixty-six per cent theoretical studies and thirty-three per cent school work. In the second year which is only undertaken if the year one examination (concours) is passed, then this ratio is reversed and the students spend two thirds of their time in school and a third of their time at the IUFM. Students are paid on the teacher salary scale during this time. There is now an all-graduate entry or, in the case of the vocational secondary training, the equivalent vocational qualification.

In all, primary student teachers spend nineteen weeks in school during the two years. For eight of these the student much take responsibility for a whole class. The secondary course consists of three hundred and fifty hours of which one hundred and twenty hours is shared with the primary students. During the second year of the course students receive two visits from an inspector and two visits from staff at the IUFM. They receive their licence to teach after passing the examination at the end of year one.

In France, therefore, greater attention is paid to pedagogic issues whereas in the United Kingdom there has been a decrease in these throetical studies in favour of more subject-based work and increased monitoring by teachers in schools.

V. Post Initial Training

In most European countries in-service training is separate from initial teacher education. Furhermore, the arrange-ments for INSET are usually determined by administrative bodies, such as school board and local authorities, rather than the schools themselves. Such a strategy conflicts with the findings of the school effectiveness movernent which suggests that school-based training, based on the results of school appraised, is more effective than sending teachers on externally organised courses (Reynolds et al, 1994).

In many Europen countries there is an on-going debate about the entitlement of teachers to INSET training and whether it should be voluntary or compulsory. Most INSET training takes place in the teachers' spare time but there is a growing argument that each teacher should be given an entitlement to a certain amount of retraining throughout his or her career. Against this view, however, is an emerging critique of the school effectiveness movement which accounts for less than 20 per cent of the variation in pupils' progress. Such variation is much less than that which often exists between teachers within the same school. This suggests that school-based models of training, by providing a programme based on the perceived school goals, may neglect the individual needs of teachers since these are likely to very considerably within any institution (Turner 1996). Hence the debate on the balance between school-based in-service training and courses organised to meet particular needs of teachers remains a vibrant one. In particular, the question of induction, that is the transition from student teacher to the self-directing professional, is claimed to be "the great omission in education" (Vonk in Galton and Moon, 1994). However, in those countries where there has been a shift towards greater amounts of school-based initial training, increased attention has focused on the role of the school mentor and this has carried over from initial training into induction. Currently, there appears to be a debate between whether the mentor should primarily be the transmitter of practical knowledge and skills to the new teacher or, through process of action research, be seen as a partner in developing personal theories of teaching (Vonk in Galton and Moon, 1994).

Because there is no little systematic study of the effects of in-service training, there are many questions to be answered before it becomes possible to create a developmental model in which new teachers learn to teach and experienced teachers learn to teach better but these questions, identified by the Association of Teacher Education in Europe's (ATEE. 1989) survey include the selection of new teachers for both training and for their first teaching post, the selection of experienced teachers for posts of responsibility, particularly school leadership, and the necessary training programmes for headship. Even less information is available concerning the teacher trainers themselves. Little is known of the qualities used to select teacher trainers for their posts. In most countries, once a selection is made, there is very little training for the post and in many cases the appointment to a post guarantees a job for life without any requirement for further re-training.

VI. Some Key Issues for the Future

The present position, therefore, is one of considerable flexibility. The main reason for the divergent approaches to the problem of improving teaching, according to Eisenhart et al (1991), is that there are no adequate theories of how teachers learn to teach. Without such a theoretical base it is difficult to plan a coherent programme of professional development which move teachers successively through initial training, then induction until finally they become experienced competent teachers. Recent reviews in the United States (Reynolds. 1992) have attempted to develop such models of professional development. Such approaches call seriously into question the present paradigm of the "reflective practitioner" which is commonly used as the basis for teacher training programmes. Critics of these developmental models, however, argue that they undervalue the importance of subject expertise. Research on the links between pedagogy and subject knowledge is not well developed.

Within this debate the growing importance of new technology, both in providing closer links between teachers and pupils in different countries but also for its capacity to organise and control knowledge, has only begun to be investigated. The use of technology such as e-mail and video conferencing will undoubtedly play a part in creating more effective, coherent and efficient teacher training systems in the future.

The question of the reflective practitioner still occupies a considerable amount of the literature on teacher training. Those who argue for the model of professional development based on growth of expertise argue that novice teachers are only able to reflect at technical and practical levels but not at a critical level as assumed by some. By this it is meant that it is not possible for such teachers to develop their own professional theories of how to teach but merely to make decisions about whether what they did during the lesson was technically correct and practically effective. Depending on one's point of view, therefore, the question of who makes the best mentor will vary. Those who believe in the reflective practitioner theory argue that it is the expert teacher that makes the best mentor because they have the flexibility and the necessary inspirational qualities to look at problems arising in the classroom in a number of different ways. However, those who reject this view argue that it is the competent teacher who largely problem solves through the use of rules (or maxims) who is of most use to the student teacher because the major purpose of initial teacher training is to induct the student into basic routines. Undoubtedly, this debate will continue but if it is to be resolved then there is a need for researchers across Europe to begin to work more co-operatively together in order to carry out comparative studies of different systems. Only in this way will it be possible to arrive at some broad principles which will help future policy makers when they engage in the reform of teacher education. Such broad agreement is essential now that teacher mobility within European countries, particularly those within the European Union, has become a reality.

Bibliography

Association of Teacher Education in Europe (ATEE) (1989) *The Selection and Professional Development of Trainers for Initial Teacher Training: Case Studies.* Strasbourg : CDCC [CC-TE (89) 22]

Council of Europe CDCC (1987) *New Challenges for Teachers and their Education.* Report on the Standing Conference of European Ministers of Education, Helsinki, 5-7 May, 1987. Strasbourg: CDCC [MED-15-19]

Eisenhart, L., Behm, L. and Romagnano, L. (1991) learning to Teach: Developing Expertise or Rite of Passage? *Journal of Education for Teaching,* (17) 1, pp 51-71.

Galton. M and Moon, B. (1994) *Handbook of Teacher Training in Europe.* London: David Fulton for the Council of Europe.

Judge, H. (1992) Teacher Education' in Clark, B and Neave, G [eds] *The Encyclopaedia of Higher Education.* Oxford: Pergamon Press.

Reynolds, A. (1992) What is Competent Beginning Teaching ? A Review of the Literature. *Review of Educational Research,* (62) 1, pp 1-36.

Reynods, D., Creemers, B.P.M., Nesselrodt. P.S., Schaffer, E.C., Stringfield, S., Teddlie, C. (1994) *Advances in School Effectiveness Research and Practice.* Oxfored: Pergamon.

Turner, J. (1996) *The State and the School: An International Perspective.* London : Flamer Press.

Paper presented at the Eeropean Preparatory Meeting on the UNESCO's 45th Session of the International Conference on Education, 1996.

Courtesy : International Bureau of Education, UNESCO, Geneva, Switzerland.

National reports presented at the forty-third (1992) and forty-fourth (1994) sessions of the International Conference on Education organized in Geneva by the International Bureau of Education.

Forty-third session

Bulgaria. *The Development of Education 1990-1992, National Report of the Republic of Bulgaria.* Sofia, Ministry of Education and Science, 1992.

Czech and Slovak Federal Republics. *Development of Education 1990-1992.* Bratislava, 1992.

Poland. Ministry of National Education. *The Development of Education in Poland in 1990-1991.* Warsaw, 1992.

Russian Federatioon, *The Development of Education National Report from the Russian Federation.* Moscow, Ministry of Education, 1992.

Slovakia. *Development of Education 1992-1994.* Bratislava, Institute of Information and Prognoses of Education, Youth and Sports, 1994.

Slovenia. *The Development of Education in the Republic of Slovenia 1990-1992.* Ljubljana, Ministry of Education and Sport, 1992.

Ukraine. *Development of Education in Ukraine in 1990-1991.* Kiev, Ministry of Education. 1992.

Federal Republic of Yugoslavia. Yugoslav Commission for Unesco; Ministry of Education and Culture. *Development of Education in the Federal of Yugoslavia, 1990-1991.* Belgrade, 1992.

Forty-fourth session

Reports on the Development of Education have been used presented by the following countries: Armenia, Bulgaria, Czech Republic, Estonia, Hungry, Poland, Romania, Russian Federation, Slovakia, Slovenia, Ukraine.

In addition, recent documents sent to the IBE or to the Bulgarian National Commission for UNESCO in December 1995 by the following Member States have been used: Albania, Belarus, Bulgaria, Estonia, Latvia, Romania, Russian Federation, Slovakia, Uzbekistan.

Other sources

Arends, R. *Learning to Teach.* New York, Random House, 1988.

Association for Teacher Education in Europe. Working 4; Information and Communication Technology for teacher Education. *In.* Libotton, A., ed. *Visions and* Realisations. Brussels, ATEF, 1993.

Birzea, C. *The Process on Educational Reform of the Countries in Transition.* Speech given at the Symposium on 'Educational Reforms in Central and Eastern Europe : Processes and Outcomes', September 1995. Strasbourg, Council for Cultural Co-operation, 1995.

Carte Blanche of the Reform of Education in Romania. Bucharest, Ministry of Education 1995.

Cole, M. ed. *Education for equality.* London; New York, Routledge, 1989.

Symposium on 'Contents and Methods in Secondary Education: a Secondary Education for Europe', Porsgrunn, Norway, October 1993. *General Report* by Francine Dugast Portes. Strasbourg, Council of Europe, 1994.

Economic Development of Slovakia in 1994. Bratislava, 1995. (Study prepared on behalf of the United Nations European Economic Commission for Europe.)

Foucher, M. *The Faces of Europe: a Secondary Education for Europe.* Strasbourg, Council for Cultural Co-operation, Council of Europe, 1995.

Galton, M.; Blyth, A., eds. *Handbook of Primary Education in Europe.* London, David Fulton, 1989.

Holly, M.L.; McLoughlin, C.S., eds. Perspectives on Teacher Professional Development. London, The Falmer Press, 1989.

Joint ILO-UNESCO Committee of experts on the Application of the Recommendation Concerning the Status of Teachers. *Report.* Geneva, ILO, 1994.

Lawn, M.; Grace, Gerald, eds. *Teachers; The Culture and Politics of Work.* London, The Falmer Press, 1987. (An Open University book.)

Lawson, R., ed. *Changing Patterns of Secondary Education: an International Comparison.* Calgary, Alberta, The University of Calgary Press, 1987.

Ministère de l' enseignement. *Le système de l' èducation.* Bucharest, 1994.

Osnovnoye itogi 1994-1995 ichebnogo goda I piti v obnovleniya obrazovaniya v Rossii. Moscow, Ministerstvo Obrazovaniya Rossii, 1995.

Poland. Ministry of National Education. *Education in a Changing Society.* Warsaw, TEPIS Publishing House, 1995.

Quality and Accountability: the Programme for Development of the Education system in the Czech Republic. Prague, Ministry of Education, Youth and Sports, 1994.

Rogers, R., ed. *Education and Social Class.* London, The Falmer Press, 1986.

Romania. *The New Education Law in Romania.* Bucharest, Public Information Department. 1994.

Seminar on 'School Legislation: Dialogue on the Reforms in Central and Estern Europe', Brussels, December 1993. *General Report* by Cesar Birzea. Strasbourg, Council for Cultural Co-operation, Council of Europe, 1994.

Symposium on 'Science and Technology Teacher Training: What Training for What Type of Teaching?' Paris March-April 1994. *General Report* by M.J. de Vries. Strasbourg, Council for Cultural Co-operation, Council of Europe, 1994.

Ukrainian Economic Trends. *Monthly Update.* August 1995.

UNESCO. *World Education Report.* Oxford, OUP, 1995.

Wilson, J., ed. *The Effectiveness of In-service Education and Training of Teachers and School Leaders.* Report of the Fifth All-European Conference of Directors of Educational Research Institutions, Triesenberg, October 1998. London; New York, Taylor & Francis, 1989.

World Statistics in Brief. New York, United Nations, 1993. (Statistical PocketBook.)

Reference Paper Prepared for the European Consultation to the 45th Session of the International Conference on Education, 1996.

Courtesy: Internationa Bureau of Education, UNESCO, Geneva Switzerland.

PART—V

Conclusions of The European Consultation Preparatory to The forty-fifth Session of the International Conference on Education "Strengthening the Role of Teachers in a Changing World"

I. Introduction

The Consultation was organized in Varsaw, Poland from 25th to 27th April 1996 under the auspices of the Polish Ministry of Education, the Polish National Commission for UNESCO, the Council of Europe and the UNESCO International Bureau of Education (IBE), and was attended by participants from 39 countries in the region. Representatives of the International Labour Office (ILO), Education International (EI), the Group of Educational NGOs at the Council of Europe, and the Standing Committee of NGOs at UNESCO also participated is observers.

The meeting was opened by Mr. Wojciech Falkowski, Secretary General of the Polish National Commission for UNESCO.

Participants w^re welcomed by Mr. E. Wiatr, Minister for Education of Poland, Mr. Jacek Wozniakowski, Vice-President of the Polish National Commission for UNESCO, Mr. M. Stobart. Deputy Director of Education, Culture and Sport of the Council of Europe, and Mr. J.C. Tedesco, Director of the International Bureau of Education.

Mr. A. Janowski (Poland) was elected Chairman of the meeting and Mr. P. Luisoni (Switzerland), Rapporteur.

Mrs. J. Savova and Mr. J.A. Fermandez, IBE consultants, introduced their papers analysing the situation of teachers in Central and Eastern Europe and in Western Europe respectively. The consultant from the Council of Europe, Mr. M. Galton, described the Council's work on problems and trends in teacher training.

The main results of the meeting's discussions were contained in an *oral report* and a series of proposals for the *drafting of a Declaration and recommendations to the 45th session of the International Conference of Education (ICE)*. The meeting endorsed the Rapporteur's proposal that the reference documents submitted to the Consultation by the aforementioned experts should form part of the meeting's report and consequently be used as reference material by the IBE which preparing the texts for submission to the ICE.

II. Oral Report by Rapporteur General

At this moment, I feet as though I am taking part in the French television programme called *''L' Heure de Vérite''* (The Moment of Truth). This is what happens to Rapporteurs at the end of meetings! Before commencing the serious business, I would like to tell a little joke if I may: this morning I suggested to Mr. Tedesco that the two main conclusions of our meeting should be: firstly, to postpone the Conference until next year; and secondly, to change the theme. He seemed to agree with this...

Ladies and Gentlemen, if I had had to give this report a title, I think I would have called it. ''The constraints and the grandeur of the unfinished'', and my choice would have been motivated by my two contrasting feelings. One is the feeling of frustration that, despite all my efforts, I have not managed to bring before you a finished, neatly constructed report, in the form of well-drafted conclusions, for example. I also feel frustration because I am well aware of the shortcomings of my efforts. But as you know—because many of you wished me well last night and I am grateful for that— the task awaiting the Rapporteur is extremely difficult, even impossible, taking into account the time constraints. I would therefore first and foremost crave your indulgence.

I am also prey to another feeling, which is the opposite of those just described. This is the feeling of satisfaction that I have not managed to present a finished product. Even though Mr. Tedesco quite rightly said that the 45th ICE starts here, I should like to remind you that we are in fact only starting to prepare for the Conference. Texts will have to be drawn up on the basis of regional consultations. Member States will have to consider them, express their views and amend them; and then there will be a meeting of government experts just before the Conference to amalgamate all these efforts and, finally, the ICE will take its decisions. This means that the floor is still wide open and it is thus an open report that I would like to submit to your today so that here and now you can complete, contest and add to it, in other words, your can appropriate it. First of all, I shall endeavour to present to you orally some of my thoughts at the conclusion of our discussions and then we shall circulate a draft text that puts down some ideas—and I lay special emphasis on the word ''ideas''—for the Declaration and the recommendations to be drawn up on the basis of the regional consultations.

Still as an introduction. I should like to underline two points: I think that the methodology adopted for the preparation of this ICE is better than the previous one. The notion of using an exchange of ideas and a discussion stimulated by experts' reports as a basis is excellent because it prevents any premature concentration on the texts to be amended. I believe that our discussions were enriching and lively, which proves that the proposed methodology was correct. A second point that I think should be underlined concerns the experts' reports. I believe that we all recognize—and many of you emphasized this—that these were of high quality. One regret perhaps is that during our discussions we did not really refer to the reports explicitly in order to emphasize the key ideas, discuss them and bring out those we wished to see used in discussions at the Conference. It is therefore important to make a first recommendation to the IBE, namely, that the content of these reports should be an integral part of the meeting report and, as such, should be a concrete inspiration and a reference when drawing up the texts to be submitted to the ICE.

Now I come to the discussions themselves. To make it easier, the report is based on the four underlying themes, namely, changes in society and the new dimensions of the teaching profession, participation, partnership, new technologies and training challenges.

I. Changes in society and the new dimensions of the profession

As an introduction, I should like to quote a text by Jacques Lesourne, whom you perhaps know. He is the former director of the newspaper "Le Monde" and the author of an important work written several years ago entitled "Education et societe: les defis del l'an 2000" (Education and society: the challenges of the year 2000). I should like to refer to this text because it seems to me not only to summarize our thoughts, but also the thinking that underpinned our meeting and even our overall outlook on the issues. Jacques Lesourne writes: "*Education is man's transformation by man, it would therefore be paradoxical if, at a time when enterprises discover—some might say at last—that people constitute their wealth forward-looking thinking on education did not focus on problems relating to the essential resources of any education system, the teaching corps.*

In order to develop schools, is it not first of all necessary above all to guarantee the satisfactory renewal of this corps, its training, its motivation, the adquacy of the means allocated to it, the satisfaction of its major aspirations, so that it can take up the task entrusted to it, respond immediately to demands from society as a whole, become the catalyst for change?" Later on, Jacques Lesourne adds *"No profession has, in the long term, such an important impact on the future of society"*.

As we saw during our discussions, however, the world has changed and both the experts' reports and our debates identified some of the changes that may be termed major or significant and I will summarize them briefly here: the increasing diversity of those attending school, the growing demand by society for more comprehensive general training, the societies and micro-societies to be found in classes that are increasingly mixed—multicultural—the information explosion and its dissemination through new technologies, the mobility of persons, exchanges that are increasingly at the global level, difficult and occasionally conflicted relations between education and the economic world, widespread crises in government finance, the weakening or even elimination of a number of reference points in terms of standards or values, in both Western as well as Central and Eastern Europe, a generalized trend towards the redistribution of power and responsibilities in the form of delocalization or decentralization (the word employed is not so important), and finally, a loss of confidence in education systems in general and, within the systems, a loss of confidence in teachers. I think that these summarize well the factors that emerged both in the debate and in the experts' reports as changes in society at the close of the 20th century.

I think we can say that the realities of the teaching profession have always been complex and difficult. I should like to recall briefly exactly what a teacher does by quoting Antoine Prost: *"When one speaks of a teacher's activity, a series of verbs immediately comes to mind: the teacher takes a class with all that this implies, preparation, content; he organizes the pupils' work, gives lessons, homework and talks; he corrects papers and attributes marks; he engages the interest of his class and motivates it; he cooperates with colleagues and with the administration: he meets parents who so request; he provides pupils with information and advice on their future: whenever necessary, he helps pupils with any problems they bring to him, etc., and so it is that, in various forms and to a greater or lesser degree, all these activities form part of the profession and it is essential for them to be fulfilled satisfactorily if the teacher is to be effective. This was probably true of teachers yesterday and is certainly true of teachers today''.*

I believe it is also true, however, that the teacher of tomorrow will have to do even more, even better, and above all do it differently. Here again I would like to quote Antoine Prost because I think he summarizes better than I could the content of our discussions: ''*The teacher of tomorrow will have to explain why a particular subject is taught, define its importance and scope so that pupils become interested in it. Lessons will be more readily accepted if teachers are capable of placing the subject in a global context. The welcome decompartmentalization of different subjects should modify the way in which each is taught. In addition to mastering their own particular subject, teachers will have to find a way of opening up to other subjects. The probable changes in the way pupils' work is organized are even more important. They will become increasingly necessary because pupils are less motivated and less uniform, which means there must be more variety in their lessons and work. As far as assessment is concerned, the criteria used in marking and the aims of each lesson will have to be clearly explained. There will also have to be greater collaboration with the administration and other colleagues. This means that, alongside adult/youth relationships, which are by far the most important in the profession, adult/adult relationships will develop. Lastly, teachers have to respond to pupil's demands because a growing number of pupils are making new demands. Among all the probable developments in the profession, whether one likes it or not, this is undoubtedly one of the most worrying and most sensitive issues*''. Antoine Prost continues by stating: ''*Underlying this description is a new concept of teaching. A job that is no longer defined as the remunerated provision of individual knowledge along the lines of other professions but as participation in the production apparatus, with attribution of responsibilities resulting from the joint sharing of tasks. Teaching is no longer at the individual level, pupils' learning process is the result of the synergy of all the time spent in school, it is the school or university enterprise which gives them the sum of the services they have come to seek there and this is never simply an arithmetical addition of all the classes attended. It is an overall product, made up it is true of separate components, but it should bear the trademark of the place of learning. Cars are not sold in kits, neither is education''.* This text of Antoine Prost seems to me to be extremely intersting and if he had not written it sometime ago one might imagine that it was the outcome of our two days of discussions.

If one looks closely at the history of teaching, it can be seen that the profession has developed in line with at least four concepts which I think it is useful to recall. At the beginning, in ancient times for example, there was the intellectual model of the master who possessed knowledge and did not need any training because his charisma sufficed, it over-rode everything else. It was said that teaching was an art. Another model then emerged, but much later on, with teacher training colleges in the 19th century. Teachers were trained using an ''imitation'' method, on the basis of the knowledge imparted by an experienced teacher. The trainer was an experience model practitioner and this is what one may term the *traditional method.* In the third model, which emerged in the 1960s, the teacher bases himself on scientific input from the human sciences; he rationalizes the practice and applies the theory. He is trained by theoreticians, teaching becomes a *genuine profession* that can be learned. Now there is a fourth model in which the interrelationship among the action, the issue and the knowledge has replaced the theory-practice dialectic and the teacher becomes a thoughtful *professional* capable of analysing his practices, resolving problems and inventing strategies; this is partly true today and should certainly be the case in the future. With regard to these four concepts, it should perhaps be emphasized—and this consideration is to be found in the OECD report before you entitled *''The teacher today''*— that this typology is useful and interesting but it is not definitive and the four concepts and not mutually exclusive. For example, they may apply to certain teachers rather than others, in particular situations, or at certain levels of teaching and not at others.

The OECD report states that, while the concept of professionalism or making teachers more professional is no longer in doubt, there should be *"clarification of roles and responsibilities needed rather than strict definition of 'professions' and 'professionalism'."* This consideration, although not spelled out, has been implicit in many of our discussions: one could spend, and I might add even waste, a considerable amount of time on questions of terminology and vocabulary and lose sight of the objective. During these two days a great deal has been said about professionalism, the constraints of the profession and the respect shown to teachers. I think that there is a degree of tension among these three components and it is not a question of adopting one or the other, for example, considering solely professionalism or professional constraints or respect. These are three indissoliable aspects of teaching policy and the measures to be taken cannot be conceived outside a global education policy. The question of respect, or perhaps I should say the lack of respect, shown to teachers must be taken very seriously because it is unfortunately a fairly general phenomenon.

Perhaps some of you took part in the Conference of Education Ministers held in January in the context of the OECD Education Committee. I did not myself attend, but I have been told that Ministers spoke rather harshly of teachers, complaining of their excessive demands, their lack of flexibility, considering them mainly responsible for the current difficulties in education systems. I think this is worrying because it is the symptom of unrest that not only affects society but is also symptomatic of the crisis of reciprocal trust between politicians and teachers: in the present situation of financial stringency, as mentioned earlier, teachers reproach the authorities with betraying education to a certain extent, failing to fulfil their social responsibilities, neglecting quality, dismantling the education system; the authorities, on the other hand, reproach teachers with ignoring the economic realities of education, lacking civic responsibility, remaining attached to their benefits, which concern privileges rather than quality, as a corporate reaction. This is barely a caricature; last week I was with the French community in Belgium, in Liège, where teachers have been on strike for two months, and when talking to some of those in charge of education I was told: "These teachers are on strike because the teacher/pupil ratio is to rise from 15 to 17". Whereas if one spoke to the teachers, they said: "...the increase from 15 to 17 is not the problem, but it would mean 3,000 fewer jobs in the French community!"

During our discussions here emphasis was also laid on the need to set aside the stereotypes of teachers as guilty parties or victims. I do not think that they are either, they are in fact actors, and if you will allow me to use a somewhat bold image, they are actors in a play called education in a theatre named society. However, they are only one element in its success; it is in fact very rare for actors in the theatre to save a play that is badly written, badly directed, acted in the wrong costumes in an unsuitable theatre. In the theatre, the public must have some talent as well... Another image was used by Mr. Fernandez in his report, namely the black box. I would like to replace this by the title of a film "Is there a pilot on board?". We all know that, by definition, the black box records all the details of a flight and that the behaviour of the pilot is only one of these elements.

Another consideration that emerged during our discussions relates to teachers themselves. We quite rightly emphasized that they are not an abstract body, but first and foremost are individuals, persons with their own qualities and limitations, they are individuals/persons in contact with particular pupils in a particular place; their task is not the same in cities or the countryside, in kindergartens, primary schools, secondary schools, vocational training or higher education institutes, and as someone said they are not all doing the same job, and this is quite true. On the other hand, teachers—that is to say the *teaching profession,* and I think this term is significant—are a body, a corporation, and are also voters.

Another issue seemed to emerge from our discussions and I hope you will forgive once again the somewhat "impressionist" nature of this report. This concerns the way in which schools and teachers view the outside world. Perhaps schools and teachers have for too long had the illusion that they are a separate entity, cut off from the upheavals outside, a closed and preserved world, a sort of ivory tower while the rest of the world is agitated, and perhaps they still foster this illusion. In the course of the debate on violence in schools some time ago a minister spoke of the need to "resanctify" schools. I would be tempted to agree if this means once more giving schools the role that churches—the buildings—had *inter alia* in times gone by, a place of sanctuary without discrimination, a safe haven for all. I would agree if it means resanctifying schools in the sense of focusing on their role as a community of life and peace and not death and war, which they should be. I would say no, however, if resanctifying means withdrawing into a sort of impregnable castle, even if it is Scottish, cut off from the world. The question posed is the following: do we want to make schools as educational establishments real live places?

In this connection. an important consideration also came to the fore. *Schools-educational establishments* (with a hyphen naturally) are themselves micro-societies and as such have economic components, they are places where education is produced, but they are also places where one lives together and where one must learn to live together. Schools-educational establishments as micro-societies have an undeniable social role, they are educational communities where everyone feels a sense of both independence and responsibility and when I say everyone I mean not only the pupils but also the teachers or the heads, independent and responsible, individuals and members of a community, alone but together. This leads to a rightful demand for training teachers as persons, training in ethics, tolerance, creativity, solidarity and participation; this demand is becoming increasingly evident and has been underlined during our discussions. It has even been stated that these qualities and in indispensable prerequisite for exercising the profession and this is an interesting point, I might even say a reversal of priorities. For a very, very long time, the priority or indispensable prerequisite for the profession has been that one must have been a good pupil oneself, in other words, have been well adapted to the education system. I believe that this changed perspective has consequences, especially on recruitment, methods of recruitment and the selection of future teachers. It has often been noted that good pupils themselves become teachers, or as someone said, teachers tend towards salf-duplication and I am well placed to speak of this because my father was a teacher, my wife is a teacher, I was a teacher and my son is a teacher. This does not however only confer advantages...

I should now like to refer to some key points that I think emerged from our discussion of this first part, the first chapter. The first consideration was the fundamental nature and at the same time the complexity of the transformations today. Without being alarmist, but simply being aware that changes or reform alone will not suffice and that there needs to be a far-reaching transformation, and I might even say a reorganization of education systems, rebuilding of their very bases. This means, in particular, that the objectives, and possibly above all the limits, of education have to be redefined. There should also be a rational refocusing of expectations of schools and teachers.

To me it is obvious that this "restructuring" can only be achieved through consultation—our discussions strongly underlined this—so as to deal not only with the deadlock and the resistance to change imposed from outside but also corporatist pressure. The current situation and the future imply the emergence of a new concept of schools: schools as centres of apprenticeship, collective enterprises where everyone possesses their own individual abilities but no one person has all the competence.

Another element which I believe we emphasized was the need for education systems as a whole and for schools to draw closer to the economic world and, as we stressed, it should be possible together to find a new consensus based on the current convergence we can see, convergence towards objectives in which overall culture and training for life constitute both for schools and the economic world a common denominator of skills in order to learn how to work, live and coexist.

Another element that emerged during our debates was the need to redefine the basic orientation of teaching programmes, highlighting knowledge of course, but also the skills required of citizens today and I believe that the basic tenets of the Delors report can provide a solid basis. I would remind you of the four cornerstones: learning to know, learning to do, learning to live together—I might say learning how to want to live together—and learning to be.

Yet another element that emerged was the new emphasis that should be laid on schools-educational establishments, school management processes and methods, the autonomy of the educational team and collaboration among all the actors. Obviously, as a consequence, there will have to be a redefinition of the roles, the profile and the training of teachers, who are the major factor for success, change and reform. At the heart of this—and I would once again underline this aspect—is naturally the question of enhancing the professionalism of teachers, with its implications in terms of scientific or disciplinary skills, teaching, personal and social skills, and also a sense of responsibility and autonomy.

Another element that we emphasized was the need to take into account in training both here and now and in the future the globalization of relations and the mobility of persons. Summarizing somewhat rapidly, I think that this concerns the whole issue of introducing into schools what are called the European dimension and the global dimension; the two are obviously not mutually exclusive and are based on the same fundamental principles. Schools must learn to understand and accept cultural differences, acknowledge the promotion of common values, seek out problems common to the education system and find harmonious solutions, open up to the outside, cooperate by means of joint projects, links and exchanges, whether within or outside the school, involving society in these. I shall not dwell on these any longer because you will find a number of the elements I have mentioned in the proposals made in the texts and we shall have an opportunity to return to them later.

2. Participation and partnership

I now come to the second part of our debates, which concerns participation and partnership. Someone said during the discussion that this subject is in fact at the very heart of the Conference. This is true, because the Conference's theme is strengthening the role of teachers in a changing world. I believe, however, that this issue is not simply at the heart of the Conference but also at the heart of the whole problem of the functioning and operation of the education system.

To summarize, it seemed to me that our discussions underlined a number of points, for example, that partnership or partnerships are not an additional or complementary element but are the very basis of what might be termed—and I leave this expression in quotation marks—*"a modern government for schools or good government of schools"*. It has been stressed that this is a highly political matter; experience shows that in fact government is no longer through decrees—was it ever?—but that the system must operate closer to the grassroots and with the grassroots.

It was also emphasized that operation of an education system through a partnership is demanding because it means first of all that the State has to agree to share power and that teachers, or the actors in the system, have to agree to exercise it. The latter aspect is not self-evident; agreeing to exercise power means agreeing to assume responsibility, and I might add it also means being accountable. It is sometimes much easier to be able to say "this has been imposed on us, we have not been consulted, we do not take the decisions". Exercise of power in partnership in fact means an extremely important strengthening and enriching of the role of teachers.

It has been stated that partnership is not static but is a movement and that it would be more appropriate to speak of partnership dynamics in schools, which implies an active commitment on the part of all.

The framework criteria for the success of partnership were highlighted, and they can be summarized as follows: firstly, reciprocal political will, secondly suitable organizations and structures. And here arises the question of decentralization and the sharing of responsibilities. A precise definition of the fields of competence and mutual roles, clear agreements and the commitment to respect the different fields of competence, the establishment of consultation forums and structures, and making the necessary time available. The time factor is one of the most important.

It was also emphasized that, although partnerships make demands, they also have a certain number of advantages and as a participatory and cooperative approach they make it easier to find effective solutions to problems, assimilate the changes and reforms and ensure their correct implementation because partners no longer feel they are the objects but the subjects of decisions. Partnerships also motivate the partners better and strengthen their commitment; they help to ensure better training because, as one person stressed "training takes place through action". Partnerships also allow democracy to be practised actively and help to reinforce mutual trust and investment in a common endeavour.

It has been stressed that genuine partnership cannot be confined to the execution of projects or reforms, but must also necessarily encompass initiation, launching, preparation, implementation, and of course assessment. It has been pointed out that partnership takes up time, although in the long term it is capable of increasing the educational potential of society as a whole, whether parents, the authorities, enterprises or the media.

Attention has also been drawn to the diversity of partnerships, both in terms of the diversity of the partners themselves or the levels at which such partnerships operate and here anything is possible; one can work in partnership at the local, regional or national levels, either directly or through representatives, in the same way as democracy.

Finally, in connection with partnerships, it was emphasized that their complexity and demands imply an adequate level of training.

3. New Technologies

The third subject of our discussions was new technologies. There are four main types of attitude relating to new technologies and education. The first might be termed the sceptical attitude, people say "in any case, it is only a fashion, computing or new technologies can only do what has always been done anyway, but they do it quicker"; the second attitude is hostility, asserting that new technologies are dangerous for the intellect and above all dangerous for culture. On the other hand, there is the attitude of those who are fascinated by new technologies and confer on them all the virtues: not only do they inform but they also place everyone on an equal footing, ensure education for all, everywhere, resolve problems of failure at school, and even promote democracy. Then there is a fourth attitude, which is mainly that of commonsense, let us call it the pragmatic attitude, which recognizes the extraordinary contribution made by these technologies but also recognizes their limits and places teaching and quality at the centre. I think that our discussion was clearly situated in the third category.

The elements that emerged during the discussions can be summarized as follows: We clearly underlined the vast potential of the new technologies for improving education. We also emphasized the vital need for the education system to integrate them to learn how to master them so as to prevent any technological, cultural or even economic servitude, as well as any marginalization of schools compared to the outside world.

The positive impact of the new technologies was emphasized, for example, when preparing the work of teachers and pupils, for individual work, access to information, meeting the need for different levels of teaching, developing cooperation, opening up to the world through networking.

A number of criteria for their successful use were mentioned, in particular, that they should be seen not in purely technical terms but also in terms of their teaching potential. The complementarity of the new technologies and other approaches was underlined, whether in the classroom and teaching or in relation to lifelong training of teachers, for example, the use of distance learning.

Strong emphasis was laid on the irreplaceable role of teachers, which is two-fold. On the one hand, their role is to arrange the information so that it can be transformed into knowledge, make choices and exercise their critical faculties, preserve the meaning of quality and, on the other, they play a vital role in transmitting culture in way that was defined by a participant yesterday as "the way of life of human beings". Teachers' role is irreplaceable in establishing personal and social relationships, encouraging approaches to others and contact with them, living together and awareness of common values.

Finally, emphasis was laid on the need to develop the search for and sharing of information, for example, on the impact, role and limitations of new technologies in education, as well as the need to promote cooperation among institutions, to encourage comparative studies and, lastly—this is perhaps the main recommendation to be made to the IBE—to take into account the recent studies mentioned here, especially those carried out by the European Union, and the outcome of the second UNESCO Congress on Education and Informatics, to be held in Moscow in July 1996.

The potential of these new technologies is awesome; as someone said yesterday, they appear to indicate that the only frontiers that will remain will be cultural frontiers and these must be preserved. One consequence is that it is important to develop high-quality software in different languages in accordance with different approaches, not only to avoid being submerged by "other worlds" but also to prevent them taking over our cultures; this does not only concern other worlds, but above all software designers because this is where the danger lies as it is well known that they care little about culture or social justice and they can scarcely be reproached for this...

4. The challenges of initial and lifelong training

Now, Mr. Chairman, Ladies and Gentlemen, I come to the last point: challenges in training. This is what we might term the overall summary. When thinking about training, one should ask oneself "What are the consequences of all these considerations and what are the requirements as far as training is concerned?" This does not mean drawing up an identikit picture of the teacher of the future or his or her training, but identifying the key elements around which this training should be built.

Many of the elements related to training that have to be taken into account stem naturally from the above considerations, but certain points should be emphasized briefly and I shall rapidly refer to the main elements that you will find later in the douments.

The first place where training issues arise is in relation to recruitment. Recruiting teachers mainly means two things: attracting the best and keeping the good ones. If one wishes to be realistic, one should add another: being capable of letting go the less good. This can only remain theoretical unless there is a careers policy, which involves a number of aspects and one must have the courage to mention them: salary scales, promotion possibilities, the time span, in other words, career plans.

There is another requirement related to recruitment and that is selection. I referred to it briefly earlier on; one can no longer—nor should one— select teachers solely on the basis of their intellectual capabilities. It is necessary to find a way of taking into account all the qualities required for this 'new profession''. This offers interesting possibilities for development: encouraging access to teaching by persons from other professional fields, which is sometimes called access to teaching as a second career. I am convinced that in all our countries there is a reservoir of highly capable people who, for one reason or another, have chosen a profession that does not really suit them, perhaps because they had to make a choice very early on. These people may have the aptitude required to become very good teachers. These avenues should be explored with a view to recruitment based on selection criteria and procedures that obviously differ from purely academic ones.

Regarding initial training, very briefly, I think we can simply say that its objective should be high degree of professionalism. I have already said that professionalism means disciplinary, teaching, and communication skills, working as a team, in addition to personal, cultural and social skills.

During these two days, it has been emphasized on several

occasions that initial training should seek a balance—perhaps a new balance—between the subjects taught and practical and teaching training. It has also been said that theory and practice should be better related, through courses for example, Mention has also been made of the need to develop all the dimensions of the teaching profession, especially adaptation to change, and the importance of this in today's world has been underlined frequently.

Attention should be paid to the way in which training is given during the initial training period. I shall explain this using a formula: future teachers should receive the teaching that they will subsequently be asked to put into practice themselves, in other words, apprenticeship teaching, teaching through active methods. Unfortunately, I believe that almost everywhere teacher training remains very academic, face-to-face, whereas there should be stimulation and teachers are asked—or even required—to teach very differently later on.

A few words on lifelong training. It has been stressed that, even though it does not play the major role, it should at least be equivalent to initial training and should be permanent any systematic. It has also been stated that lifelong training should be considered as both a right and an obligation, as a mutual commitment between teachers and public authorities. I think that this is an important element that should be included in what might be called the new contract between teachers and public authorities.

Stress was also laid on the need to encourage lifelong training through incentives, perhaps in career terms or even in financial terms. Another important element is that in the ''schools-apprenticeship enterprises'' context, lifelong training should focus on what is done within schools themselves.

It has been stated that lifelong training should be closely linked to initial training establishments. It was also emphasized that special attention should be paid to the early days of a teacher's career because this is a decisive period for the future; difficulties and discouragement quickly stifle enthusiasm and encourage a rapid return to old habits. As I mentioned earlier, it was also stated that lifelong training should use to the utmost the potential of new technologies and distance learning in particular.

Another aspect was underlined and I fear that it is too often neglected when speaking of teacher training, namely, the training of trainers. It has been said that trainers should themselves be trained to meet the demands of change, that they should be convinced of the need for change and should seek to prepare teachers to train themselves, and I emphasize ''themselves'' because this is very important.

It has been suggested that trainers should participate in training in schools themselves and not only in their own institutions, which are often far away, not necessarily in terms of miles but in real terms. Emphasis has also been laid on the special role of trainers in respect young teachers, not only in providing support and helping them but also because this would help trainers to assess realistically the actual effects of initial training on classroom practices.

Lastly, attention was drawn to research. At the end of the 20th century, teacher training as a whole should be closely linked to research, whether research by teachers themselves during their training or research on teachers and their training. In connection with research, mention was also made of the importance of developing research on effectiveness and above all efficiency, in other words, the cost-effectiveness ratio of various forms of lifelong training.

Mr. Chairman, Ladies and Gentlemen, this is what I wished to say to you this morning, once again with the feeling that I have perhaps weakened the substance of our bedate. This is may report to data, it is now up to you to take it over and complete it because the report of our meeting should be your report. Before concluding, I should like to thank three people most warmly: Maitland Stobart, Alison Cardwell and Sally Paton, who not only kept me company in the flesh and the spirit last night, but also undertook the translation into English and the typing of the texts we shall consider shortly. I should also like to thank you all for having been good and patient students, and for having listened to me right up until the end.

Warsaw, 27 April, 1996.

III. Proposed Elements to be Taken into Account in the Declaration

In the first part, mention should be made of the important changes that characterize society at the end of the 20th century and have an impact on education systems, namely :

* the growing search for answers to questions relating to daily life, together with increased demand for democratic participation, especially on the part of society;
* the increasing disversity of the school population due *inter alia* to the emergence of societies—and the microsocieties to be found in classes—that are more and more multicultural; recognition of the important role schools can play as a factor for integration;
* growing social demand for more comprehensive training;
* the information explosion and its dissemination using new technologies;
* the sometimes difficult relationship between education and the economy; growing unemploy-ment among the young;
* widespread crises in government finance;
* the danger of weakening or eliminating reference points in terms of values or standards, which can encourage feelings of intolerance and violence *inter alia*;
* a generalized movement towards the redistri-bution of power and responsibilities (deloca-lization, decentralization);
* re-emergence of the debate on "human development through education";
* a certain lessening of confidence in education systems and teachers in general, despite the large number of positive innovations and the outstanding commitment of a large number of educators.

The second part of the declaration should bring out the main points of the 'response' that can be made by education systems, particularly teachers, underlining the following:

* the fundamental nature and the complexity of the current changes implies adaptation, reform and sometimes far-reaching 'restructuring' of education systems;
* this means redefining objectives and rational refocusing of expectations of schools and teachers;
* such a redefinition can only be the result of consultation so as to control as far as possible the resistance to change and/or corporatist pressures;
* the emergence of a new concept of schools as centres of apprenticeship and collective enterprises to which each must

contribute his or her personal skills, even if these do not necessarily cover all areas;

* Limitation of the application of free enterprise economic principles to education systems: for example, profitability, competitiveness and the danger of applying them blindly;
* the need for public authorities to play fully their role in respect of equal opportunities, access to education, social cohesion and the promotion of democratic values;
* the need to draw closer to the economic world by searching for a new consensus based on convergence towards objectives in which general culture and training for life constitute a common denominator of skills for learning to work, live and coexist;
* the benefits of developing educational research, comparative studies and research-action directly related to the situation in schools, by increasing contacts with teacher training institutions;
* one of the tasks of such research and of the work of relevant national and international institutions would be to analyses and disseminate information on the positive benefits and innovatory experiments of the best schools and teachers;
* redefinition of the basic orientation of teaching programmes, specifying the knowledge and above all the skills needed by citizens today: learning to know, to do, to (wish to) live together, to be (see the report of the UNESCO Commission on education in the 21st century);
* new emphasis on schools as establishments, the processes and methods of educational management, the autonomy of the education team and collaboration among all the actors;
* redefinition of the roles, profile and training of teachers, the major factor in the success of the changes and reforms;
* restoration of society's confidence in teachers' action and an appeal to teachers to be the agents for progress in school and society;
* obligation for schools and teachers to place values at the centre of their concerns and to develop among students a spirit of openness, receptive to ideas of peace, tolerance and respect for human dignity;
* at the regional and international levels, streng-thening of exchanges and existing networks, promotion of solidarity among teachers.

IV. Proposed Elements to be Taken into Account in the Recommendations

Changes in society and the new dimensions of the teaching profession

The recommendations could deal with the following issues:

— enhancing the professionalism of teachers and its implications both in terms of competence in the subjects taught and teaching personal and social skills; teacher's responsibilities and autonomy;
— opening up schools and teachers towards the outside world;
— taking into account during training the globalization of relations and increased personal mobility, which requires the introduction of a European—and global—dimension into schools: understanding and acceptance of cultural differences, acknowledgment and promotion of common values, learning languages, identification of problems common to education systems and the search for convergent solutions, opening up to others and cooperation through joint projects, links and exchanges both within and outside school; all of society (parents, associations, NGOs, etc.) should participate in the latter;
— training in intercultural education;
— training for team work, autonomy and solidarity;
— teaching values and training for democratic citizenship;
— assessment of teachers and establishments;
— expectations of school and teachers and the need to establish new contracts with them that can reasonably be fulfilled.

2. Partnerships

The recommendations could focus on the following points:

— partnership constitutes the very basis of "modern government of schools";
— this is a highly political issue : experience shows that "one can no longer govern by decree" alone, but that action must be taken at the grassroots before any decisions are made;
— for the State, operating an education partnership means sharing power and for teachers it means both accepting the exercise of

power and sharing it. This represents significant strengthening of the role of teachers within the framework of democratic management of schools and also a high degree of responsibility;

— partnership is not a static method of operation but a dynamic one, continually being adapted, and it calls for an active commitment on the part of all;

— the criteria for the success of partnerships can be summarized as follows:
  * mutual political will;
  * suitable organizations and structures (decentra-lization, delocalization);
  * precise definition of the fields of competence and respective roles;
  * clear contracts and the commitment to respect the relevant fields of competence;
  * the establishment of forums and structures for consultation;
  * availability of the time required.

— pratnership as a participatory and cooperative approach permits:
  * the most effective solution of the problems;
  * assimilation of the changes and reforms so as to ensure their better implementation because people feel that they are subjects and not objects of decisions;
  * motivation of partners and strengthening of their commitment;
  * better training of all the parties concerned through effective action and participation;
  * effective practice of democracy;
  * strengthening of mutual trust and implication in a common endeavour.

— partnership cannot be limited to the execution phase of projects or reforms but necessarily also encompasses their initiation, preparation, launching, implementation and assessment;

— the establishment of an effective partnership takes time, but is capable of increasing the educational potential of the main actors (parents, families, authori-ties, enterprises, media etc.) and of society as a whole and, ultimately, of enhancing the quality of education;

— partnership is a method of operation so it not only concerns schools but also the local, regional and national levels; it is effected either directly (by teachers themselves) or through representation (by their professional associations);

— partnership is complex and demanding so it requires adequate training.

New technologies

Recommendation in this area should underline in particular:

— the vast potential of new information and communi-cation technologies for the improvement of education;

— the vital need for the education system to integrate these technologies and to learn how to master them so as to prevent any technological, cultural or economic servitude and any marginalization of schools in comparison with other sectors;

— the positive impact of the new information and commu-nication technologies on the preparation of the work of teachers and pupils, access to information, response to individual needs, the development of cooperation, opening up to the world through networking;

— the criteria for their successful utilization are that they must not be seen in purely technical terms but in terms of their teaching potential, must utilize pupils' languages, develop partnerships among institutions for the design of software, provide access to new information and communication technologies outside usual school hours, develop an enlightened environ-ment that allows choice, establish participation strategies, accessibility and networking;

— the complementarily of the new technologies and other approaches, both in classrooms and in teaching activities or in the lifelong training of teachers;

— the irreplaceable role of teachers, which consists on the one hand of arranging information so that it can be transformed into knowledge, making choices and developing critical faculties, preserving the meaning of quality and, on the other, transmitting culture, which is "the way of life of human beings", establishing personal and social relationships, encouraging approaches to others, living together and awareness of differences and common values;

— the need to develop the search for and sharing of information on the impact, role and limitations of the new information and communication technologies in education;
— the need to promote cooperation among institutions, at the national and international levels, and to encourage comparative studies;
— taking into account recent studies on policies related to the introduction of new information and communi-cation technologies in education (European Union) and the outcome of the 2nd UNESCO Congress on Education and Informatics (Moscow, July 1996).

The challenges of training

Several basic recommendation concerning training stem naturally from the preceding chapters. More specifically, these recommendations should relate to:

Recruitment

— attracting the best elements and keeping the good ones, but also finding solutions for those who are less good. This means in particular a career policy that covers several aspects: salary scales, promotion possibilities, the time span, etc.;
— selecting future teachers taking into account all the qualities required and not simply intellectual capabilities;
— searching for a better balance between women and men in the teaching profession at all levels;
— encouraging access to teaching for persons from other professions by establishing adequate recruitment and training procedures.

Initial training

— aiming for true professionalism, which implies competence in the subject chosen, teaching skills, the aptitude to communicate and work as a team, as well as personal, cultural and social skills;
— relating theory to practice, finding a balance between mastery of the subjects taught and psychopedagogical, methodological and practical training; promoting *"in situ"* training (courses, tutorials, etc.);
— developing thc ability to adapt to change;

— when training future teachers, practising with them the teaching methods they will have to put into practice (apprenticeship teaching, active methods, etc.);
— beginning with initial training, laying down the bases for the future lifelong training of teachers, it being understood that both initial and lifelong training are elements of the same process of permanent training within the framework of partnership between teacher training institutions and schools.

Lifelong training

— its status should be at least equivalent to initial training. If should be permanent and systematic;
— it should be considered both a right and an obligation and thus a mutual commitment by teachers, schools, public authorities and professional teaching bodies;
— it should be promoted through incentive measures in career or financial terms;
— from the perspective of schools as communities for apprenticeship, lifelong training should be promoted within schools themselves;
— it should involve the active participation of initial training institutions;
— special attention should be given to the begining of teachers' careers because this period is decisive for the future. Entry into the profession should be accompanied by special training which both completes the initial training and constitutes an apprenticeship for the practice of teaching; it must therefore involve training institutions and the best teachers exercising the profession;
— the potential of new technologies and distance learning should be utilized;
— with the aim of raising the overall cultural level of teachers and promoting multi- and intercultural teaching, exchanges and the initial and lifelong training of teachers in other countries in the region should be promoted.

Training of trainers

— they should themselves be trained in the demands of change;

they should believe in the changes and should prepare teachers to train themselves;
— they should take part in lifelong training in schools themselves;
— they should play a special role among young teachers; this would allow them *inter alia* to assess the effects of initial training on actual classroom practices.

Research

— training of teachers as a whole should be closely related to research, including research on teachers and their training; teachers themselves should be taught about research and should use its results to enhance the theory and practice of teaching;
— research on the results and the cost/effectiveness of various forms of lifelong training should be developed.

V. Special Remarks

The meeting noted certain positive trends in the development of education in European countries, for example, increased political stability, a larger number of and more open exchanges of experience, ideas and staff, a general movement towards a more integrated Europe, etc.

The participants expressed the hope that the Declaration of the 45th session of the ICE would take into account the broad outline of the joint ILO/UNESCO Recommendation on the status of teaching staff (1966).

On behalf of the participants, the Chairman of the Council's Working Group, Mr. Y. Brunsvick, thanked the Polish authorities for their hospitality and for the excellent organization of the Consultation's work.

At the proposal of the Chairman of the Council's Working Group, the meeting expressed the hope that participants in regional meetings would be involved in preparing the final drafts of the ICE's Declaration and recommendations.

Coustesy: International Bureau of Education, UNESCO, Geneva, Switzerland.

References

1. The following text is a straightforward transcription of the tape recording of the oral report given in Warsaw. It was not been revised from the point of view of style and should therefore be read bearing in mind the special conditions of the meeting, particularly the lack of time available for preparing the report.

Additional Reading

Bhaskara Rao, Digumarti (1994). *Scientific Aptitude.* New Delhi: Ashish Publishing House.

Bhaskara Rao, Digumarti (1995). *Animal Kingdom.* New Delhi: Discovery Publishing House.

Bhaskara Rao, Digumarti (1995). *Batracology.* New Delhi : Discovery Publishing House.

Bhaskara Rao, Digumarti (1996). *Scientific Attitude vis-a-vis Scientific Aptitude.* New Delhi : Discovery Publishing House.

Bhaskara Rao, Digumarti, ed. (1996). *Encyclopaeida of Education For All,* 5 vols. New Delhi : APH Publishing Corporation.

Vol. I Education For All : The World Conference

Vol. II Education For All : The EAP - 9 Summit.

Vol. III Education For All : Quality Education For All.

Vol. IV Education For All : Planning and Monitoring.

Vol. V Education For All : The Indian Scenario.

Bhaskara Rao, Digumarti, ed. (1996). *Global Perceptions on Peace Education,* 3 vols. New Delhi : Discovery Publishing House.

Bhaskara Rao, Digumarti, ed. (1996). *National Policy on Education,* 2 Vols. New Delhi : Anmol Publications Pvt. Ltd.

Bhaskara Rao, Digumarti, ed. (1997). *Care the Child,* 2 Vols. New Delhi : Discovery Publishing House.

Bhaskara Rao, Digumarti, ed. (1997). *Education for the 21st Century.* New Delhi : Discovery Publishing House.

Bhaskara Rao, Digumarti, ed. (1997). *Reflections on Scientific Attitude.* New Delhi : Discovery Publishing House.

Bhaskara Rao, Digumarti, ed. (1997). *Scientific Attitude.* New Delhi: Discovery Publishing House.

Bhaskara Rao, Digumarti, ed. (1997). *Success Story of a Primary Education Project.* New Delhi : APH Publishing Corporation.

Bhaskara Rao, Digumarti, ed. (1997). *World Food Summit.* New Delhi : Discovery Publishing House.

Bhaskara Rao, Digumarti, ed. (1998). *Adolescence Education.* New Delhi : Discovery Publishing House.

Bhaskara Rao, Digumarti, ed. (1998). *Community and School Nutrition Education.* New Delhi : Discovery Publishing House.

Bhaskara Rao, Digumarti, ed. (1998). *District Primary Education Programme.* New Delhi : Discovery Publishing House.

Bhaskara Rao, Digumarti, ed. (1998). *Earth Summit,* 2 vols. New Delhi : Discovery Publishing House.

Bhaskara Rao, Digumarti, ed. (1998). *National Policy on Education: Towards and Enlightened and Humane Society.* New Delhi : Discovery Publishing House.

Bhaskara Rao, Digumarti, ed. (1998). *Reforming School Education.* New Delhi : Discovery Publishing House.

Bhaskara Rao, Digumarti, ed. (1998). *Teacher Education in India.* New Delhi : Discovery Publishing House.

Bhaskara Rao, Digumarti, ed. (1998). *World Summit for Social Development.* New Delhi : Discovery Publishing House.

Bhaskara Rao, Digumarti, ed. (2000). *Education For All : Achieving the Goal.* 3 vols. New Delhi : APH Publishing Corporation.

Vol. I The Global Consensus.
Vol II Mid-Decade Review Reports of Regional Seminars.
Vol III Issues and Trends.

Bhaskara Rao, Digumarti, ed. (2000). *International Encyclopeadia of AIDS,* 11 Vols in 13 parts. New Delhi : Discovery Publishing House.

Vol. 1 Introduction to HIV/AIDS.
Vol. 2 HIV/AIDS – Issues and Challenges, 2 parts.
Vol. 3 HIV/AIDS – Socio Economic Realities.
Vol. 4 HIV/AIDS Law Ethics and Human Rights, 2 parts.
Vol. 5 AIDS and NGOs.
Vol. 6 AIDS and Home Care.
Vol. 7 STD Case Management.
Vol. 8 HIV Prevention and Care – Teaching Modules for Nurses and Midwives.

Vol. 9 HIV/AIDS Prevention Education for Educational Institutions.
Vol. 10 Instructional Modules for AIDS Education.
Vol. 11 School Health Education to prevent AIDS and STD – A Package for curriculum planners.

Bhaskara Rao, Digumarti, ed. (2000). *International Encyclopaedia of Science and Technology Education.* 11 Volumes. New Delhi : Discovery Publishing House.
Vol. 1 Science and Technology Education.
Vol. 2 Science Education in Developing Countries.
Vol. 3 Organisational Structure of Science.
Vol. 4 Science Education in Asia and the Pacific.
Vol. 5 Science and Technology Education For All.
Vol. 6 Values, Ethics, Talent and Girls in Science and Technology Education.
Vol. 7 Popularization of Science and Technology Education.
Vol. 8 Science, Power and Society.
Vol. 9 Information Technology.
Vol. 10 Teacher Training in Science and Technology
Vol. 11 Science, Technology and Society : A Curriculum Framework.

Bhaskara Rao, Digumarti, ed. (2001). *Distance Education in Different Countries.* New Delhi : APH Publishing Corporation.

Bhaskara Rao, Digumarti, ed. (2001). *Decentralised Management of Education (Management of Education in Panchayati Raj and Municipal Bodies).* New Delhi : Discovery Publishing House.

Bhaskara Rao, Digumarti, ed. (2001). *Electrochemistry for Environmental Protection.* New Delhi : Discovery Publishing House.

Bhaskara Rao, Digumarti, ed. (2001). *Global Educational Studies.* New Delhi : Discovery Publishing House.

Bhaskara Rao, Digumarti, ed. (2001). *Global Synthesis of Educational Assessment.* New Delhi : Discovery Publishing House.

Bhaskara Rao, Digumarti, ed. (2001). *International Encyclopaedia of Human Rights,* 7 volumes in 13 parts. New Delhi : Discovery Publishing House.
Vol. 1 International Instruments of Human Rights, 2 parts
Vol. 2 Regional Instruments of Human Rights.
Vol. 3 Human Rights and the United Nations, 2 parts.

Vol. 4 Fact Files of Human Rights, 2 parts.
Vol. 5 Study Stories of Human Rights, 3 parts.
Vol. 6 International Meetings on Human Rights, 2 parts.
Vol. 7 Professional Training in Human Rights.

Bhaskara Rao, Digumarti, ed. (2001). *Jomtein Decade of Education.* New Delhi : Discovery Publishing House.

Bhaskara Rao, Digumarti, ed. (2001). *Nuclear Materials : Issues and Concerns,* 2 vols. New Delhi : Discovery Publishing House.

Bhaskara Rao, Digumarti, ed. (2001). *World Conference on Education for All.* New Delhi : APH Publishing Corporation.

Bhaskara Rao, Digumarti, ed. (2001). *World Conference on Higher Education.* New Delhi : Discovery Publishing House.

Bhaskara Rao, Digumarti, ed. (2001). *World Conference on Science.* New Dęlhi : Discovery Publishing House.

Bhaskara Rao, Digumarti, ed. (2003). *Inspiring Experiences in Teacher Education.* New Delhi : Discovery Publishing House.

Bhaskara Rao, Digumarti, ed. (2003). *International Studies in Education.* New Delhi : Discovery Publishing House.

Bhaskara Rao, Digumarti, ed. (2003). *Military Conversion : Impact on Science and Technology.* New Delhi : Discovery Publishing House.

Bhaskara Rao, Digumarti, ed. (2003). *United Nations Milenium Summit.* New Delhi : Discovery Publishing House.

Bhaskara Rao, Digumarti, ed. (2002). *World Assembly on Aging.* New Delhi : Discovery Publishing House.

Bhaskara Rao, Digumarti, ed. (2003). *World Conference on Human Rights.* New Delhi. Discovery Publishing House.

Bhaskara Rao, Digumarti, ed. (2003). *World Education Forum.* New Delhi : Discovery Publishing House.

Bhaskara Rao, Digumarti, ed. (2003). *Education Employment and Human Resource Development.* New Delhi : Discovery Publishing House.

Bhaskara Rao, Digumarti, ed. (2003). *Successful Schooling.* New Delhi : Discovery Publishing House.

Bhaskara Rao, Digumarti, C.A.P. Swamy & B.S.V. Dutt (1997). *Self Evaluation in Student Teaching.* New Delhi : Discovery Publishing House.

Bhaskara Rao, Digumarti, C. Sridevi & K. Vijaya (1995).

Achievement in Social Studies. New Delhi : Discovery Publishing House.

Bhaskara Rao, Digumarti & Digumarti Pushpa Latha (1994). *Achievement in Biology*. New Delhi : Discovery Publshing House.

Bhaskara Rao, Digumarti & Digumarti Pushpa Latha (1995). *Achievement in English*. New Delhi : Discovery Publishing House.

Bhaskara Rao, Digumarti & Digumarti Pushpa Latha (1995). *Achievement in Science*. New Delhi. Discovery Publishing House.

Bhaskara Rao, Digumarti & Digumarti Pushpa Latha (1995). *Achievement in Mathematics*. New Delhi : Discovery Publishing House.

Bhaskara Rao, Digumarti & Digumarti Pushpa Latha, eds (1998). *International Encyclopaedia of Women,* 5 vols. New Delhi : Discovery Publishing House.
Vol. 1 Status of World's Women.
Vol. 2 Women, Education and Empowerement.
Vol. 3 Women Challenges and Advancement.
Vol. 4 Women and Family Health.
Vol. 5 Women and International Action.

Bhaskara Rao, Digumarti, Digumarti Pushpa Latha & Digumarti, Harshitha eds. (2001). *Biological Warfare*. New Delhi : Discovery Publishing House.

Bhaskara Rao, Digumarti & Digumarti Puspha Latha & Digumarti, Harshitha eds. (2001). *Women as Educators*. New Delhi : Discovery Publishing House.

Bhaskara Rao, Digumarti, Digumarti Harshitha (2000). *Education in India*. New Delhi : APH Publishing Corporation.

Bhaskara Rao, Digumarti & Digumarti Harshitha eds. (2001). *Assessing Learning Achievement*. New Delhi : Discovery Publishing House.

Bhaskara Rao, Digumarti & Digumarti Harshitha eds. (2001). *Energy Security*. New Delhi : Discovery Publishing House.

Bhaskara Rao, Digumarti, D. Harshitha and K.R.S.S. Rao, eds. (1999). *Advanced Biotechnology*. New Delhi : Discovery Publishgin House.

Bhaskara Rao, Digumarti & D. Sridhar (2002). *Job Satisfaction of School Teachers*. New Delhi : Discovery Publishing House.

Bhaskara Rao, Digumarti & K.R.S. Sambasiva Rao, eds. (1996).

Current Trends in India Education. New Delhi : Discovery Publishing House.

Bhaskara Rao, Digumarti and K. Vijaya (1995). *A Text Book Evaluation.* Ambala Cantt : The Associated Publishers.

Bhaskara Rao, Digumarti and N.V.M. Mohana Rao (2002). *Problems of Mentally Handicapped.* New Delhi : Discovery Publishing House.

Bhaskara Rao, Digumarti, V.V. Rao, V.V. Lakshmi and V.V. Krishna, eds. (2000). *Status and Advancement of Women.* New Delhi: APH Publshing Corporation.

Babu, P.C. and Digumarti Bhaskara Rao,ed. (2002). *Flowers of Wisdom.* New Delhi : Discovery Publishing House.

Bhagya Lakshmi, Lingineni and Digumarti Bhaskara Rao, ed. (2000). *Reading and Comprehension.* New Delhi : Discovery Publishing House.

Bhuvaneswara Lakṣhmi, G. & Digumarti Bhaskara Rao, ed. (2000). *Attitude Towards Science.* New Delhi : Discovery Publshing House.

Devraj, T.A.S. & Digumarti Bhaskara Rao, ed. (1997). *Trace Analysis of Uranium and Thorium.* New Delhi : Discovery Publishing House.

Durgani Rani, K. & Digumarti Bhaskara Rao, ed. (2000). *Educational Aspirations and Scientific Attitudes.* New Delhi : Discovery Publishing House.

Dutt, B.S.V. & Digumarti Bhaskara Rao (2001). *Empowering Primary Teachers.* New Delhi : Discovery Publishing House.

Ediger, Marlow & Digumarti Bhaskar Rao (1996). *Science Curriculum.* New Delhi : Discovery Publishing House.

Ediger, Marlow & Digumarti Bhaskara Rao (2000). *Teaching Mathematics Successfully.* New Delhi : Discovery Publishing House.

Ediger, Marlow & Digumarti Bhaskara Rao (2000). *Teaching Reading Successfully.* New Delhi : Discovery Publishing House.

Ediger Marlow & Digumarti Bhaskara Rao (2001). *Teaching Science Successfully.* New Delhi: Discovery Publishing House.

Ediger Marlow & Digumarti Bhaskara Rao (2001). *Teaching Social Studies Successfully.* New Delhi : Discovery Publishing House.

Ediger Marlow & Digumarti Bhaskara Rao (2002). *Philosophy and*

Curriculum. New Delhi : Discovery Publishing House.

Ediger Marlow & Digumarti Bhaskara Rao (2002). *Improving School Administration*. New Delhi : Discovery Publishing House.

Ediger Marlow & Digumarti Bhaskara Rao (2003). *Elementary Curriculum*. New Delhi : Discovery Publishing House.

Ediger Marlow & Digumarti Bhaskara Rao (2002). *Language Arts Curriculum*. New Delhi : Discovery Publishing House.

Ediger Marlow & Digumarti Bhaskara Rao (2003). *Teaching Language Arts Successfully*. New Delhi : Discovery Publishing House.

Ediger Marlow & Digumarti Bhaskara Rao (2003). *Teaching Mathematics in Primary Schools*. New Delhi : Discovery Publishing House.

Ediger Marlow & Digumarti Bhaskara Rao (2003). *Teaching Science in Primary Schools*. New Delhi : Discovery Publishing House.

Jayasree, Kandi & Digumarti Bhaskara Rao, ed. (1999). *Correlates of Socialisation*. New Delhi : Discovery Publishing House.

John Babu, Ch., T.J.R. Prasad, G.M. Madhukar & Digumarti Bhaskara Rao, eds. (2001). *Problem Solving in Mathematics*. New Delhi : APH Publishing Corporation.

Jyothi, Nirmala & Digumarti Bhaskara Rao, ed (2002). *Non-dentention System in Education*. New Delhi : Discovery Publishing House.

Marja. Talvi & Digumarti Bhaskara Rao, eds. (1996). *Educational Leadership and Social Changes*. New Delhi : Discovery Publishing House.

Prabhakaram, K.S. & Digumarti Bhaskara Rao, ed. (1998). *Concept Attainment Model in Mathematics Teaching*. New Delhi : Discovery Publishing House.

Prasanth Kumar, J. & Digumarti Bhaskara Rao, ed. (1998). *Effectiveness of Distance Education System*. New Delhi : Discovery Publishing House.

Prasanth Kumar, J. & Digumarti Bhaskara Rao and G. Sundara Rao, eds. (2000). *Open University Student Support Services*. New Delhi : Discovery Publishing House.

Ramatulasamma K. & Digumarti Bhaskara Rao, ed. (2002). *Job Satisfaction of Teacher Educators*. New Delhi : Discovery

Publishing House.

Rama Krishnaiah, D. & Digumarti Bhaskara Rao, ed. (1998). *Job Satisfaction of College Teachers.* New Delhi : Discovery Publishing House.

Ramesh, Ganta & Digumarati Bhaskara Rao, eds. (1998). *Environmental Education : Problems and Prospects.* New Delhi : Discovery Publishing House.

Rathaiah, L. and Digumarti Bhaskara Rao, eds. (1997). *International Innovations in Education.* New Delhi : Discovery Publishing House.

Rathaiah, Lavu, Digumarti Bhaskara Rao and Patrui Koteswara Rao. (1997). *Achievement Correlates.* New Delhi : Discovery Publishing House.

Reddy, Sudhakar & Digumarti Bhaskara Rao, ed. (2002). *Creativity in Adolescents.* New Delhi : Discovery Publishing House.

Sanjeeva Rao, P.C. & Digumarti Bhaskara Rao, ed. (1996). *A Text Book of Geology.* New Delhi : Discovery Publishing House.

Satya Narayana, V. & Digumarti Bhaskara Rao, ed. (2001). *Physical Education, Social Attitudes and Leadership Qualities.* New Delhi: Discovery Publishing House.

Srinivasulu Reddy, M., K.R.S. Sambasiva Rao & Digumarti Bhaskara Rao, ed. (1999). *A Text Book of Aquaculture.* New Delhi: Discovery Publishing House.

Vanaja, M. & Digumarti Bhaskara Rao, ed. (1999). *Inquiry Training Model.* New Delhi : Discovery Publishing House.

Valeri V. Koustiouk & Digumarti Bhaskara Rao, ed. (2002). *A Text Book of Cryogenics.* New Delhi : Discovery Publishing House.

Valeri V. Koustiouk & Digumarti Bhaskara Rao, ed. (2002). *Refrigeration and Environment.* New Delhi : Discovery Publishing House.

Veena Kumari, Balusu & Digumarti Bhaskara Rao (1996). *Operation Black Board.* New Delhi : APH Publishing Corporation.

Veena Kumari, B. & Digumarti Bhaskara Rao, ed. (2000). *Psycho Social Correlates of Achievement.* New Delhi : Discovery Publishing House.

Venkata Rao, P. & Digumarti Bhaskara Rao (1989). *A Text Book of Zoology – Junior Intermediate.* Guntur : Vignan Publishers.

Venkata Rao, P. & Digumarti Bhaskara Rao (1989). *A Text Book of*

Zoology – Senior Intermediate. Guntur : Vignan Publishers.

Venugopala Rao, K. & Digumarti Bhaskara Rao, ed. (2000). *Teacher Morale in Secondary Schools.* New Delhi : Discovery Publishing House.

Vidya, C. & Digumarti Bhaskara Rao, ed. (1996). *A Text Book of Nutrition.* New Delhi : Discovery Publishing House.

Vijaya Bharathi, D. & Digumarti Bhaskara Rao, ed. (2000). *Educational Philosophies of Swami Vivekanand and John Dewey.* New Delhi : APH Publishing Corporation.

Bhaskara Rao, Digumarti, (1986). *Dhrushya Sravana Bodhanapakaranalu* (Audio-Visual Teaching Aids). Guntur : Nagarjuna Publishers.

Bhaskara Rao, Digumarti (1993). *Jeevasashtra Bodhana* (Teaching of Biology). Guntur : Nagarjuna Publishers.

Bhaskara Rao, Digumarti (1995). *Vignanasasthra Bodhana.* (Teaching of Science). Guntur : Nagarjuna Publishers.

Bhaskara Rao, Digumarti (1997). *Vidya Manovignana Sashtram.* (Educational Psychology). Guntur : Creative Press.

Bhaskara Rao, Digumarti (1998). *DSC Study Material.* Guntur: Nagarjuna Publishers.

Bhaskara Rao, Digumarti (1998). *Upadhyayudu Vidya* (Teacher and Education). Guntur : Nagarjuna Publishers.

Bhaskara Rao, Digumarti (1998). *Vidya Dhrukpadhalu.* (Perspectives of Education). Guntur : Nagarjuna Publishers.

Bhaskara Rao, Digumarti (1999).*EdCET Teaching Aptitude.* Guntur: Nagarjuna Publishers.

Bhaskara Rao, Digumarti (2001). *Bharata Samajamulo Upadhayayudu Vidya* (Teacher and Education in Emerging Indian Society). Guntur : Nagarjuna Publishers.

Bhaskara Rao, Digumarti (2001). *Bhoutika Sastra Bodhana Padhatulu* (Methods of Teaching Physical Science). Guntur : Nagarjuna Publishers.

Bhaskara Rao, Digumarti (2001). *Jeeva Sastra Bodhana Padhatulu* (Methods of Teaching Biological Science). Guntur : Nagarjuna Publishers.

Bhaskara Rao, Digumarti (2001). *Vidya Manovignana Sastram* (Educational Pyschology). Guntur : Nagarjuna Publishers.

□□□